MAKING SENSE OF

PROGRAMMING ALGORITHMS

FOUNDATIONS

MAKING SENSE OF

PROGRAMMING ALGORITHMS

FOUNDATIONS

ROBERT SETIADI, PhD

First Edition

01-02i

ISBN: 978-0-6489636-1-5
Libraries Australia ID 75221993

A catalogue record for this work is available from the National Library of Australia

*This book is dedicated to my amazing wife Henny
and my not-so-little ones Andrew and Alice.*

CONTENTS

this page intentionally left blank

PREFACE

Making Sense of Programming Algorithms Foundations is a comprehensive introduction to computer programming. It is written for students seeking to gain a solid understanding of software engineering, as well as self-taught professionals who wish to explore careers in software development.

Programming algorithms are the fundamental blocks of software development, serving as the essential blueprint for processing inputs into outputs and automating tasks using computing devices. They are a set of well-defined, step-by-step instructions that dictate how a device should execute a specific function.

At its core, an *algorithm* is a logical sequence of steps designed to solve a particular problem or execute a specific task. Defining algorithms allows us to break down complex challenges into manageable components that can be solved systematically.

To define an algorithm, a software developer uses *logic* as the high-level reasoning behind the steps. Logic is used as an abstract to define the problem-solving approach, the triggers for actions, the states of computations and the overall flow of the algorithm.

A computer (or other computing device) executes instructions presented in machine language, which consists of binary and hexadecimal characters. These instructions are not meant to be understood by humans. Programming languages are created so that humans can create instructions for machines without having to go to the level of machine-level binary instructions.

Low-level programming languages such as Assembly Language use simple human-readable instructions but are still aimed to communicate directly with hardware. High-level programming languages (C++, Java, Python, etc.) introduce several abstractions to make it easier for humans to design an algorithm for machines to execute. This is the most common form of programming used in modern computing.

Code represents the concrete implementation of an algorithm using a specific programming language. It is the tangible form of logic instructions that can be executed by a computer. Each line of code represents a specific step in the algorithm flow. A *compiler* translates code into machine instructions before a program runs. An *interpreter* translates code as it runs, line-by-line.

Computer *programming* is an activity that transforms abstract logic into tangible code using a specific programming language so that it can be executed (or interpreted) by a computer. For example, the code written for Python will not work with the C++ compiler.

One common misconception about programming study is the over-focus on a specific language or technology stack. Quite often, mastering the syntaxes of some programming languages is used as a measurement of someone's competency. While knowing the syntaxes of multiple programming languages is indeed an impressive feat on its own, it does not necessarily align with one's ability to write good and efficient code in those languages.

A person can spend long years doing programming in 8 different languages, but all he was doing was repetitive work without any real challenge to do significant optimisation. Another person could only do 1 programming language and only have 2 years' experience. However, during those 2 years, he has successfully improved a certain module in a system that normally takes 4 hours execution every night, down to 20 minutes. Arguably, the second person is a better software engineer.

Many programming books in the market provide comprehensive knowledge of a specific programming language or technology platform. This book chooses to focus on the logic behind those codes. Discussions of algorithms in this book are presented in the form of *pseudocode* instead of code from any specific programming language. This will make this book valuable for people learning different technology stacks, and allow readers to focus on algorithms and its logic instead of syntax and libraries of certain programming languages.

Pseudocode is different from code specific to a programming language. It is an informal language that helps in the process of developing logic in algorithms. There is no precise syntax for pseudocode. Instead, it uses text-based lines to describe an algorithm, including selections, loops, and modules. In loose definition, we can position pseudocode somewhere in between plain English and proper code.

This book has 10 chapters divided into 3 sections. Quick reading for a high-level understanding of the overall topics will take approximately 16-24 hours, whereas comprehensive reading could take a few weeks to a few months depending on time commitment.

The first section is intended for absolute beginners in programming algorithms, thus helping everyone to learn the basics. The second section has the main discussions of various algorithm topics. As the title suggests, this book only covers the foundation level of programming algorithms.

Parts of this book's content are inspired by the author's earlier (non-English) book published in 2008, about programming algorithms for university students. Even though some chapters inherit similar structures, this book exclusively delivers more value through improved contents and new chapters.

Several algorithm topics are grouped by the base logic behind them. Divide and conquer techniques break down a problem into multiple smaller pieces of sub-problems. Greedy algorithm techniques make one choice at a time and always choose the best immediate option for that choice. Dynamic programming techniques split a problem into multiple overlapping sub-problems and then evaluate overlapping sub-problems to consider the impacts of one decision to other decisions. Huffman coding focuses on representing data with smaller sizes of binary values. Search tree techniques aim to make choices in multiple stages.

Each technique is explained with examples. Most examples are presented with great details and step-by-step calculations, thereby helping readers to make sense of the algorithm. Pseudocodes and illustrations are used where relevant, to make this book as easy as possible to understand.

Section three is aimed at transitioning readers to the next learning steps. The chapter on algorithm analysis presents discussions about algorithms complexity, understanding worst-case scenarios expressed in Big O notation, and a step-by-step example to analyse and improve an algorithm.

The chapter on algorithm testing introduces some basic terms and concepts in testing, along with understanding the principles of test coverage. Some examples of control flow coverage, data flow coverage, logic coverage and input space partitioning would effectively help in understanding the tester role and the preparation of test cases.

Final chapter provides short summaries of a few topics beyond basic algorithms: database queries, libraries and frameworks, low-code platforms, and artificial intelligence. There, topics are chosen to help readers to connect how the knowledge of basic algorithms links to some real-world applications with some modern trends in software development.

Finally, this book is written in Australian English, which means it follows the conventions and spellings specific to Australian use. It means you will see *optimise* instead of *optimize*, *customise* instead of *customize*, *colour* instead of *color* and so on. These differences in spelling do not alter the meaning or content of the book.

GETTING TO KNOW

01. ALGORITHMS

Humans and machines think differently. To be more accurate, machines do not actually think. They process large set of instructions within a short time, sometimes creating the impression similar to what humans normally referred to as thinking.

Any problem-solving or complex calculation that a computer can do is essentially the result of the set of instructions created by humans for that computer to execute. In a way, the problems need to be resolved by a machine is already defined by humans, including step-by-step instructions of what to do. All computer needs to do is taking the inputs from its users, then run it against the set of instructions commonly known as software or app, then display results depending on the instructions.

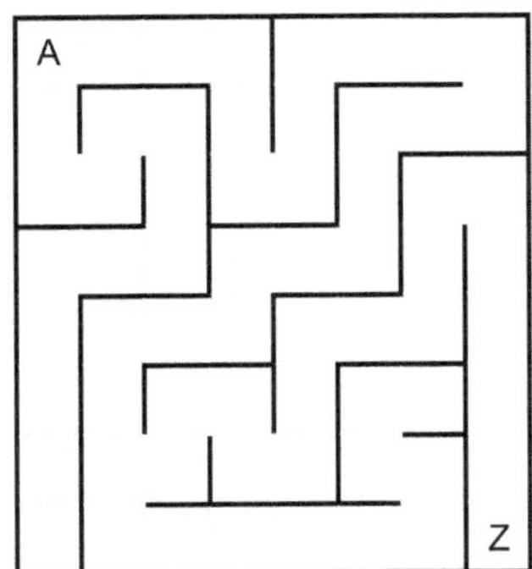

Using human brain, we can quickly find a path from A to Z in the above maze. Thick lines represent maze walls, and one could not travel through them.

Young children will use their pencils to trace a path, then backtrack when there is no further path. Older kids and adults can quickly see if a potential path will end up blocked before deciding which path to take.

Instead of drawing the path using a pencil, computer algorithm sees the above problem as a series of movement choices. From each position, there are 4 possible moves: up (U), down (D), left (L) and right (R). Some moves are invalid when the move is blocked by a wall. Avoiding all the walls, the solution from A to Z is {R, R, R, D, D, R, U, U, R, R, R, D, L, L, D, D, L, L, D, L, L, D, D, R, U, R, D, R, U, U, R, R, U, U, R, D, D, D, D, D}. This could look more complicated than simply drawing a path using pencil, but this serves as a good first introduction to show how human brain and computer processing work differently.

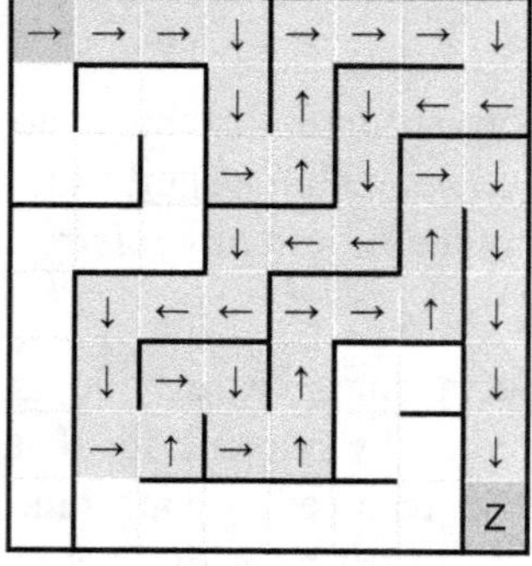

By giving the solution to a computer, we can give instruction for computer to move from A to Z. However, getting the computer to find the solution is what we will learn throughout this book.

An algorithm normally takes some inputs, does some processing and calculations, then produces outputs. A *good algorithm* would produce the correct outputs within the shortest possible time, using the minimum possible computing resources. A *correct algorithm* would produce correct outputs for ALL possible inputs, including error handling of all invalid inputs. Even though an algorithm handles 99% of possible inputs correctly, if it produces wrong results for the remaining 1%, the algorithm is said to be incorrect. Just like a computer processes binary data of 1 and 0, an algorithm is either correct or incorrect, there is no such thing as almost correct. This is the biggest challenge of designing an algorithm.

Pseudocode

Instead of using specific programming language, this book uses *pseudocode* to represent an algorithm. Pseudocode sits between algorithm logic abstraction and its implementation in code. It is a high-level, human-readable description of an algorithm, commonly used during design and planning phase, allowing a software engineer to outline the steps of an algorithm and communicate with other team members. Pseudocode lacks the syntax-level precision of code, but its lack of language-specific details allows more focus on conveying algorithm's logic.

```
1 show "Hello World"
```

Algorithm 01-A Hello World

The very first algorithm in this book simply tells the computer to show "Hello World" message on the screen. This line of pseudocode is well understood by humans and can be implemented in different programming languages.

Unlike programming languages that have specific syntax, pseudocode does not have restrictive rule. Instead of `show`, we can also use `display` or other words with similar meaning. It is not even restricted to English because speakers of other languages can simply choose words from their own languages.

Components of Algorithm

It is important to understand the core components which define the structure and functionality of an algorithm. By understanding these components, a software engineer gains comprehensive understanding of how it works to tackle a wide range of computational challenges.

Core components:
- Statement / instruction
- Sequence
- Variable and values
- Selections (branches)
- Iterations (loops)

Statement is a single logical instruction, a basic unit of an algorithm. It ranges from simple instructions to display plain text messages, assigning values to variables, getting user inputs, performing calculations, or evaluating conditions. It can also be used to describe more complex instructions such as reading data from a file or displaying outputs in specific format.

The *sequence* of statements within an algorithm determines how the instructions are being executed. When designing algorithm, it is important to ensure that statements in the algorithm is sequenced in a logical and coherent manner, with each statement is building upon the results of the previous ones. It defines the flow of execution and algorithm's quality and correctness.

```
1 show "How are you?"
2 show "Good morning"
```

Algorithm 01-B Algorithm Sequence (1)

```
1 show "Good morning"
2 show "How are you?"
```

Algorithm 01-C Algorithm Sequence (2)

Both algorithms above have the same set of statements but listed in different sequence. Algorithm 01-B will show the message "How are you?" first and then "Good morning". Algorithm 01-C will show the message "Good morning" first and then "How are you?". The difference might not mean much when both statements are simple instruction to display plain text messages. However, if we combine it with other core components (selection and iteration), sequence difference can impact calculations and have significant downstream impacts.

Variables are used to store and manipulate data within an algorithm. Imagine them as empty boxes that can be filled in with items (values). Just like empty boxes can be filled with wide variety of items, variables can represent wide range of data, from text, number, and more complex data types.

Selections introduce decision making capability into algorithms. They enable algorithms to choose different paths depending on some conditions. Also known as *branches*, the most common form of selection is `if-else` construct. This core component is essential to allow an algorithm the capability to handle different inputs.

Iterations (also known as *loops*) is a construct to allow an algorithm to repeat some statements multiple times. This component of algorithm is very important to handle repetitive tasks, such as processing a list of data, or to repeat some calculations until certain conditions are met.

Sequence

The sequence of statements in an algorithm impacts the flow and result. To help understanding this concept, the below illustration shows a rabbit trying to get a carrot. It starts from top left position. Each move brings the rabbit up, down, left, or right. Diagonal moves are not valid. There are rocks in the middle of the field, forcing the rabbit to take the path around them.

There are two possible paths the rabbit can take. It can go from the top, then going down, or it can go down first then move right.

Possible solutions for the problem are {R, R, R, R, D, D, D, D} and {D, D, D, D, R, R, R, R}. Note that each solution has 8 moves. In the form of pseudocode, movement of the rabbit can be written with 8 lines following the sequence of the solution.

```
1 move right
2 move right
3 move right
4 move right
5 move down
6 move down
7 move down
8 move down
```

Algorithm 01-D Rabbit Path (Option 1)

```
1 move down
2 move down
3 move down
4 move down
5 move right
6 move right
7 move right
8 move right
```

Algorithm 01-E Rabbit Path (Option 2)

If we swap lines #4 and #5 from Algorithm 01-E, the sequence will bring the rabbit to locations with rock. This makes the algorithm to be incorrect.

```
1 move down
2 move down
3 move down
4 move right
5 move down
6 move right
7 move right
8 move right
```

Algorithm 01-F Rabbit Path (Incorrect Solution)

A change on the problem will change the solution. If additional rock appears somewhere on solution #1 (see below illustration), the path {R, R, R, R, D, D, D, D} is no longer valid because it is now blocked by a rock. Algorithm 01-D cannot be used as a correct solution anymore.

Algorithm 01-E is still a valid solution for the revised problem because there is no rock blocking this path.

Variables, Values and Data Types

Variables are containers to store and manage data. An easy way to understand the concept of variable is to think of it as boxes that can contain items in it. Items in a box is the value stored in a variable.

There are different types of boxes to handle different types of items. A box to store a fishing rod will have different shape from a box to store a hat. Storing liquid requires box to be made of certain materials to prevent leaking. Similar concept applies for variables. Different types of values need different types of variables. Numeric values go into variables with numeric data types so that the programming language can apply various arithmetic operations on it. Text (string) values will not need multiplication operations, but they might need concatenation, scanning or inserting.

Some programming languages requires software developers to declare variables with name and type before using them. Some others allow the use of variable name without creating it first. Different software developers have different preferences for naming, but generally it needs to be consistent, readable, and representative. Variable names should help us to understand an algorithm with minimum effort.

Data types can be implemented differently by programming languages. Below are examples of numeric data types to store whole numbers in Java:

Data Type	Length	Value Range	Memory
byte	8 bits	- 128 to 127	1 byte
short	16 bits	- 32,768 to 32,767	2 bytes
int	32 bits	- 2,147,483,648 to 2,147,483,647	4 bytes
long	64 bits	- 9,223,372,036,854,775,808 to 9,223,372,036,854,775,807	8 bytes

Other data types:

Data Type	Description	Memory
float	Stores fractional numbers, up to 6 or 7 decimal digits.	4 bytes
double	Stores fractional numbers, up to 15 decimal digits.	8 bytes
Boolean	Stores *true* or *false* values.	1 byte
char	Stores a single character or symbol.	2 bytes

A *Boolean* variable technically only needs 1 bit of data to store true or false value. However, Java implements it using 1 byte in memory (8 bits). Other programming languages might have different implementations. *Char* variable requires 2 bytes instead of 1 to cover Unicode characters.

Arrays and Strings

Multiple variables with the same data type can be stored using a single name using *array* data structure. Individual components (and the values in them) are called *elements*.

Elements in an array can be accessed using numeric *index*. There are 2 approaches of index numbers for array with *n* elements:
- 0 to n−1
- 1 to n

Index that starts with 0 maps naturally with memory address, hence it is more commonly used in many programming languages. However, index that starts from 1 maps closer to natural human language, excluding programmers who are influenced by their work. When someone has 3 apples, it is more likely to count them with one, two, three instead of zero, one, two. Some programming languages such as COBOL, R and Matlab start array index from 1. Some others allow custom definition of array index.

> **IMPORTANT**: This book uses array index starting from 1 to align closer to human language.

An example of array A with 7 elements:

index	1	2	3	4	5	6	7
value	16	25	22	3	14	9	23

Each element has integer data type and holds its own values. These values can be manipulated as part of iterations, or it can be accessed independently.

```
1 show A[5]
2 A[6]=A[2]-4
```

Algorithm 01-G Accessing an Element in Array

The first line from the above pseudocode instructs the computer to show the value currently hold by element #5 of array A. The value is currently 14. Line #2 takes the value in element #2 (25), subtract 4 from it (25 − 4 = 21), and then put the result of calculation (21) into element #6.

Values of array A after the execution of Algorithm 01-G:

index	1	2	3	4	5	6	7
value	16	25	22	3	14	21	23

Arrays can have more than one dimension. Two-dimensional arrays have indexes arranged in (x, y), three-dimensional arrays have indexes of (x, y, z) and so on. Technically, there is no limit of how many dimensions an array can have. However, it is advised to plan the structure of an array wisely because arrays with more dimensions will require more memory and more difficult to manage.

There are many ways to implement arrays, from storing a simple list of user inputs to representing problems to solve. For example, the 5x5 board with a rabbit trying to reach a carrot can be modified into a more challenging problem that the rabbit needs to drink potion to destroy ball-shaped rock before it can reach the goal.

To represent the board, each possible object in a cell needs to be mapped into a value:

- 0 for empty squares
- 1 for the rabbit's initial location
- 2 for the normal (indestructible) rock
- 3 for the round-shaped rock that can be destroyed
- 4 for the potion
- 5 for the carrot (goal)

With the mapping, the above board can be represented using a two-dimensional array:

1	0	2	0	0
0	2	4	2	0
0	0	0	0	2
0	2	0	2	0
2	0	0	3	5

A *string* is a special form of array to store text data. Each element in a string contains a single character value. Instead of assigning individual elements with characters, it is more common to assign text value to the whole string variable.

An example string S:

index	1	2	3	4	5	6	7
value	M	a	c	h	i	n	e

Instead of assigning 'M' to S[1], 'a' to S[2] and so on, it is more common to assign the whole text to the variable: S = "Machine".

String variable can handle dynamic length, depending on its current value. In some programming languages, the first character in a string uses index 1 instead of 0. This is because element #0 in a string variable usually contains the length of the string. In the above example, the value in S[0] is 7.

Record (Structure)

Record (also known as *structure* or *compound*) is data structure that groups a fixed number of fields. Each field in a record has its own identifier (field name) and can have different data type.

For example, an algorithm can have a variable named `Employee` to store name, date of birth, job title and position level of an employee:
- `Name` field is a string variable.
- `Date of Birth` is a date variable.
- `Job Title` is a string variable.
- `Position Level` is an integer variable.

It is common to use record data type with arrays to build a logical list that can be manipulated in an algorithm.

Selections (Branches)

Selection, often referred to as *branching* or *conditional* statements, is a fundamental concept in programming language that empowers algorithms to make decisions based on specific conditions. Using selection, an algorithm can calculate different formulas or execute different sets of instructions depending on which criteria are met.

Let us consider a simple scenario of an algorithm that will take a numeric value from user, then shows the word "small" if the input value is smaller than 5 and the word "big" if it is bigger than or equal to 5.

```
1 show "Please enter a value: "
2 read A
3 if A<5 then
4    show "Small"
5 else
6    show "Big"
7 end if
```

Algorithm 01-H Selection Example (1)

The `else` part of an `if-then` instruction is optional. An algorithm can be designed to do nothing if certain conditions are not met. It is also possible to check different conditions using `else if` clause before the final `else` catch-all.

```
if <conditions> then
   ...
   ...
end if

if <conditions> then
   ...
   ...
else
   ...
   ...
end if

if <conditions> then
   ...
   ...
else if <conditions> then
   ...
   ...
else
   ...
   ...
end if
```

Structure of Selection using IF

The below algorithm will take a whole number value, then shows whether that value is a positive number, negative number or zero.

```
1 show "Please enter a value: "
2 read A
3 if A>0 then
4    show "Positive"
5 else if A<0 then
6    show "Negative"
7 else
8    show "Zero"
9 end if
```

Algorithm 01-I Selection Example (2)

Sometimes, an `if-then` statement needs to evaluate multiple conditions. When multiple conditions are involved, `if-then` statement will evaluate each condition and apply the operators between those conditions. No matter how many conditions are involved, the selection part of `if-then` statement always evaluates to either *true* or *false*.

The most common operators between `if-then` conditions are AND and OR. AND operator will only evaluate as *true* if both conditions are *true*. OR operator will only evaluate as *false* if both conditions are *false*.

```
true   AND true  = true
true   AND false = false
false  AND true  = false
false  AND false = false

true   OR true   = true
true   OR false  = true
false  OR true   = true
false  OR false  = false
```

AND and OR Operators

Another common operator is NOT. This operator takes only 1 operand and will negate the value of its operand.

```
NOT true  = false
NOT false = true
```

NOT Operator

When multiple operators are involved, programming languages will evaluate the conditions based on the order of precedence: NOT, then AND, then OR. Grouping with brackets take higher precedence. Therefore, we can use brackets to design evaluation order of any complex conditions.

There are total of 7 logical operators. Most algorithms only need AND, OR and NOT. Operators XOR, NAND, NOR and XNOR are not frequently used. They are included here for completion.

Operand 1 (A)	Operand 2 (B)	NOT A	A AND B	A OR B	A XOR B	A NAND B	A NOR B	A XNOR B
T	T	F	T	T	F	F	F	T
T	F	F	F	T	T	T	F	F
F	T	T	F	T	T	T	F	F
F	F	T	F	F	F	T	T	T

Each structure of `if-then` statement is a building block of an algorithm. It can be combined with any other components, including more `if-then` statements in sequential or nested structures.

A different selection technique uses `switch-case` instead of `if-then` statement. Selection with `switch-case` structure evaluates the value of a variable instead of conditions.

```
switch <variable>
   case 1 : ...
   case 2 : ...
            ...
            ...
   case 3 : ...
            ...
   else   : ...
            ...
end switch
```

Structure of Selection using SWITCH-CASE

The below algorithm will take a whole number value, then shows the name of a two-dimensional shape with that many sides.

```
 1 show "Please enter the number of sides: "
 2 read A
 3 switch A
 4    case 3 : show "Triangle"
 5    case 4 : show "Rectangle"
 6    case 5 : show "Pentagon"
 7    case 6 : show "Hexagon"
 8    case 7 : show "Heptagon"
 9    case 8 : show "Octagon"
10    else :
11      if A>8 then
12         show "Polygon"
13      else
14         show "Not a valid two-dimensional shape"
15      end if
16 end switch
```

Algorithm 01-J Switch-Case Example

Line #3 starts the `switch-case` selection structure. Algorithm will then use the value of variable A and execute instructions based on it. Lines #4 to #9 cover some of the common two-dimensional shapes from triangle to octagon. Shapes with more than 8 sides are simplified as polygon in this example.

Value other than 3 or 4 or 5 or 6 or 7 or 8 cannot be assumed as greater than 8 because there is a possibility that user might put 0, 1, 2 or even negative number. Therefore, an `if-then` statement is needed inside the `else` block from this `switch-case` structure.

If line #11 evaluates as *true*, algorithm will execute line #12 because the number entered by user is greater than 8. There is no valid two-dimensional shape with less than 3 sides, this is covered by the else clause from line #14.

Iterations (Loops)

Iterations or *loops* are fundamental constructs in programming languages that enable the repetitive execution of a set of instructions. They play a crucial role in automating tasks, processing lists, and iterating arrays or other data structures. By using iterations, algorithms become more maintainable with the significant reduction of redundancies.

There are 3 basic techniques to do iterations:
- Iteration with `for-do`
- Iteration with `repeat-until`
- Iteration with `while-do`

Iteration with `for-do` uses a counter variable, start and end limits. Let us consider the bunny path from Algorithm 01-E. Instead of repeating the same instruction multiple times, iteration can help to simplify the algorithm.

```
1 for i=1 to 4 do
2   move down
3 end for
4 for i=1 to 4 do
5   move right
6 end for
```

Algorithm 01-K Rabbit Path Option 2 with Iteration

Using iteration simplifies the algorithm from requiring 8 lines in Algorithm 01-E into 6 lines in Algorithm 01-K. The benefit of using iteration becomes more evident when the required repetitive actions is greater.

If the bunny example is modified to have 8×8 board instead of 5×5, the bunny will need to do more moves before it can reach the carrot. Since the path of {R, R, R, R, R, R, R, D, D, D, D} is blocked by a rock, the only valid path is {D, D, D, D, D, D, D, R, R, R, R, R, R, R}. This would require an algorithm with 14 lines (and a grumpy software developer), or this can be solved using iteration with only 6 lines.

```
1 for i=1 to 7 do
2    move down
3 end for
4 for i=1 to 7 do
5    move right
6 end for
```

Algorithm 01-L Rabbit Path in Larger Board with Iteration

Algorithm 01-L is almost identical to Algorithm 01-K. The only difference is the number of repeats defined in the `for-do` statements. Even if the board for bunny problem is enlarged to 100x100 (with similar pattern of rocks blocking the middle area of the board), a path going from top left to bottom left, then going to bottom right will still require 6 lines.

```
for <var> = <start> to <end> do
   . . .
   . . .
   . . .
end for
```

Structure of Iteration using FOR-DO

The counter variable used in `for-do` statement is usually a variable with numeric data type (whole numbers). The `start` and `end` limits determine how many repetitions will happen. Direct values can be used for these limits, or it can be variables that hold values from other calculations. Some programming languages allow increasing or decreasing steps of the counting variable.

One of the most useful characteristics of iteration using `for-do` is the fact that the value of its counting variable will change during each cycle. This can be used as part of formula or other processes, including combining selections and iterations, or doing nested iterations.

```
1 for i=1 to 3 do
2    for j=7 to 8 do
3       show "The value of i = ",i," and j = ",j
4    end for
5 end for
```

Algorithm 01-M Nested Iteration with For-Do

Executing the above algorithm will produce the following results:

```
The value of i = 1 and j = 7
The value of i = 1 and j = 8
The value of i = 2 and j = 7
The value of i = 2 and j = 8
The value of i = 3 and j = 7
The value of i = 3 and j = 8
```

Iteration with `repeat-until` uses conditions instead of counter variable. During execution, instructions within a `repeat-until` structure are being repeated until the conditions evaluate as *true*.

```
repeat
  . . .
  . . .
  . . .
until <conditions>
```

Structure of Iteration using REPEAT-UNTIL

```
1 x=1
2 repeat
3   show "The value of x = ",x
4   x=x+5
5 until x>12
```

Algorithm 01-N Iteration with Repeat-Until

Executing the above algorithm will produce the following results:

```
The value of x = 1
The value of x = 6
The value of x = 11
```

In Algorithm 01-N, lines #3 and #4 are executed repeatedly until the value of x is greater than 12. This condition is only evaluated once per cycle, at the end of the cycle when line #5 is executed.

Steps of execution:
- In the first iteration, the value 1 is displayed, then x becomes 6.
- 6 is not greater than 12. Therefore, line #5 evaluates as *false*, the whole block is repeated.
- In the second iteration, the value 6 is displayed, then x becomes 11.

- 11 is not greater than 12. Therefore, line #5 evaluates as *false*, the whole block is repeated.
- In the third iteration, the value 11 is displayed, then x becomes 16.
- 16 is greater than 12. Therefore, line #5 evaluates as *true*, this ends the `repeat-until` iterations.

Iteration with `while-do` uses conditions evaluated at the beginning of each cycle. During execution, instructions within a `while-do` structure are being repeated as long as the conditions evaluate as *true*.

```
while <conditions> do
   . . .
   . . .
   . . .
end while
```

Structure of Iteration using WHILE-DO

```
1 y=2
2 while y<12 do
3    show "The value of y = ",y
4    y=y+5
5 end while
```

Algorithm 01-O Iteration with While-Do

Executing the above algorithm will produce the following results:

```
The value of y = 2
The value of y = 7
```

In Algorithm 01-O, lines #3 and #4 are executed repeatedly while the value of x is less than 12. This condition is only evaluated once per cycle, at the beginning of the cycle when line #2 is executed.

Steps of execution:
- Initial value of y is 2. It is less than 12. Therefore, line #2 evaluates as true, the first iteration begins.
- The value 2 is displayed, then x becomes 7.
- 7 is less than 12. Therefore, line #2 evaluates as *true*, the second iteration begins.
- The value 7 is displayed, then x becomes 12.
- 12 is not less than 12. Therefore, line #2 evaluates as *false*, this ends the `while-do` iterations.

It is important to note that there is a possibility that instructions inside a `while-do` structure are not executed at all. This can happen if the conditions evaluate as false right from beginning, causing total of 0 cycle. In contrast, instructions inside a `repeat-until` structure are executed at least once because the conditions are evaluated at the end of each iteration.

Modules and Parameters

Several lines of algorithm that work together to achieve one logical purpose can be grouped into *modules*. Creating modules help to manage complex system with several algorithms. If certain functions are used multiple times in an algorithm, it makes sense to put them as modules so that future changes to those functions do not need to be updated in multiple locations.

```
1 module myGreeting
2    show "Good morning"
3 end module
4
5 show "Hello, how are you?"
6 myGreeting
7 show "It is nice to meet you."
```

Algorithm 01-P Simple Module

Lines #1 to #3 define a module called *myGreeting*. Lines #5 to #7 are the main algorithm. Main algorithm can call any module that has been previously defined. In this example, line #6 instructs the computer to execute module *myGreeting*.

Executing the above algorithm will show the following results:

```
Hello, how are you?
Good morning.
It is nice to meet you.
```

Sometimes a module needs some input values to be processed. This can be achieved using the concept of *parameters*, also known as *arguments*. The ability to pass values into a module allows better code flexibility and reusability. Different inputs can trigger different calculations in algorithms. In a similar way, parameters allow software engineers to customise the behaviour of a module to process different data.

Parameters can come in various data types, from simple types that hold single value (byte, Boolean, char) to more complex data types (such as arrays or abstract data types). By passing values through parameters, a module becomes independent and self-contained. It is easier to control what values are passed as parameters during module call instead of always monitoring the values of global variables.

```
 1 module calculatePlus(P1,P2)
 2   Total=P1+P2
 3   show "The result is ",Total
 4 end module
 5
 6 show "Please enter the value of A : "
 7 read A
 8 show "Please enter the value of B : "
 9 read B
10 calculatePlus(A,B)
11 show "End"
```

Algorithm 01-Q Module with Parameters

Lines #1 to #4 define a module called *calculatePlus* which takes 2 parameters: P1 and P2. Lines #6 to #11 are the main algorithm. In this example, line #10 instructs the computer to execute module *calculatePlus* using the 2 parameters that has been previously assigned value by user.

Executing the above algorithm will show the following results:

```
Please enter the value of A : 7
Please enter the value of B : 5
The result is 12
End
```

When we pass a parameter *by value*, module caller sends some values into parameters, but those parameters will then be treated as local variables within the module. If the values of those parameters change during module execution, it will stay local without impact to the caller.

In the Algorithm 01-G above, line #10 does not send variables A and B to *calculatePlus*. Instead, it sends values 7 and 5 into the module. Whatever happens to P1 and P2 during module execution will have no impact to the caller.

Parameters can also be used to pass some values (module's outputs) back to the caller. This technique is called passing parameter *by reference*. It allows caller to tell a module the location of variables as parameters. Using the box analogy, it passes the location of boxes instead of the items inside. The module will then use whatever items (values) in the boxes (variables) during execution. If the calculation changes values of those variables, new items will be put into the boxes and the caller will be able to see what are in those boxes after module is executed.

```
 1 module calculateAdd(P1,P2,P3)
 2    P3=P1+P2
 3    show "The result is ",P3
 4 end module
 5
 6 show "Please enter the value of A : "
 7 read A
 8 show "Please enter the value of B : "
 9 read B
10 C=0
11 calculateAdd(A,B,C)
12 show "Value of C is ",C
13 show "Value of P3 is ",P3
14 show "End"
```

Algorithm 01-R Module with Pass-By-Value Parameters

Lines #1 to #4 define a module called *calculateAdd* which takes 3 parameters by value: P1, P2 and P3. Lines #6 to #14 are the main algorithm. In this example, line #11 instructs the computer to execute module *calculateAdd* using the 3 parameters. A and B received their values from user. C is assigned initial value of 0.

Executing the above algorithm will show the following results:

```
Please enter the value of A : 7
Please enter the value of B : 5
The result is 12
Value of C is 0
Value of P3 is #Error
End
```

Why the value of C stays 0 after module *calculateAdd* completed? Line #11 sends the value of 0 during module calling. Module then assigns the value of 0 into parameter P3 and treats it as local variable within the module. Any change to P3 is not reflected back to variable C because *calculateAdd* never knew this variable. Line #13 returns error because P3 does not exist in the main algorithm.

Programming languages have different ways to implement pass-by value and pass-by-reference. For the purpose of pseudocode in this book, symbol & before a parameter is used to indicate that the parameter is passed by reference.

```
 1 module calculateAddByRef(P1,P2,&P3)
 2   P3=P1+P2
 3   show "The result is ",P3
 4 end module
 5
 6 show "Please enter the value of A : "
 7 read A
 8 show "Please enter the value of B : "
 9 read B
10 C=0
11 calculateAddByRef(A,B,C)
12 show "Value of C is ",C
13 show "Value of P3 is ",P3
14 show "End"
```

Algorithm 01-S Module with Pass-By-Reference Parameters

Lines #1 to #4 define a module called *calculateAddByRef* which takes 3 parameters by value: P1, P2 and P3. Lines #6 to #14 are the main algorithm. In this example, line #11 instructs the computer to execute module *calculateAddByRef* using the 3 parameters. A and B received their values from user. C is assigned initial value of 0.

Executing the above algorithm will show the following results:

```
Please enter the value of A : 7
Please enter the value of B : 5
The result is 12
Value of C is 12
Value of P3 is #Error
End
```

The value of C is updated to 12 after module is completed. Since module *calculateAddByRef* takes parameter P3 by reference, line #11 sends location of variable C during module calling. Module then creates an alias P3 to represent C from caller based on its location. This P3 is treated as local variable within the module. However, updating value in this location will also update the value of C because they are located at the same memory location. Any change to P3 is reflected back to variable C. Line #13 returns error because P3 does not exist in the main algorithm.

Some modules can return values through their own names. Different programming languages have different implementation of this concept. In this book, if a module has local variable named `Result` in it, the value will be returned to the caller when module execution finishes.

```
 1 module calculateAddResult(P1,P2)
 2    result=P1+P2
 3    show "The result is ",result
 4 end module
 5
 6 show "Please enter the value of A : "
 7 read A
 8 show "Please enter the value of B : "
 9 read B
10 C=calculateAddResult(A,B)
11 show "Value of C is ",C
12 show "End"
```

Algorithm 01-T Module with Return Value

Lines #1 to #4 define a module called *calculateAddResult* which takes 2 parameters by value: P1 and P2. Lines #6 to #12 are the main algorithm. In this example, line #11 instructs the computer to execute module *calculateAddResult* using the 2 parameters. A and B received their values from user.

Executing the above algorithm will show the following results:

```
Please enter the value of A : 7
Please enter the value of B : 5
The result is 12
Value of C is 12
End
```

Since *calculateAddResult* has a local variable named `result` in it, at the completion of execution, the name of the module itself contains value from `Result`. Line #10 updates the value of C is updated to 12 from the return value in module name.

Are parameters the only method to communicate values between a module and its caller? It is possible to use A, B and C directly in both main algorithm and module. This approach is called using *global variables*.

```
 1 module calculateAddGlobal
 2    C=A+B
 3    show "The result is ",C
 4 end module
 5
 6 show "Please enter the value of A : "
 7 read A
 8 show "Please enter the value of B : "
 9 read B
10 C=0
11 calculateAddGlobal
12 show "Value of C is ",C
13 show "End"
```

Algorithm 01-U Module with Global Variables

Lines #1 to #4 define a module called *calculateAddGlobal* which uses global variables A, B and C instead of passing parameters. Lines #6 to #13 are the main algorithm. A and B received their values from user. C is assigned initial value of 0. In this example, line #11 instructs the computer to execute module *calculateAddGlobal* and directly uses A, B and C.

Executing the above algorithm will show the following results:

```
Please enter the value of A : 7
Please enter the value of B : 5
The result is 12
Value of C is 12
End
```

Since both the module and its caller uses the same global variables, the value of C is updated to 12 after module is completed. This approach is not recommended for most real-world implementations. Calling *calculateAddGlobal* from different parts of algorithm will create different results without an easy way to control its inputs. The module is no longer independent and cannot be implemented in other algorithms that have different use of variables A, B and C. This defeats the main purpose of creating modules in the first place.

Using local variables for each module is generally considered as best practice. It allows easier debugging in the event of issues because the values of variables within a module is contained.

Recursion

In a similar way that selections can be combined with iterations and an algorithm can have nested selections and nested iterations, a module can also call itself in a technique commonly referred to as *recursion*.

Recursion is based on the idea of breaking down a complex problem into smaller and more manageable sub-problems. A recursive module consists of two parts: a stopping state and a recursive path. The *stopping state* defines the simplest scenario in which the module can directly calculate a result without further recursion. In contrast, the *recursive path* defines how the module should call itself to process smaller instances of the problem, gradually moving towards the stopping state (also known as the *base case*). This process continues until the stopping state is reached, and then the module starts to combine the results from each recursive call to solve the original problem.

The below algorithms take a value from user, then calculates factorial of that input. To show a comparison between two techniques, Algorithm 01-V uses iteration to calculate the factorial while Algorithm 01-W uses recursion.

```
1 show "Please enter a positive number: "
2 read N
3 R=1
4 for i=2 to N do
5    R=R*i
6 end for
7 show "Factorial of ",N," is ",R
```

Algorithm 01-V Factorial with Iteration

```
 1 module Factorial(X)
 2    if X=1 then
 3       Result=1
 4    else
 5       Result=X*Factorial(X-1)
 6    end if
 7 end module
 8
 9 show "Please enter a positive number: "
10 read N
11 R=Factorial(N)
12 show "Factorial of ",N," is ",R
```

Algorithm 01-W Factorial with Recursion

Using iteration technique, an algorithm starts with initial value of 1 because factorial of 1 (1!) is 1 and the problem statement defines that this algorithm is intended to calculate factorial of positive number. Lines #4 to #6 perform iterations from 2 to N and multiply the last value of R with the counter variable. If N is 4, this will calculate $1\times2\times3\times4$, which is the correct formula for 4!.

Recursion technique uses mathematical formula of $N! = N \times (N-1)$. The $X=1$ in line #2 is the stopping state. It is the simplest scenario that the module can calculate without doing further recursion because $1! = 1$. Line #5 is the recursive path. If the module is called using value of X greater than 1, it needs to recursively call itself with smaller parameter value.

If user executes Algorithm 01-W and puts value of 4 into N, the following steps will happen during the recursion:
- First call of *Factorial*
    - $X = 4$
    - Line #2 evaluates as *false*
    - Result = $4 \times$ *Factorial*(3), this triggers another call
- Second call of *Factorial*
    - $X = 3$
    - Line #2 evaluates as *false*
    - Result = $3 \times$ *Factorial*(2), this triggers another call
- Third call of *Factorial*
    - $X = 2$
    - Line #2 evaluates as *false*
    - Result = $2 \times$ *Factorial*(1), this triggers another call

- Fourth call of *Factorial*
  - X = 1
  - Line #2 evaluates as *true*
  - Result = 1, this value is returned to the third call
- Return to third call
  - Result = 2 × 1 = 2, this value is returned to the second call
- Return to second call
  - Result = 3 × 2 = 6, this value is returned to the first call
- Return to first call
  - Result = 4 × 6 = 24, this value is returned to the initial caller
- Return to initial caller in the main algorithm:
  - R = *Factorial*(4) = 24

Recursion technique can be very useful to solve some types of problems, but it also carries the risk of infinite recursion if the stopping state is not properly defined. Careful consideration of when and how to do recursion is essential to harness its power effectively without causing issues.

02. ABSTRACT DATA TYPES

Abstract Data Type (ADT) is a fundamental concept in software development that allow algorithms to define certain data structures independently of their implementation details. These provide a high-level, abstract interface for organising and manipulating data, promoting modularity, encapsulation, and code reusability.

By defining a specific data model to encapsulate a concept, ADTs empower teams to work on different parts of a large solution independently. For instance, a team member responsible for implementing a stack data structure can work on performance optimisation while ensuring that the stack's interface remains consistent for other team members to use. This separation of concerns improves code readability, simplifies code maintenance and debugging, as changes to ADT implementation can be made without affecting the rest of the solution.

This chapter discusses 6 abstract data types: stack, queue, tree, binary tree, heap, and graph. Some of the concepts will be explored in more details in later parts of this book.

Stack

Stack is an abstract data type that represent a pile of data structured in a stack format. Imagine a pile of books stacked on a desk. When we need to retrieve a book, we need to start from the book at the top of the pile. When we add more books to the pile, we would add them to the top.

In computer programming, a stack has 3 basic operations:
- PUSH X (adding a new data with the value of X into the stack)
- POP (remove the top element from the stack and retrieve its value)
- EMPTY (clear the stack)

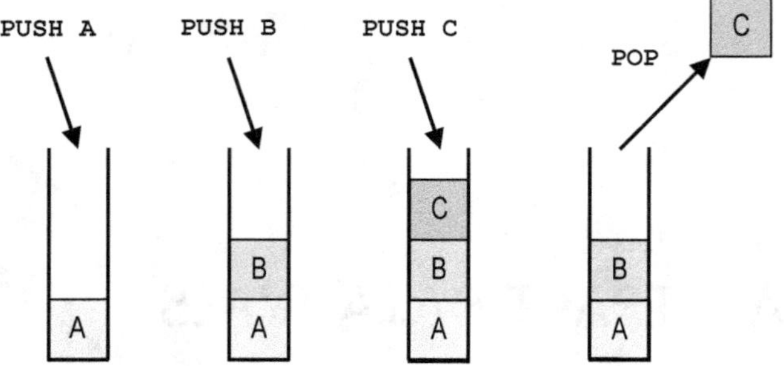

The above illustration shows value A being pushed into an empty stack. A is placed at the bottom of the stack because there is no existing element. When B is pushed into the same stack, it is placed on top of A. Similarly, pushing C puts it on top of B. Pop operation will remove the top element in the stack. In this particular example, it is element C.

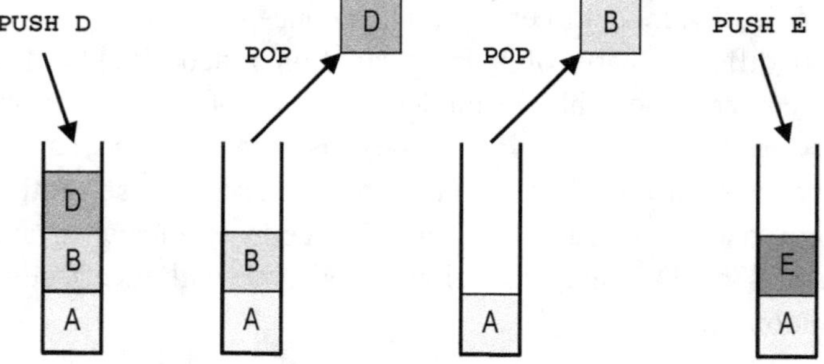

Continuing from the previous illustration, element D is pushed into the stack. Since C was already removed, D is placed on top of B. The next pop operation would remove D from the stack. If pop operation is executed one more time, element B would get removed. Only element A remains. Pushing new element E will put it on top of A.

Stack uses the principle of LIFO (Last In First Out) . The most recent element is the first element that will get removed with pop instruction. Depending on its implementation, stack can have unlimited number of elements, or an algorithm can specify the maximum capacity of a stack.

Queue

Queue is an abstract data type that represent a set of data structured in a queue format. Imagine the queue to buy tickets to a cinema. Visitors who arrive first get earlier positions in the queue and will be able to get their tickets before people who come later. When someone joins a queue, that person will have to join from the back end of the queue. Ticket officer will sell tickets to people in front of the queue.

In computer programming, a queue has 3 basic operations:
- PUSH X (adding a new data with the value of X into the queue)
- POP (remove the oldest element from the queue and retrieve its value)
- EMPTY (clear the queue)

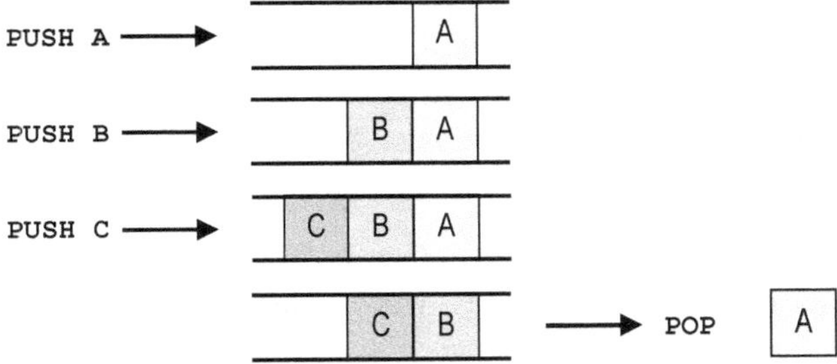

The above illustration shows value A being pushed into an empty queue. A is placed at the front of the queue because there is no existing element. When B is pushed into the same queue, it is placed behind A. Similarly, pushing C puts it behind B. Pop operation will remove the front element in the stack. In this example, it is element A. Note that after A is removed, B needs to move to the front of the queue (formerly A's position), and then C needs to move one step forward.

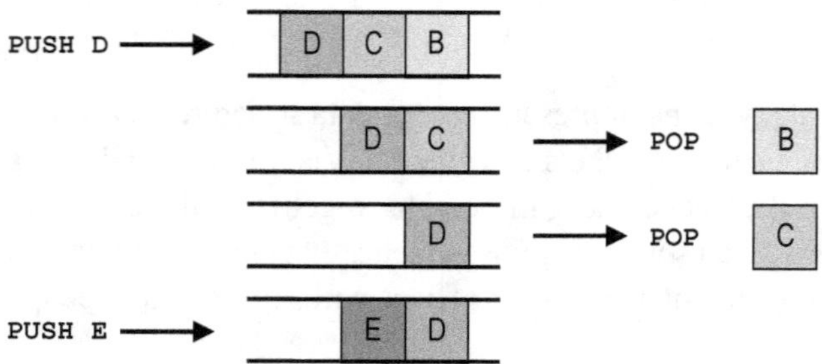

Continuing from the previous illustration, element D is pushed into the queue. It is placed at the back (end) of queue. The next pop operation would remove B from the queue. If pop operation is executed one more time, element C would get removed. Only element D remains. Pushing new element E will put it behind D.

Stack uses the principle of FIFO (First In First Out) . The oldest element in the queue is the first element that will get removed with pop instruction. Depending on its implementation, queue can have unlimited number of elements, or an algorithm can specify the maximum capacity of a queue.

Queue ADT can also implement priorities. Elements with normal priority values are treated as normal queue element. However, elements with higher priority gets moved faster. This is similar to the concept of check-in queue at the airport where there are lines for normal passengers and there are (faster) priority queue for first class passengers.

Comparing the example for stack and queue, the same instructions were sent to the ADTs: PUSH A, PUSH B, PUSH C, POP, PUSH D, POP, POP and PUSH E. From the 3 POP instructions, stack retrieves the values of C, D and B. Queue retrieves the values of A, B and C.

Tree

Tree is an abstract data type that represent nodes and edges in a hierarchical structure. The topmost node called *root* is the starting point of a tree. Each node except for root has exactly one parent node. Each node can have any number of child nodes. Nodes without child nodes under them are called *leaf* nodes.

Due to its nature, tree can be used to model various decision-making problems in algorithms. This makes tree one of the most popular ADTs. Because of its wide range of possible implementations, there are many operations to explore and manage a tree.

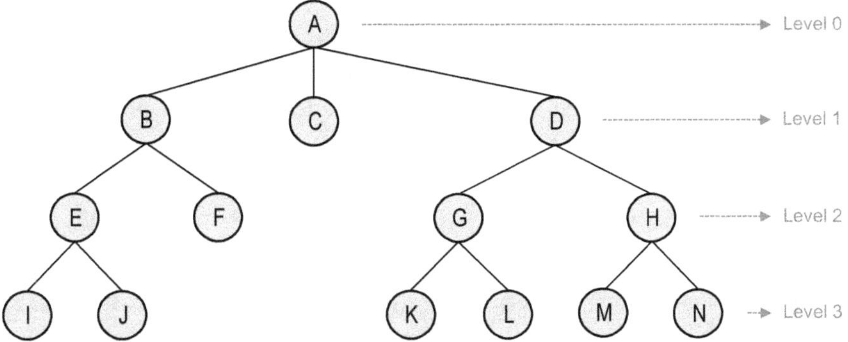

The above example of tree shows 14 nodes. Root node is A. Leaf nodes are I, J, K, L, M and N. Node levels represent the distance from a node to root. Root node is on level 0. All direct child nodes from root are said to be on level 1. The children of level 1 nodes are level 2 nodes, and so on.

When used in decision-making algorithm, the nodes of a tree could represent decision points while the edges connecting that node with its children represent the possible choices.

Binary Tree

Binary tree is a special type of tree with specific characteristics. In binary tree, each node has either 0 or 2 child nodes.

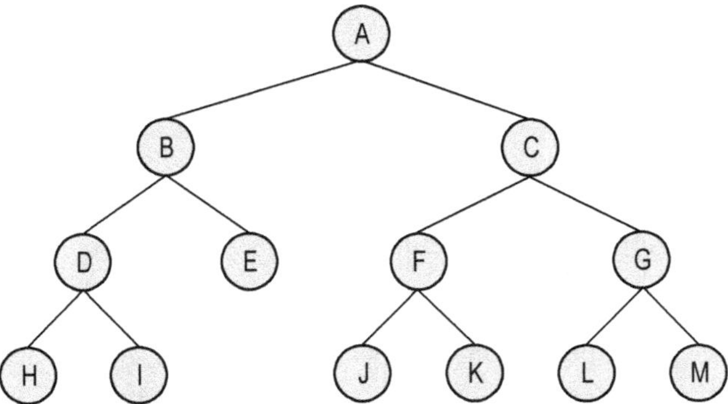

Because of these special characteristics, the maximum number of nodes in each level of binary tree can be calculated using a formula. If the level of root node is 0, the maximum number of nodes in level k is 2^k.

Some common implementations of binary tree include data storage, search algorithm and expression evaluation. Binary tree also serves as the foundation of more specific tree-based ADTs, such as heap and self-balancing binary search tree (also known as AVL).

Heap

Heap is a binary tree that meets some additional characteristics. In a heap, nodes with child nodes are called *internal nodes*. They are used to store values. Nodes without child nodes are called *external nodes*.

In computer programming, a heap has 3 basic operations:
- INSERT X (adding a new node with the value of X into the heap)
- REMOVE (remove the root node from heap, retrieve its value and then rearrange heap to meet the required characteristics)
- EMPTY (clear a heap)

There are two main forms of heap: minimum heap and maximum heap. In *minimum heap*, the value stored in a parent node is smaller than the values of its left child and right child. For *maximum heap*, the parent node's value is greater than the values of its two child nodes.

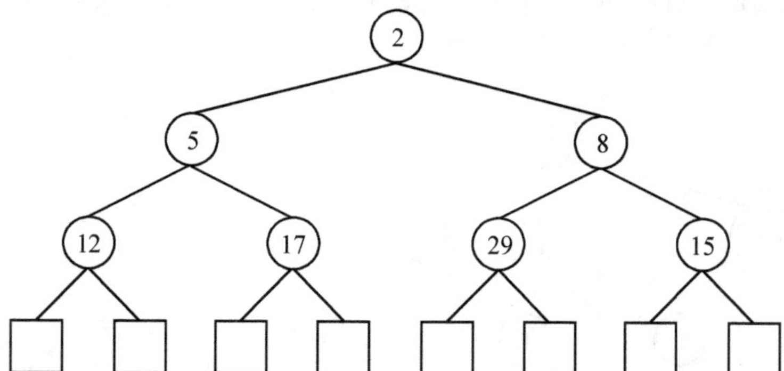

The above heap is an example of minimum heap. Internal nodes are represented with circles and external nodes are represented with squares. The value in each parent is always smaller than the values of its child nodes.

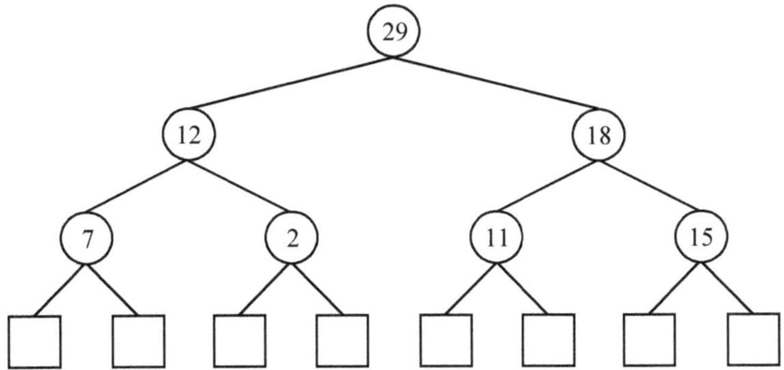

The above heap is an example of maximum heap. It carries the same characteristics as minimum heap except that value in each parent is always greater than the values of its child nodes.

Heaps are often used together with priority queue. Each internal node in a heap stores the priority value and some other data. The mechanism of heap will move the data following the characteristics of minimum or maximum heap, allowing the data with smallest or largest priority value to always be stored at the root of heap.

A detailed example of inserting and removing nodes from heap are discussed in chapter 03 as part of heap sort implementation.

Graph

A graph is an abstract data type with a set of nodes and edges. This ADT is commonly used to model relationships between objects or data. Depending on its implementation, graph ADT can be utilised to solve several complex problems such as route planning and network analysis.

An edge can connect a node with itself. This type of edge is called a *loop*.

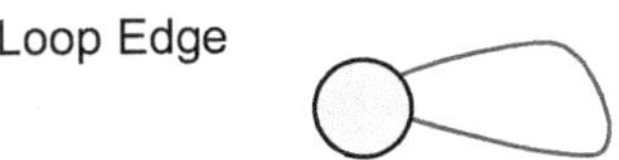

In *directed graph*, edges represent one-way connections from one node to another. Basic graph without edges showing one-way connection is known as *undirected graph*. It is possible for a graph to have a mix of plain edges and edges with specific directions.

Directed Graph

Undirected Graph

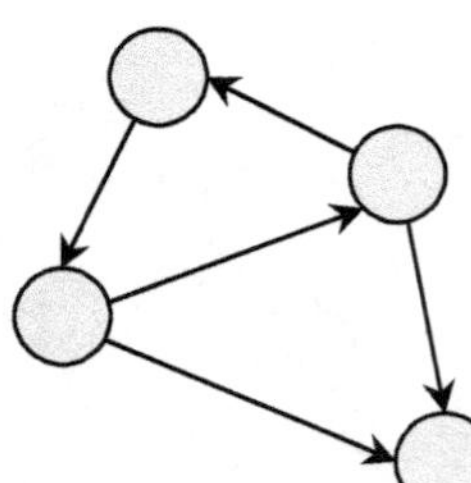

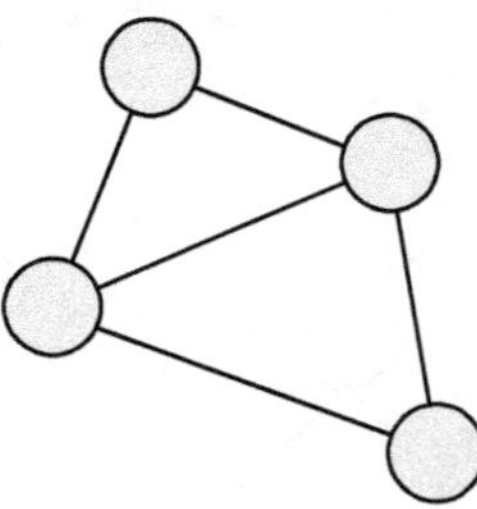

Further classification of graph differentiates between *weighted graph* (where each edge is associated with certain weight/cost) and *unweighted graph* (edges have no associated weight).

Weighted Graph

Unweighted Graph

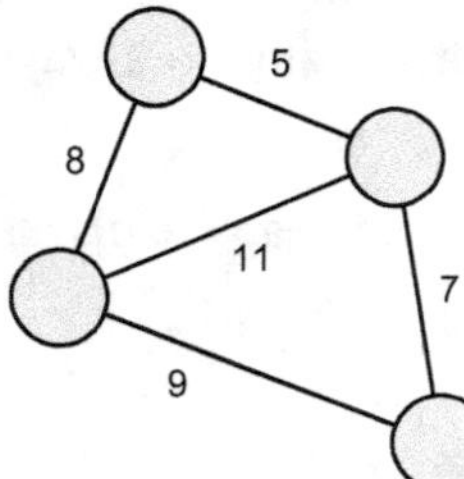

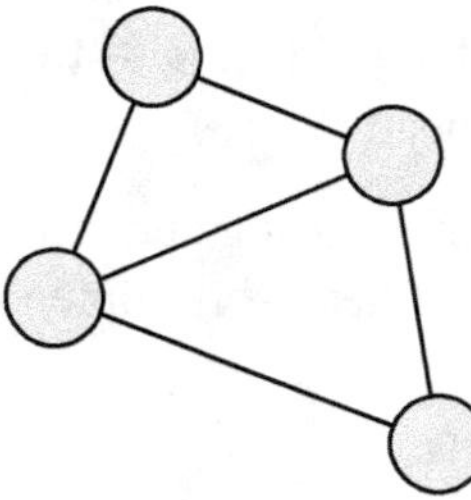

For an undirected graph, degree of a node is the number of edges connected to that node. Nodes in directed graph have two different degrees:

- *Out-degree* of node X is the number of edges with that node as the starting point.
- *In-degree* of node X is the number of edges with that node as the destination point.

A graph node is considered as *source node* if it has 0 in-degree and positive number of out-degree. Similarly, a *sink node* has no edge coming out of it (0 out-degree) and greater-than-zero in-degree.

One of the popular implementations of graph in algorithm uses adjacency matrix. Any two nodes with one or more edges connecting them are said to be adjacent. An *adjacency matrix* maps which nodes in a graph have edges between them. This matrix serves as a lookup table, where a value of non-zero represents an edge that exists. The rows and columns of the matrix model the nodes in the graph.

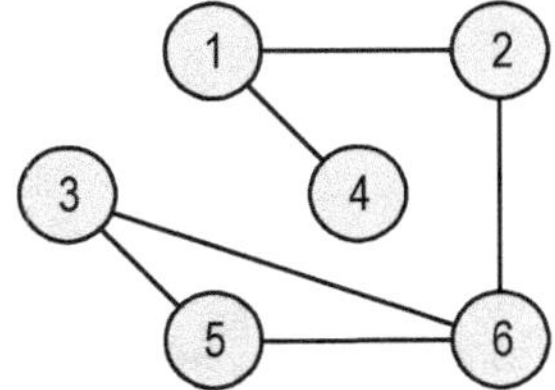

An adjacency list can be produced from the above graph:
- Node 1 does not have loop edge. Therefore, A[1,1]=0.
- Edge between nodes 1 and 2 exists. Therefore, A[1,2]=1.
- Edge between nodes 1 and 3 does not exist. Therefore, A[1,3]=0.
- Edge between nodes 1 and 4 exists. Therefore, A[1,4]=1.
- Edge between nodes 1 and 5 does not exist. Therefore, A[1,5]=0.
- Edge between nodes 1 and 6 does not exist. Therefore, A[1,6]=0.
- In undirected graph, adjacency lists between two nodes are reversible. Therefore A[2,1]=A[1,2].
  There is no need to list adjacency elements that can be obtained by swapping the pair of nodes.
- Node 2 does not have loop edge. Therefore, A[2,2]=0.
- Edge between nodes 2 and 3 does not exist. Therefore, A[2,3]=0.
- Edge between nodes 2 and 4 does not exist. Therefore, A[2,4]=0.
- Edge between nodes 2 and 5 does not exist. Therefore, A[2,5]=0.
- Edge between nodes 2 and 6 exists. Therefore, A[2,6]=1.
- Node 3 does not have loop edge. Therefore, A[3,3]=0.
- Edge between nodes 3 and 4 does not exist. Therefore, A[3,4]=0.
- Edge between nodes 3 and 5 exists. Therefore, A[3,5]=1.
- Edge between nodes 3 and 6 exists. Therefore, A[3,6]=1.
- Node 4 does not have loop edge. Therefore, A[4,4]=0.
- Edge between nodes 4 and 5 does not exist. Therefore, A[4,5]=0.
- Edge between nodes 4 and 6 does not exist. Therefore, A[4,6]=0.
- Node 5 does not have loop edge. Therefore, A[5,5]=0.
- Edge between nodes 5 and 6 exists. Therefore, A[5,6]=1.
- Node 6 does not have loop edge. Therefore, A[6,6]=0.

Adjacency matrix is created using the values from adjacency list.

A[1,1]	A[1,2]	A[1,3]	A[1,4]	A[1,5]	A[1,6]
A[2,1]	A[2,2]	A[2,3]	A[2,4]	A[2,5]	A[2,6]
A[3,1]	A[3,2]	A[3,3]	A[3,4]	A[3,5]	A[3,6]
A[4,1]	A[4,2]	A[4,3]	A[4,4]	A[4,5]	A[4,6]
A[5,1]	A[5,2]	A[5,3]	A[5,4]	A[5,5]	A[5,6]
A[6,1]	A[6,2]	A[6,3]	A[6,4]	A[6,5]	A[6,6]

It can be observed from the table that adjacency matrix is divided into 3 areas. The top-right triangle (darker colour) represents normal edges between nodes. The diagonal line from top-left to bottom-right (white background) represents loops. The bottom-left triangle (lighter colour) represents the other direction from the edges in top-right triangle. In undirected graph, this area will mirror the values from top-right triangle.

Undirected Graph

Adjacency Matrix

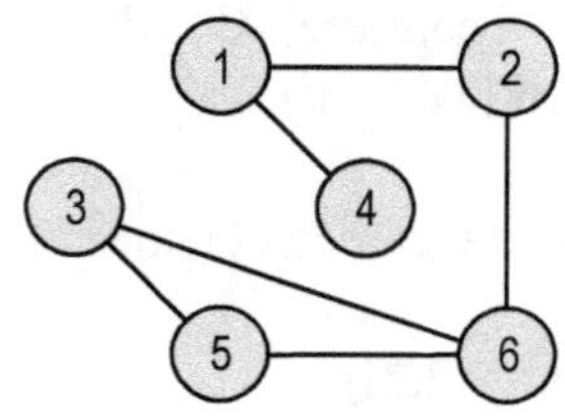

Directed Graph

Adjacency Matrix

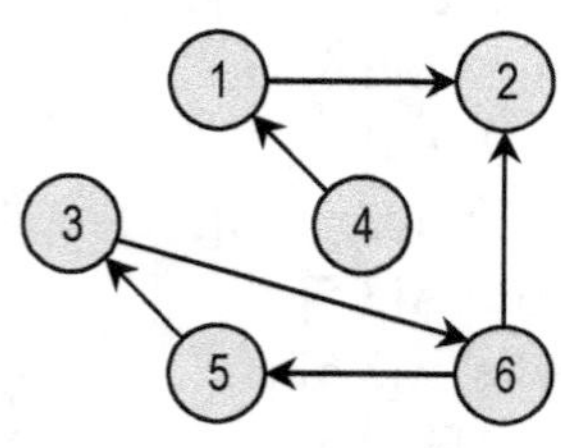

Directed-Undirected Mixed Graph

Adjacency Matrix

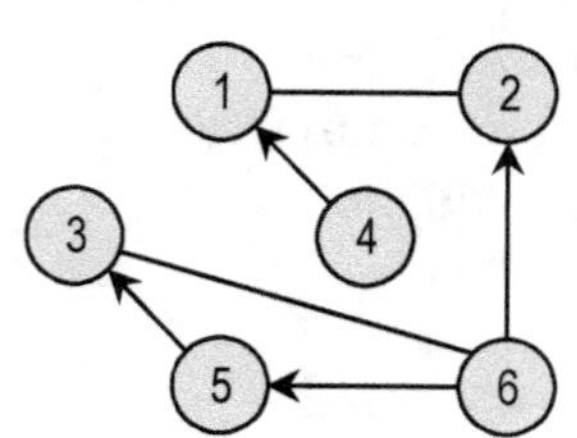

Mixed Graph with Loop

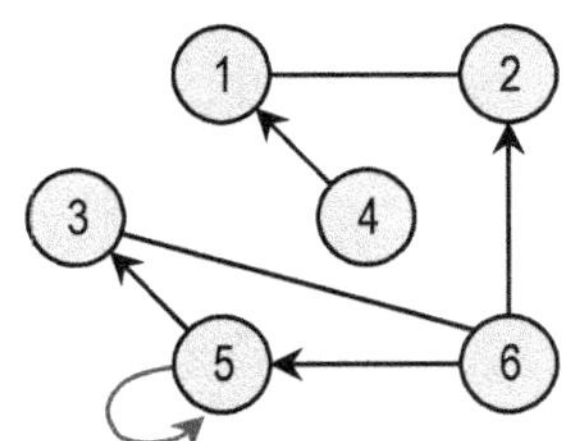

Adjacency Matrix

0	1	0	0	0	0
1	0	0	0	0	0
0	0	0	0	0	1
1	0	0	0	0	0
0	0	1	0	1	0
0	1	1	0	1	0

Weighted Graph

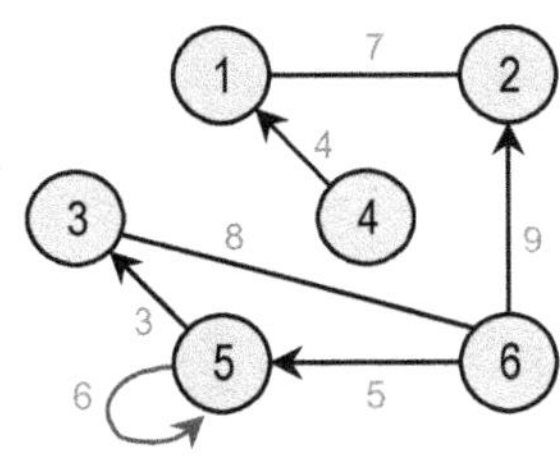

Adjacency Matrix

0	7	0	0	0	0
7	0	0	0	0	0
0	0	0	0	0	8
4	0	0	0	0	0
0	0	3	0	6	0
0	9	8	0	5	0

Weighted Graph

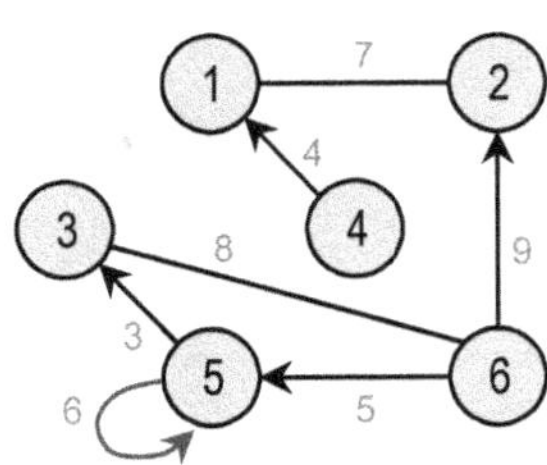

Cost Matrix

∞	7	∞	∞	∞	∞
7	∞	∞	∞	∞	∞
∞	∞	∞	∞	∞	8
4	∞	∞	∞	∞	∞
∞	∞	3	∞	6	∞
∞	9	8	∞	5	∞

Cost matrix uses the concept of distance instead of adjacency. In adjacency matrix, if there is no node between two nodes, it is said that the nodes are not adjacent, thus the cell value is zero. In cost matrix, if there is no edge between two nodes, it is said that the cost (or distance) between those nodes is infinite.

LEARNING ALGORITHMS

03. DIVIDE AND CONQUER

Divide-and-conquer is one of the popular topics to learn basic algorithm. As the name suggests, this technique focuses on solving a problem by breaking it down into multiple smaller pieces of sub-problems.

The division into smaller sub problems could happen repeatedly in a loop, or recursively, until it is no longer possible to break them down into anything smaller. After each unit of small sub-problems are solved, an algorithm will use the solutions to reconstruct a complete solution for the original problem.

Not all problems can be solved using divide-and-conquer. Two common examples of problems that can be solved using divide-and-conquer are sorting and searching.

Most modern programming languages already have built-in functions to perform sort and search functions. Why do we need to learn more about how they work? They serve very good purpose to illustrate basic algorithm in a way that is easy to understand.

As a reminder, for array with n elements, this book uses index 1 to n instead of 0 to $n-1$. Please read chapter 01 for refresher.

Selection Sort

Sorting algorithm has one purpose: to sort data. It could be in ascending order (from the smallest to the largest) or descending order (from the largest to the smallest). This book discusses ascending sort using different algorithms. Minor modifications can be applied to the algorithms to turn them into descending sort.

Selection sort is one of the easiest versions of sorting algorithm. It breaks the main problem (sort) into smaller sub-problems:
- Find the smallest value, put it in the right position.
- Find the second smallest value, put it in the right position.
- Find the third smallest value, put it in the right position.
- and so on.

Suppose we have a series of numeric values stored in array A. There are total n elements in array A.

```
1 for i=1 to n-1 do
2   minIndex=i
3   for j=i+1 to n do
4     if A[j]<A[minIndex] then
5       minIndex =j
6     end if
7   end for
8   swap(A[i],A[minIndex])
9 end for
```

Algorithm 03-A Selection Sort Algorithm

The basic principle of the algorithm is repeating the process of finding the ith smallest value during each iteration. First, the algorithm compares every value in the array and remember the location of the smallest value (`minIndex`). The smallest value will be swapped with whatever value originally located in element #1. Next, the algorithm ignores the first element because it already has the right value, and proceed with comparing every value from element #2 to element #n. This process is repeated until the element of $n-1$. After element #1 to element #$n-1$ are processed, the last element would always have the highest value.

Example:

Array A has 7 elements. The values of each element are shown below. Selection sort algorithm is used to sort the values in ascending order.

index	1	2	3	4	5	6	7
value	16	25	22	3	14	9	23

The first iteration (i=1) tries to find the smallest value. It starts with assumption that element #1 (`minIndex`) is where the smallest value is located. Then it creates another loop of j, comparing the value of element `minIndex` against values of elements #2 to #7. If smaller value is found, the location of the smallest value (`minIndex`) is updated. After comparing value 16 with 25, 22, 3, 14, 9 and 23, it was discovered that 3 is the smallest value, located in element #4. Therefore, the algorithm swaps the value in element #1 (i) with the value of element #4 (`minIndex`).

index	1	2	3	4	5	6	7
value	3	25	22	16	14	9	23

The second iteration (i=2) tries to find the second smallest value. It starts with assumption that element #2 (`minIndex`) is where the second smallest value is located. Then it creates another loop of j, comparing the value of element `minIndex` against values of elements #3 to #7. If smaller value is found, the location of the second smallest value (`minIndex`) is updated. After comparing value 25 with 22, 16, 14, 9 and 23, it was discovered that 9 is the second smallest value, located in element #6. Therefore, the algorithm swaps the value in element #2 (i) with the value of element #6 (`minIndex`).

index	1	2	3	4	5	6	7
value	3	9	22	16	14	25	23

The third iteration (i=3) tries to find the third smallest value. It starts with assumption that element #3 (`minIndex`) is where the third smallest value is located. Then it creates another loop of j, comparing the value of element `minIndex` against values of elements #4 to #7. If smaller value is found, the location of the second smallest value (`minIndex`) is updated. After comparing value 22 with 16, 14, 25 and 23, it was discovered that 14 is the third smallest value, located in element #5. Therefore, the algorithm swaps the value in element #3 (i) with the value of element #5 (`minIndex`).

index	1	2	3	4	5	6	7
value	3	9	14	16	22	25	23

The fourth iteration (i=4) tries to find the fourth smallest value. Using similar process, it was discovered that 16 is the fourth smallest value, located in element #4. Since the swap instruction does not check if i=`minIndex`, this algorithm will still perform the swap of value in element #4 (i) with the value of element #4 (`minIndex`). No change happens, but computing calculation was spent.

index	1	2	3	4	5	6	7
value	3	9	14	16	22	25	23

The fifth iteration (`i=5`) tries to find the fifth smallest value. Using similar process, it was discovered that 22 is the fifth smallest value, located in element #5. This algorithm will still perform the swap of value in element #5 (`i`) with the value of element #5 (`minIndex`).

index	1	2	3	4	5	6	7
value	3	9	14	16	22	25	23

The sixth iteration (`i=6`) tries to find the sixth smallest value. Using similar process, it was discovered that 23 is the sixth smallest value, located in element #7. Therefore, the algorithm swaps the value in element #6 (`i`) with the value of element #7 (`minIndex`).

index	1	2	3	4	5	6	7
value	3	9	14	16	22	23	25

Note that there is no need to perform the seventh iteration because the last remaining value (the seventh smallest value) is the highest value.

index	1	2	3	4	5	6	7
value	3	9	14	16	22	23	25

The algorithm name (selection sort) comes from the fact that the algorithm works by selecting the smallest value and putting it in the right location. This technique is classified as divide-and-conquer because it divides the problem of sorting array with n elements into smaller arrays with n−1 elements.

Insertion Sort

Insertion sort is another technique to sort data. Like selection sort, this algorithm takes an array A with n elements, then sort the values in ascending order (from smallest to largest). Minor modification is required to handle sort with descending order.

As the name suggests, this algorithm inserts a value to the right position during its iterations. For every iteration, the algorithm will insert a value to the correct location by comparing it to other values to the left side.

```
1 for i=2 to n do
2    valueInsert=A[i]
3    j=i
4    while (j>1) and (A[j-1]>valueInsert) do
5       A[j]=A[j-1]
6       j=j-1
7    end while
8    A[j]=valueInsert
9 end for
```

Algorithm 03-B Insertion Sort Algorithm

Example:

Array A has 7 elements. The values of each element are shown below. Insertion sort algorithm is used to sort the values in ascending order.

index	1	2	3	4	5	6	7
value	16	25	22	3	14	9	23

The first iteration ($i=2$) checks the value in element #2. The value (25) is stored in `valueInsert` variable. Next, the algorithm will check from the position to the left to insert the value (25) to the correct location. Since the value in element #1 (16) is already smaller than 25, no insertion is executed.

index	1	2	3	4	5	6	7
value	16	25	22	3	14	9	23

The second iteration ($i=3$) checks the value in element #3. The value (22) is stored in `valueInsert` variable. Next, the algorithm will check from the position to the left to insert the value (25) to the correct location.

- Value 25 is greater than 22, so it gets copied into element #3.
- Value 16 is smaller than 22, so it does not get copied.
- Instead, value 22 from `valueInsert` variable is copied to element #2.

index	1	2	3	4	5	6	7		valueInsert
values	16	25	22	3	14	9	23		22
	16	25	25	3	14	9	23		22
	16	22	25	3	14	9	23		22

The third iteration ($i=4$) checks the value in element #4. The value (3) is stored in `valueInsert` variable. Next, the algorithm will check from the position to the left to insert the value (3) to the correct location.

- Value 25 is greater than 3, so it gets copied into element #4.

- Value 22 is greater than 3, so it gets copied into element #3.
- Value 16 is greater than 3, so it gets copied into element #2.
- At last, value 3 from `valueInsert` variable is copied to element #1.

index	1	2	3	4	5	6	7	valueInsert
values	16	22	25	3	14	9	23	3
	16	22	25	25	14	9	23	3
	16	22	22	25	14	9	23	3
	16	16	22	25	14	9	23	3
	3	16	22	25	14	9	23	3

The fourth iteration (`i=5`) checks the value in element #5. The value (14) is stored in `valueInsert` variable. Next, the algorithm will check from the position to the left to insert the value (14) to the correct location.

- Value 25 is greater than 14, so it gets copied into element #5.
- Value 22 is greater than 14, so it gets copied into element #4.
- Value 16 is greater than 14, so it gets copied into element #3.
- Value 3 is smaller than 14, so it does not get copied.
- Instead, value 14 from `valueInsert` variable is copied to element #2.

index	1	2	3	4	5	6	7	valueInsert
values	3	16	22	25	14	9	23	14
	3	16	22	25	25	9	23	14
	3	16	22	22	25	9	23	14
	3	16	16	22	25	9	23	14
	3	14	16	22	25	9	23	14

The fifth iteration (`i=6`) checks the value in element #6. The value (9) is stored in `valueInsert` variable. Next, the algorithm will check from the position to the left to insert the value (9) to the correct location.

- Value 25 is greater than 9, so it gets copied into element #6.
- Value 22 is greater than 9, so it gets copied into element #5.
- Value 16 is greater than 9, so it gets copied into element #4.
- Value 14 is greater than 9, so it gets copied into element #3.
- Value 3 is greater than 9, so it does not get copied.
- Instead, value 9 from `valueInsert` variable is copied to element #2.

index	1	2	3	4	5	6	7	valueInsert
values	3	14	16	22	25	9	23	9
	3	14	16	22	25	25	23	9
	3	14	16	22	22	25	23	9
	3	14	16	16	22	25	23	9
	3	14	14	16	22	25	23	9
	3	9	14	16	22	25	23	9

The sixth iteration (i=7) checks the value in element #7. The value (23) is stored in valueInsert variable. Next, the algorithm will check from the position to the left to insert the value (23) to the correct location.

- Value 25 is greater than 23, so it gets copied into element #7.
- Value 22 is smaller than 23, so it does not get copied.
- Instead, value 23 from valueInsert variable is copied to element #6.

index	1	2	3	4	5	6	7	valueInsert
values	3	9	14	16	22	25	23	23
	3	9	14	16	22	25	25	23
	3	9	14	16	22	23	25	23

After all values have been inserted to the correct locations, the array would already have sorted values.

index	1	2	3	4	5	6	7
value	3	9	14	16	22	23	25

Insertion sort algorithm is classified as divide-and-conquer because it divides the problem of sorting into several sub-problems, namely shorter array. The sub-solutions from the sub-problems build the overall solution to the main problem.

Bubble Sort

Bubble sort takes inspiration from bubbles. It does not select nor insert values. Instead, bubble sort achieves the sorting end goal by bubbling up values. Every value is treated as bubble, which will go up to float above anything "heavier".

This algorithm takes an array A with n elements, then sort the values in ascending order (from smallest to largest). Minor modification is required to handle sort with descending order.

```
1 for i=2 to n-1 do
2    for j=n to i-1 do
3       if A[j-1]>A[j] then
4          swap(A[j-1],A[j])
5       end if
6    end for
7 end for
```

Algorithm 03-C Bubble Sort Algorithm

Example:

Array A has 7 elements. The values of each element are shown below. Bubble sort algorithm is used to sort the values in ascending order.

index	1	2	3	4	5	6	7
value	16	25	22	3	14	9	23

The first iteration ($i=1$) aims to bubble the smallest value to element #1. It starts by comparing each pair of values from the last element, down to the first element.

Compare 9 with 23. 14 is smaller, no swap is required.

index	1	2	3	4	5	6	7
value	16	25	22	3	14	9	23

Compare 14 with 9. 14 is greater, swap the values.

index	1	2	3	4	5	6	7
value	16	25	22	3	14	9	23
	16	25	22	3	9	14	23

Compare 3 with 9. 3 is smaller, no swap is required.

index	1	2	3	4	5	6	7
value	16	25	22	3	9	14	23

Compare 22 with 3. 22 is greater, swap the values.

index	1	2	3	4	5	6	7
value	16	25	22	3	9	14	23
	16	25	3	22	9	14	23

Compare 25 with 3. 25 is greater, swap the values. We can start to observe that value 3 is being "bubbled up" to the left.

index	1	2	3	4	5	6	7
value	16	**25**	**3**	22	9	14	23
	16	**3**	**25**	22	9	14	23

Compare 16 with 3. 16 is greater, swap the values.

index	1	2	3	4	5	6	7
value	**16**	**3**	25	22	9	14	23
	3	**16**	25	22	9	14	23

This marks the end of first iteration. Value 3 was bubbled up from element #4 to element #1.

index	1	2	3	4	5	6	7
value	**3**	16	25	22	9	14	23

The second iteration ($i=2$) aims to bubble the second smallest value to element #2. It starts by comparing each pair of values from the last element, down to the second element.

Compare 14 with 23. 14 is smaller, no swap is required.

index	1	2	3	4	5	6	7
value	**3**	16	25	22	9	**14**	**23**

Compare 9 with 14. 9 is smaller, no swap is required.

index	1	2	3	4	5	6	7
value	**3**	16	25	22	**9**	**14**	23

Compare 22 with 9. 22 is greater, swap the values.

index	1	2	3	4	5	6	7
value	**3**	16	25	**22**	**9**	14	23
	3	16	25	**9**	**22**	14	23

Compare 25 with 9. 25 is greater, swap the values.

index	1	2	3	4	5	6	7
value	**3**	16	**25**	**9**	22	14	23
	3	16	**9**	**25**	22	14	23

Compare 16 with 9. 16 is greater, swap the values.

index	1	2	3	4	5	6	7
value	3	16	9	25	22	14	23
	3	9	16	25	22	14	23

This marks the end of second iteration. Value 9 was bubbled up from element #5 to element #2.

index	1	2	3	4	5	6	7
value	3	9	16	25	22	14	23

The third iteration ($i=3$) aims to bubble the third smallest value to element #3. It starts by comparing each pair of values from the last element, down to the third element.

Compare 14 with 23. 14 is smaller, no swap is required.

index	1	2	3	4	5	6	7
value	3	9	16	25	22	14	23

Compare 22 with 14. 22 is greater, swap the values.

index	1	2	3	4	5	6	7
value	3	9	16	25	22	14	23
	3	9	16	25	14	22	23

Compare 25 with 14. 25 is greater, swap the values.

index	1	2	3	4	5	6	7
value	3	9	16	25	14	22	23
	3	9	16	14	25	22	23

Compare 16 with 14. 16 is greater, swap the values.

index	1	2	3	4	5	6	7
value	3	9	16	14	25	22	23
	3	9	14	16	25	22	23

This marks the end of third iteration. Value 14 was bubbled up from element #6 to element #3.

index	1	2	3	4	5	6	7
value	3	9	14	16	25	22	23

The fourth iteration ($i=4$) aims to bubble the fourth smallest value to element #4. It starts by comparing each pair of values from the last element, down to the fourth element.

Compare 22 with 23. 22 is smaller, no swap is required.

index	1	2	3	4	5	6	7
value	3	9	14	16	25	22	23

Compare 25 with 22. 25 is greater, swap the values.

index	1	2	3	4	5	6	7
value	3	9	14	16	25	22	23
	3	9	14	16	22	25	23

Compare 16 with 22. 16 is smaller, no swap is required.

index	1	2	3	4	5	6	7
value	3	9	14	16	22	25	23

This marks the end of fourth iteration. Value 16 was already in the right position. However, note that value 23 and 25 are swapped as part of the process.

index	1	2	3	4	5	6	7
value	3	9	14	16	22	25	23

The fifth iteration ($i=5$) aims to bubble the fifth smallest value to element #5. It starts by comparing each pair of values from the last element, down to the fifth element.

Compare 25 with 23. 25 is greater, swap the values.

index	1	2	3	4	5	6	7
value	3	9	14	16	22	25	23
	3	9	14	16	22	23	25

Compare 22 with 23. 22 is smaller, no swap is required.

index	1	2	3	4	5	6	7
value	3	9	14	16	22	23	25

This marks the end of fifth iteration. Value 22 was already in the right position.

index	1	2	3	4	5	6	7
value	3	9	14	16	22	23	25

The sixth iteration ($i=6$) aims to bubble the sixth smallest value to element #6. It starts by comparing each pair of values from the last element, down to the sixth element.

Compare 23 with 25. 23 is smaller, no swap is required.

index	1	2	3	4	5	6	7
value	3	9	14	16	22	23	25

This marks the end of sixth iteration. Value 23 was already in the right position. The sixth iteration is also the final iteration because the last remaining value (25) can be concluded as the highest value.

index	1	2	3	4	5	6	7
value	3	9	14	16	22	23	25

Heap Sort

Heap sort is a special type of sorting technique using the unique characteristics of heap. As refresher, a heap is a tree-shaped data structure that meets the criteria of a *binary tree*; has internal nodes and external nodes; every internal node contains value; every value is either bigger or smaller than every node under it depending on the heap type. In *minimum heap*, the value in root node is always the smallest value of all the nodes under it.

Discussion of heap sort in this chapter assumes that the following functions are available for use:

- `insertNode(H,k)`, this is a function to insert a new internal node with the value of `k` into heap `H`.
- `removeNode(H)`, this is a function to remove the root node from heap `H` and recalculate the remaining nodes to maintain special characteristics of heap.

Sorting an array with `n` elements using heap sort is as simple as using `insertNode(H,k)` function n times to create heap `H`, followed by executing `removeNode(H)` function n times.

```
1 for i=1 to n do
2   insertNode(H,A[i])
3 end for
4 for i=1 to n do
5   A[i]=removeNode(H)
6 end for
```

Algorithm 03-D Heap Sort Algorithm

Example:

Array A has 7 elements. The values of each element are shown below. Heap sort algorithm is used to sort the values in ascending order.

index	1	2	3	4	5	6	7
value	16	25	22	3	14	9	23

The first loop adds each value from array A into heap H. Since the heap is empty, the first execution of `insertNode` function simply creates one internal node and two external nodes.

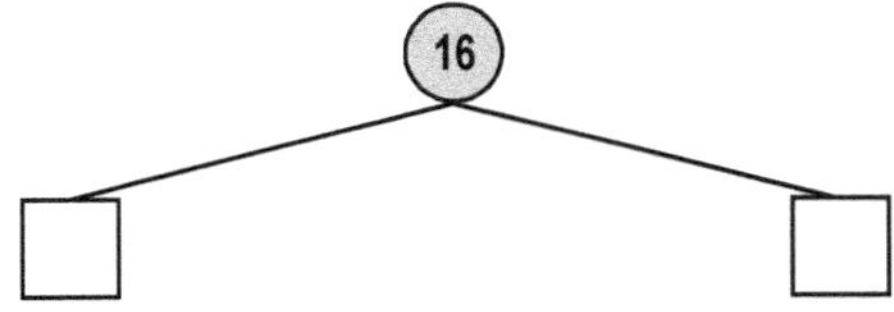

Next, adding value 25 into the heap will create new nodes. Since 25 is less than 16, no *upheap* is required.

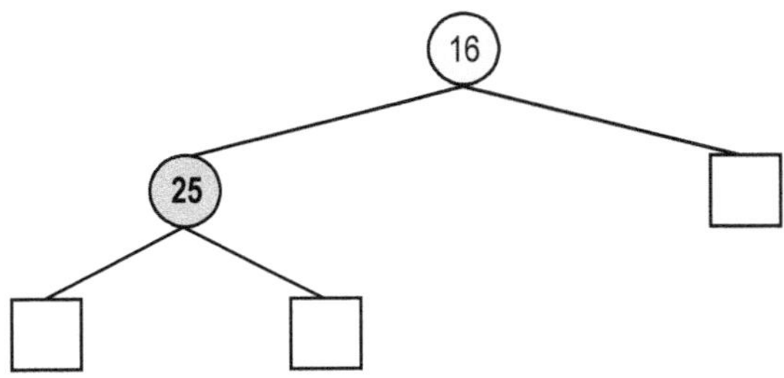

Adding 22 into heap H is another straightforward step because 16 is less than 22.

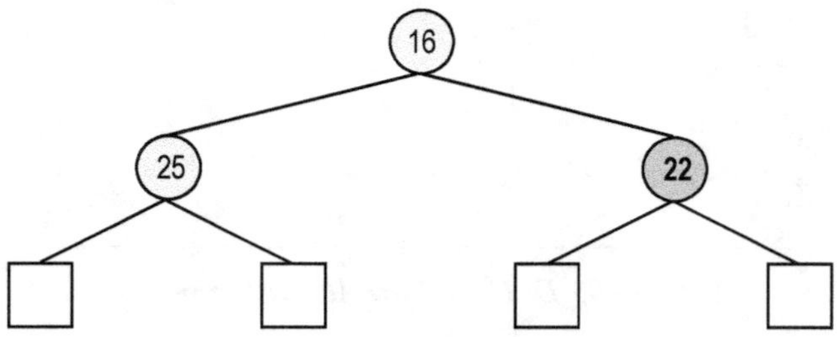

Executing `insertNode(H,3)` inserts internal node with value 3 under node 25. This violates minimum heap characteristics.

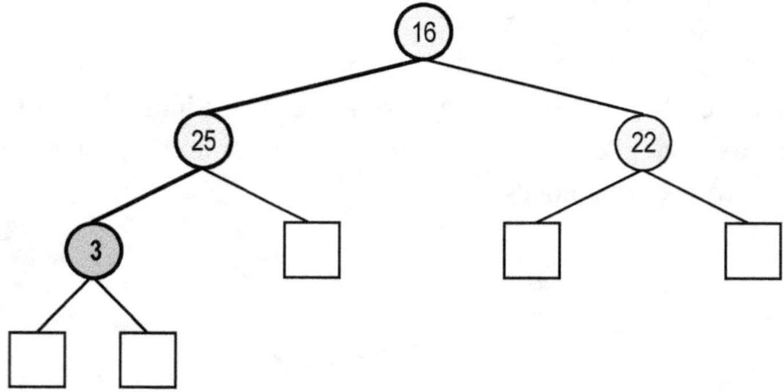

To restore minimum heap characteristics, *upheap* process is required to bring the internal node 3 up until all nodes under it has larger values.

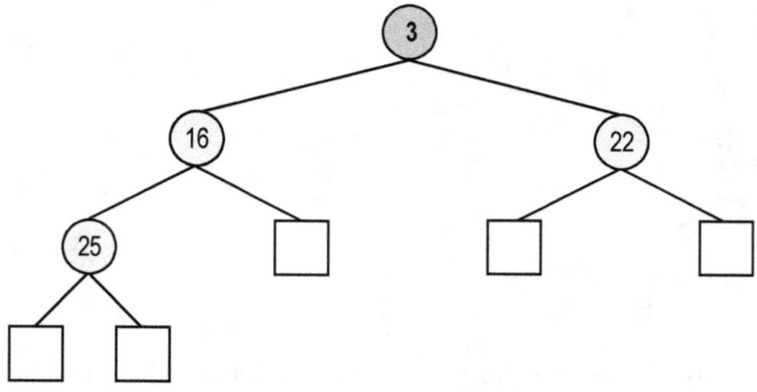

Executing `insertNode(H,14)` inserts internal node with value 14 under node 16. Again, this violates minimum heap characteristics.

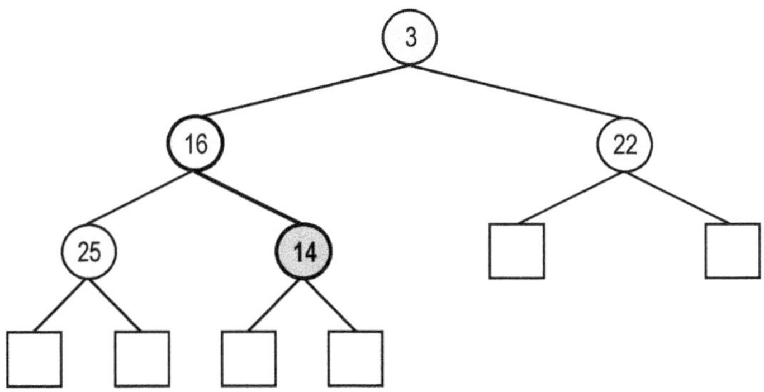

Using *upheap* process, node 14 is repositioned.

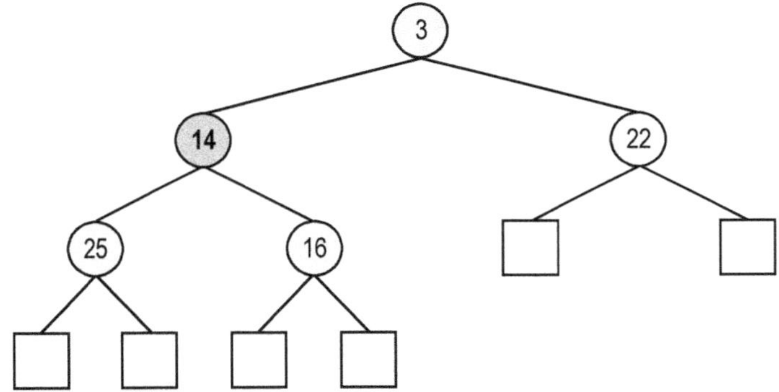

Executing `insertNode(H, 9)` inserts internal node with value 9 under node 22. This violates minimum heap characteristics because 22 is greater than 9.

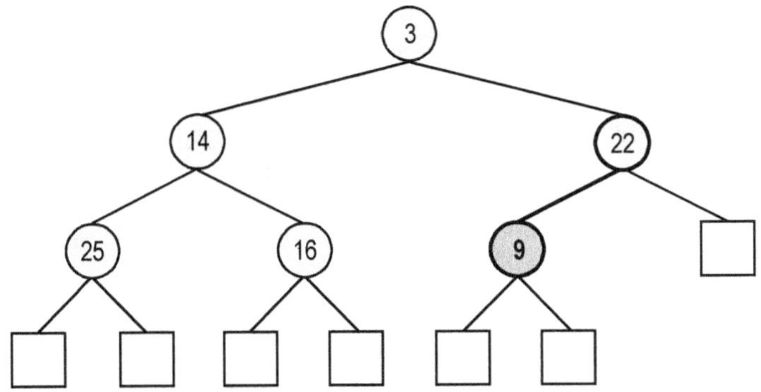

Using *upheap* process, node 9 is repositioned.

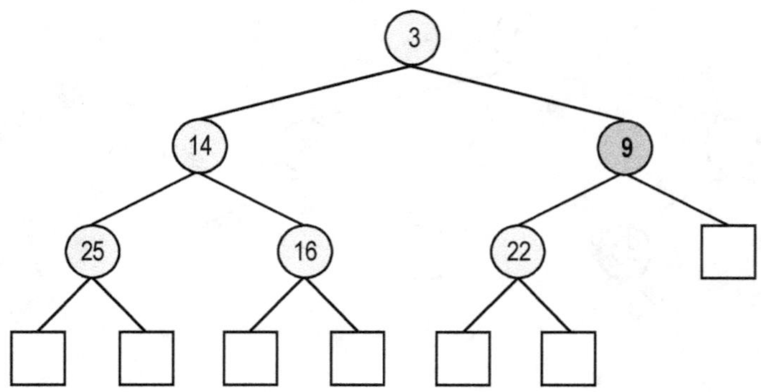

Finally, the last element of array `A` is added to heap `H` using `insertNode(H,23)` inserts internal node 23 under node 9. Since 9 is less than 23, no *upheap* is required. This concludes the creation of heap `H`.

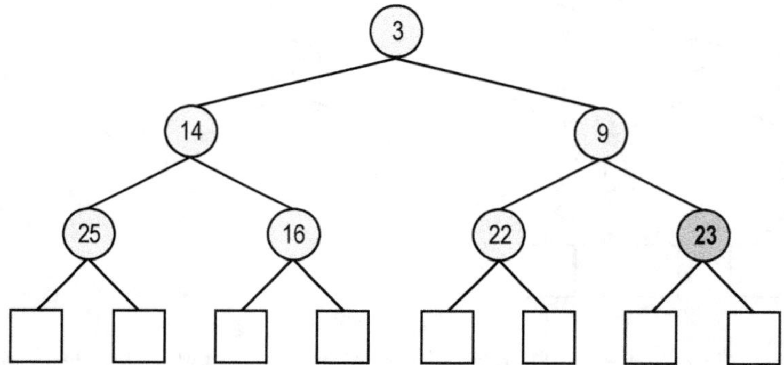

After heap `H` is created, the second loop of heap sort algorithm is executing `removeNode` function `n` times. There are different theories about reconstructing minimum heap after root removal. This book uses the technique that replaces the root node with the <u>right most node at the bottom level</u>, then performs node reposition to uphold minimum heap rule.

After node 3 (root) was removed, node 23 becomes the new root because 23 was the right most node at the bottom level.

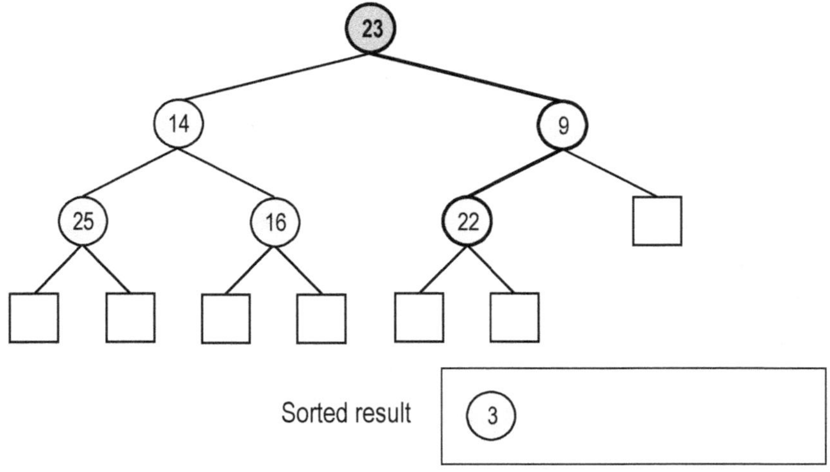

Having 23 as the new root violates the rule of minimum heap. *Downheap* swap is required. 23 needs to be swapped with the smaller value from its two child nodes, which is node 9. Then having node 23 as the parent of node 22 also violates minimum heap rule. Therefore, *downheap* swap is needed between node 23 and 22.

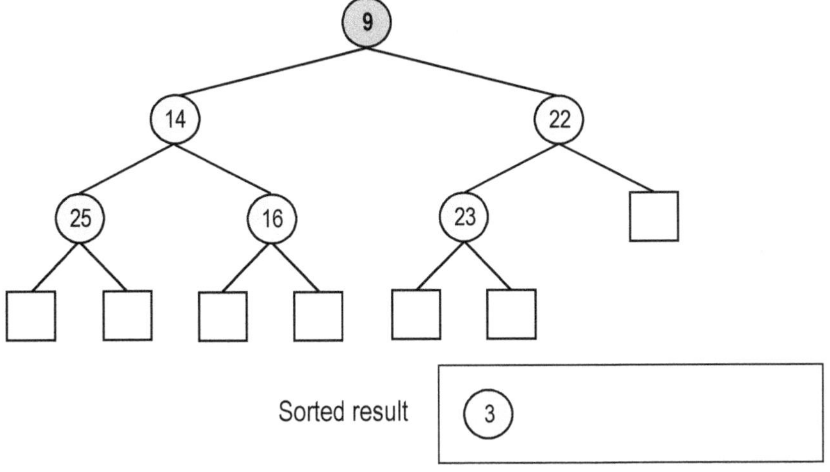

Next execution of `removeNode` function removes node 9, resulting in node 23 becomes the new root once again.

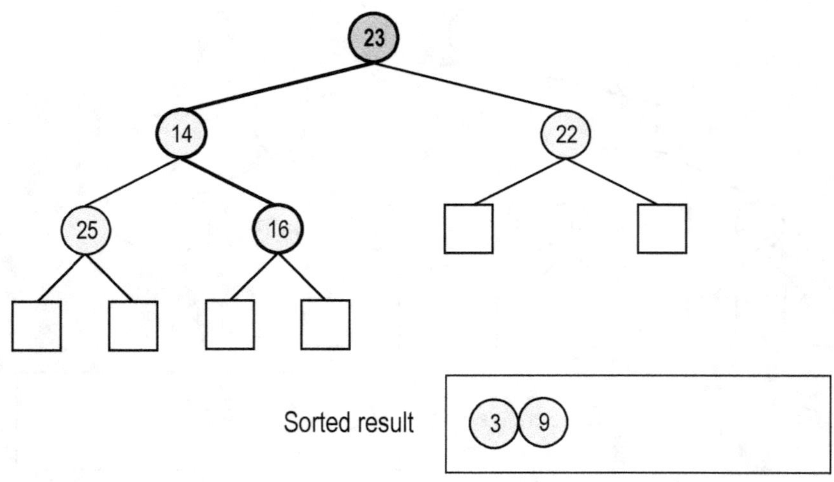

Having 23 as the new root violates the rule of minimum heap. *Downheap* swap is required. 23 needs to be swapped with the smaller value from its two child nodes, which is node 14. Then having node 23 as the parent of node 16 also violates minimum heap rule. Therefore, *downheap* swap is needed between node 23 and 16.

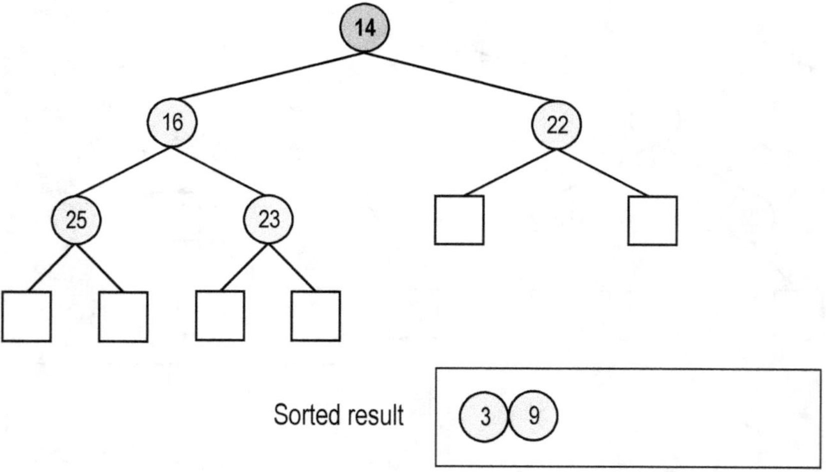

Next execution of `removeNode` function removes node 14, resulting in node 23 becomes the new root because it is the right most node at the bottom level again.

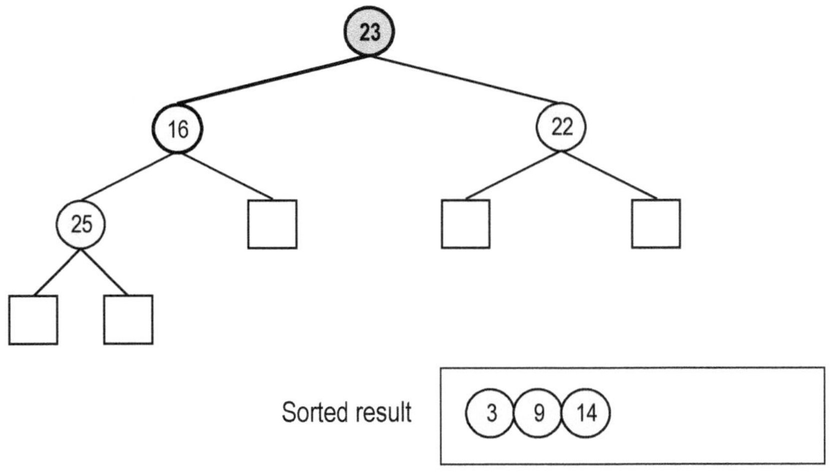

Having 23 as root node violates the rule of minimum heap. *Downheap* swap is required. 23 needs to be swapped with the smaller value from its two child nodes, which is node 16.

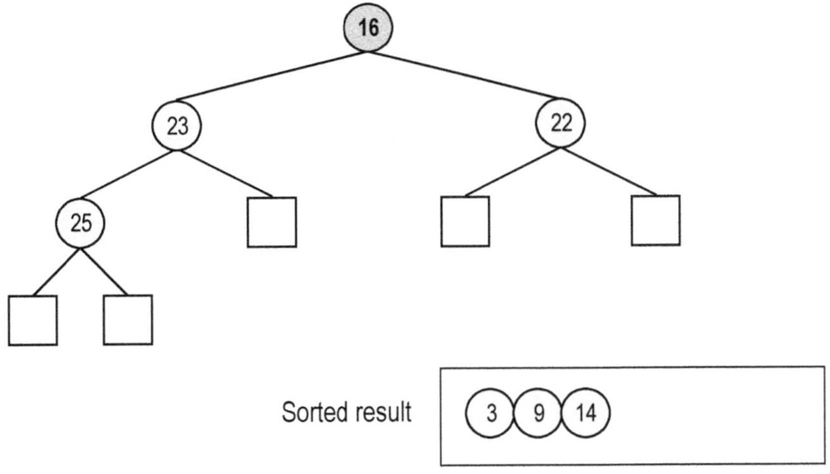

Next execution of `removeNode` function removes node 16, resulting in node 25 becomes the new root.

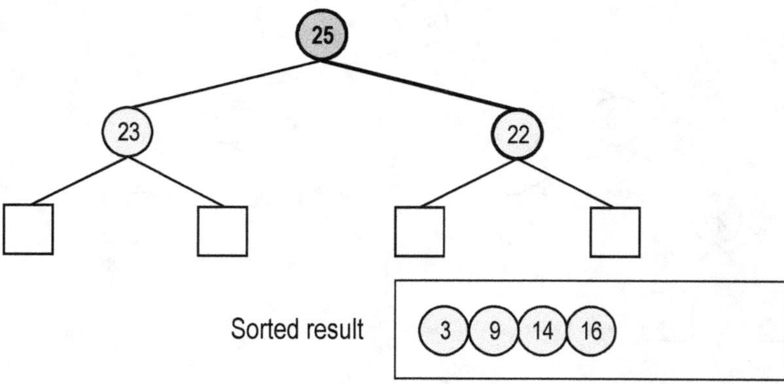

Another *downheap* process is needed to swap node 25 and 22.

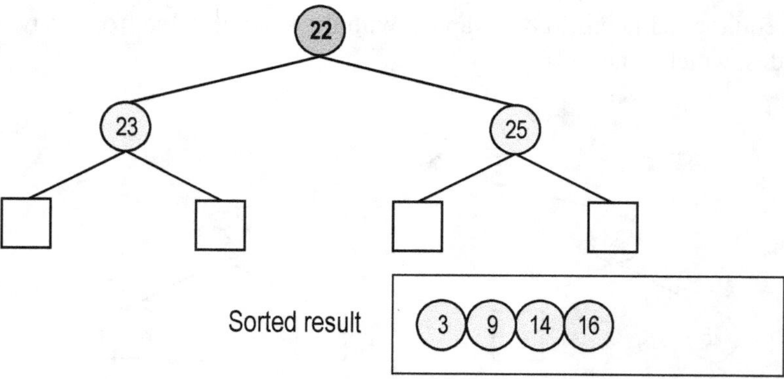

Next execution of `removeNode` function removes node 22, resulting in node 25 becomes the new root.

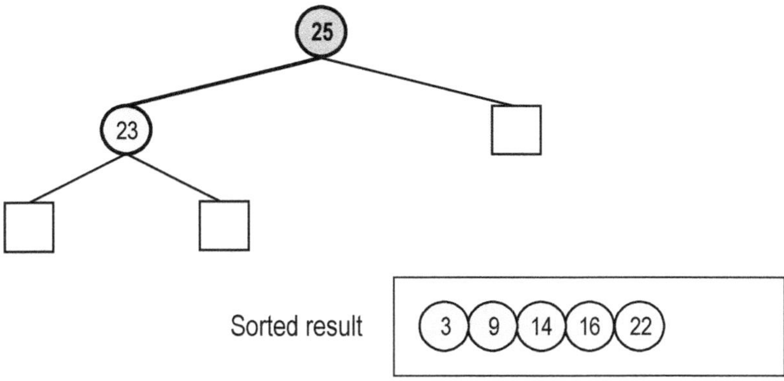

Downheap step is performed to swap node 25 and 23.

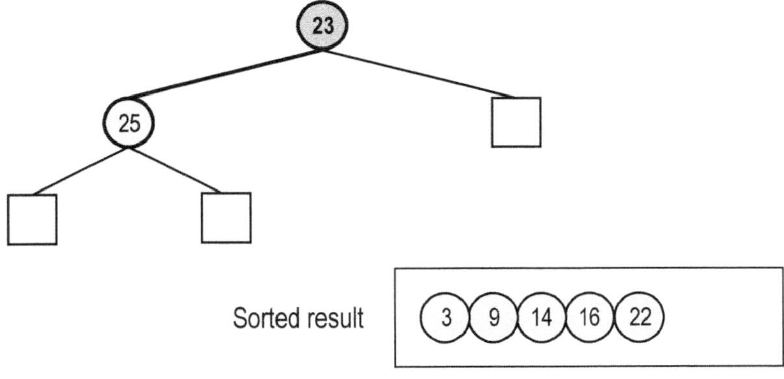

Next execution of `removeNode` function removes node 23, resulting in node 25 becomes the new root and the last internal node.

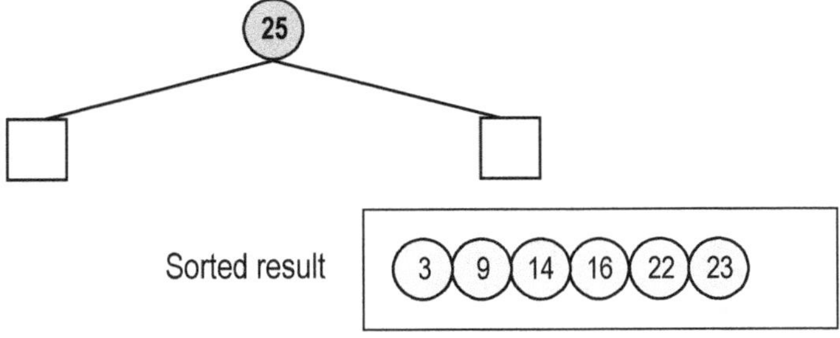

Finally, the last execution of `removeNode` function removes node 25. Heap H is now empty and array A has the sorted values.

Heap sort performs better than selection sort, insertion sort and bubble sort because it requires less calculations to sort large amount of data.

Merge Sort

Merge sort algorithm performs sorting calculation by dividing an array into smaller pieces recursively down to an array with 1 element or an empty array. From this smallest point, the algorithm builds back the sorted array by merging 2 pieces of array, each known as already sorted.

The algorithm for merge sort has two parts: the main module (`MergeSort`) that breaks down the array recursively and the module that merge the pieces back into a complete result (`MergeTwoArrays`).

```
 1 module MergeSort(A)
 2   if length(A)<=1 then
 3     result=A
 4   else
 5     idxMiddle=length(A) div 2
 6     arrayL=MergeSort(A[1..idxMiddle])
 7     arrayR=MergeSort(A[(idxMiddle+1)..length(A)])
 8     result=MergeTwoArrays(arrayL,arrayR)
 9   end if
10 end module
11
12 module MergeTwoArrays(L,R)
13   idxL=1
14   idxR=1
15   tempArray=[]
16   while idxL<=length(L) or idxR<=length(R) do
17     if idxL<=length(L) and idxR<=length(R) then
18       if L[idxL]<R[idxR] then
19         add L[idxL] to tempArray
20         idxL=idxL+1
21       else
22         add R[idxR] to tempArray
23         idxR=idxR+1
24       end if
```

```
25        else if idxR>length(R) then
26          add L[idxL] to tempArray
27          idxL=idxL+1
28        else if idxL>length(L) then
29          add R[idxR] to tempArray
30          idxR=idxR+1
31       end if
32     end while
33     result=tempArray
34 end module
```

Algorithm 03-E Merge Sort Algorithm

Module `MergeSort` works in a simple way. First, it breaks down an array into 2 parts. If an array has even number of elements, the two parts will have equal length. Otherwise, a sub-array will have one more element from the other. These two pieces are being used as passing parameter to recursively call the same module.

Each execution of a module does its own processes. When a module calls itself (recursion), each call will trigger separate process with different input array. The result of the call is returned to the caller (see line #6 and #7 from Algorithm 03-E). In this case, the result of executing `MergeSort` with left sub-array as parameter is saved into `arrayL` variable. Likewise, the result of executing `MergeSort` with right sub-array as parameter is saved into `arrayR` variable.

In line #8, `arrayL` and `arrayR` contain data that have already been sorted. However, merging two sorted arrays is not as easy as putting elements from one array after the other. Module `MergeTwoArrays` is used to merge two arrays with sorted data into one. This is easily achieved by comparing the elements from the two arrays from left to right using index (counter) variables.

Lastly, line #2 and #3 from the algorithm is the stopping criteria to prevent the recursion from running endless call. The process of breaking down an array into two parts need to stop when the input array is already an array with 1 element or an empty array.

Example:
Array `A` has 7 elements. The values of each element are shown below. Merge sort algorithm is used to sort the values in ascending order.

index	1	2	3	4	5	6	7
value	16	25	22	3	14	9	23

The root call of `MergeSort` takes array A as parameter, then breaks down A into two sub-arrays [16,25,22] and [3,14,9,23]. Next, module `MergeSort` is called again to handle each sub-array.

- The call with array [16,25,22] as parameter produces 2 sub-arrays: [16] and [25,22].
- The call with array [3,14,9,23] as parameter produces 2 sub-arrays: [3,14] and [9.23].
- The call with array [16] meets the criteria of line #2 in the algorithm, this stops the recursion from this branch.
- The call with array [25,22] as parameter produces 2 sub-arrays: [25] and [22].
- The call with array [25] meets the criteria of line #2 in the algorithm, this stops the recursion from this branch.
- The call with array [22] meets the criteria of line #2 in the algorithm, this stops the recursion from this branch.
- The call with array [3,14] as parameter produces 2 sub-arrays: [3] and [14].
- The call with array [9,23] as parameter produces 2 sub-arrays: [9] and [23].
- The call with array [3] meets the criteria of line #2 in the algorithm, this stops the recursion from this branch.
- The call with array [14] meets the criteria of line #2 in the algorithm, this stops the recursion from this branch.
- The call with array [9] meets the criteria of line #2 in the algorithm, this stops the recursion from this branch.
- The call with array [23] meets the criteria of line #2 in the algorithm, this stops the recursion from this branch.

Through recursive calls, every sub-array becomes an array with one element. From this point, `MergeTwoArrays` will merge them back into a sorted array.

- Arrays [25] and [22] are merged into [22,25].
- Arrays [3] and [14] are merged into [3,14].
- Arrays [9] and [23] are merged into [9,23].
- Arrays [16] and [22,25] are merged into [16,22,25].
- Arrays [3,14] and [9,23] are merged into [3,9,14,23].
- Finally, arrays [16,22,25] and [3,9,14,23] are merged into [3,9,14,16,22,23,25], which is the final solution for the original input array A.

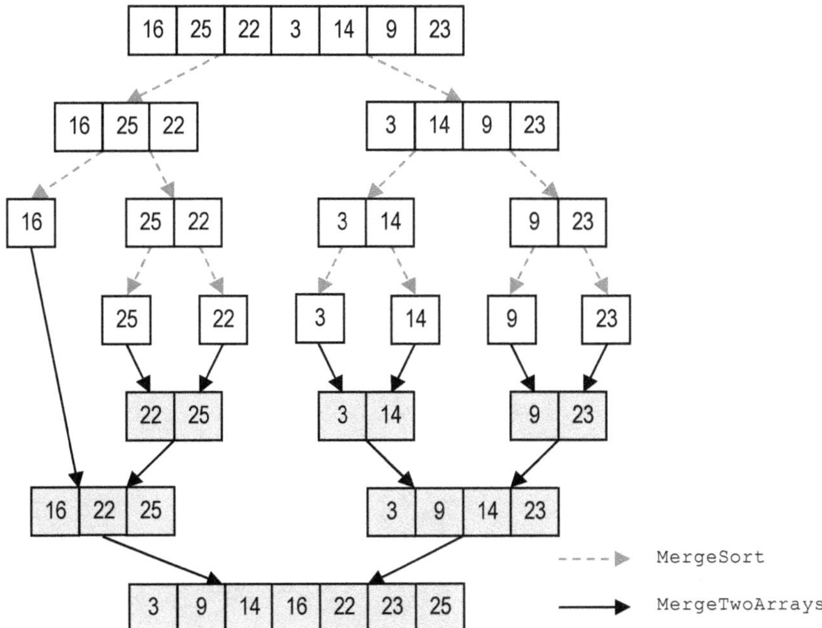

It is easy to combine [22] and [25] into [22,25]. But how does the `MergeTwoArrays` algorithm work to merge longer arrays, such as [16,22,25] and [3,9,14,23]?

If array `L` and array `R` are both sorted, we know that the smallest value of the merged array (temporarily stored in `tempArray` variable) is either the first value of array `L` or the first value of array `R`.

If the first value of `tempArray` comes from array `L`, we know that the second value is either the second value of array `L` or the first value or array `R`. On the other hand, if the first value of `tempArray` comes from array `R`, we know that the second value is either the first value of array `L` or the second value of array `R`. Repeat this process and `MergeTwoArrays` will produce the merged array using the help of variables `idxL` and `idxR` to remember which elements have been used for `tempArray`.

First, `idxL` and `idxR` are set to 1. This is to mark that the first element of the merged array is either the first element of array `L` (16) or the first element of array `R` (3).

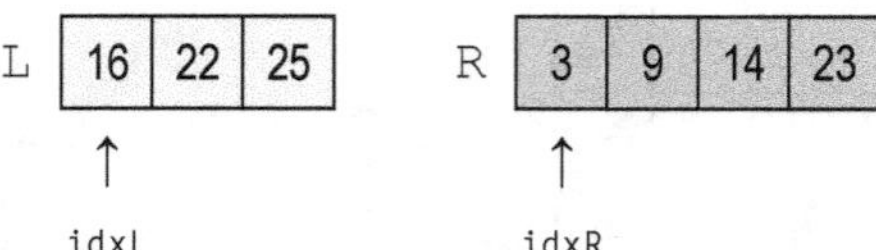

The first element of array `R` (3) is smaller. Store the value into `tempArray` and increase the index counter `idxR`.

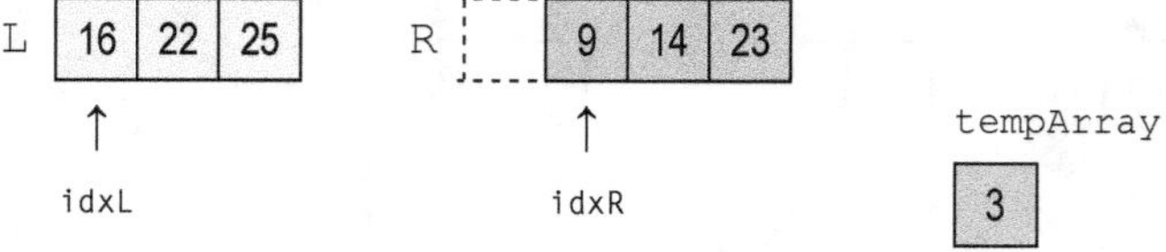

Next, compare the values of `L[idxL]` (16) and `R[idxR]` (9). Store the smaller value (9) into `tempArray` and increase the index counter `idxR` because 9 comes from array `R`.

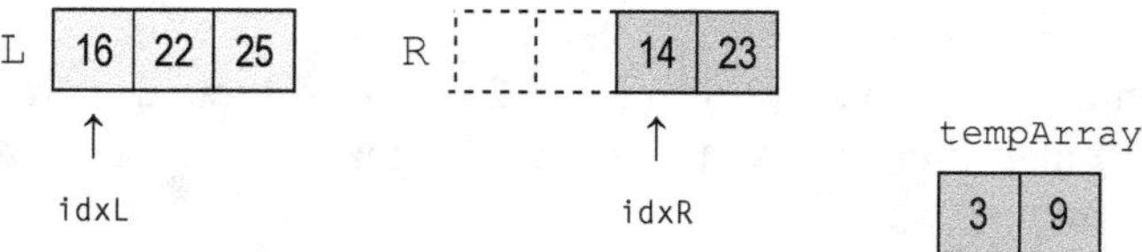

Next, compare the values of `L[idxL]` (16) and `R[idxR]` (14). Store the smaller value (14) into `tempArray` and increase the index counter `idxR` because 14 comes from array `R`.

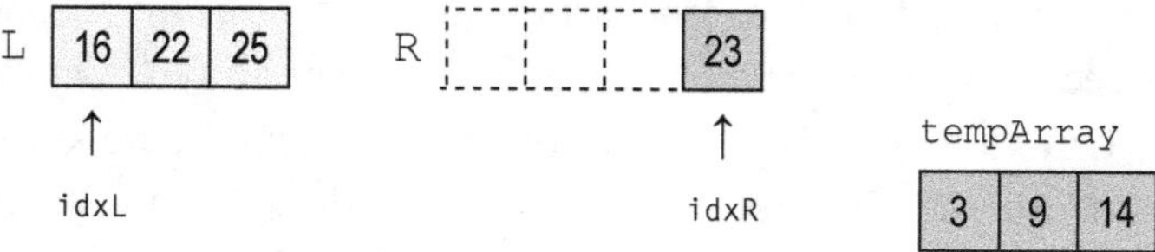

Next, compare the values of `L[idxL]` (16) and `R[idxR]` (23). Store the smaller value (16) into `tempArray` and increase the index counter `idxL` because 16 comes from array `L`.

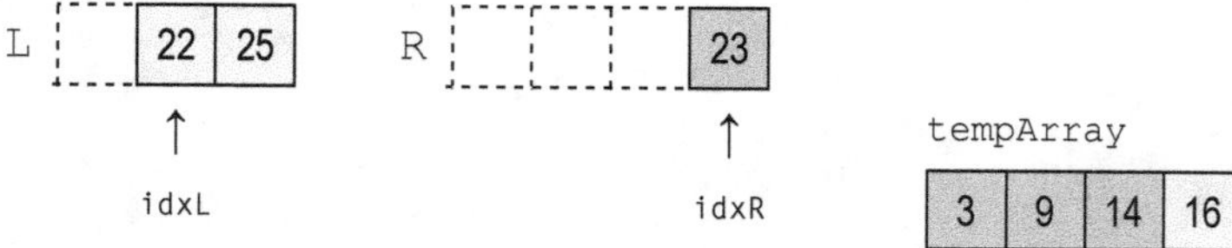

Next, compare the values of `L[idxL]` (22) and `R[idxR]` (23). Store the smaller value (22) into `tempArray` and increase the index counter `idxR` because 22 comes from array L.

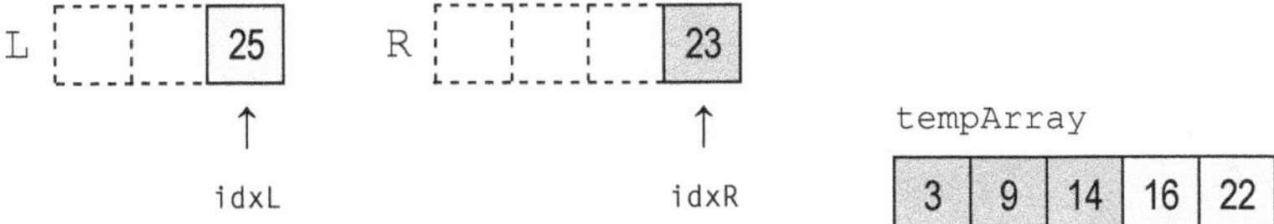

Next, compare the values of `L[idxL]` (25) and `R[idxR]` (23). Store the smaller value (23) into `tempArray` and increase the index counter `idxR` because 23 comes from array R.

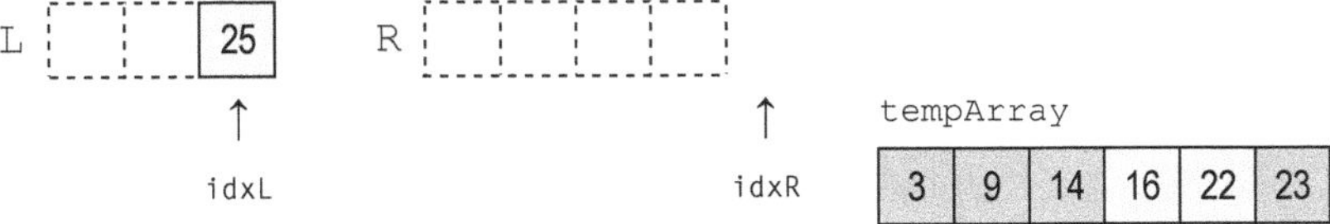

There is no element left from array R because `idxR>length(R)`. Store the `L[idxL]` (23) into `tempArray` and increase the index counter `idxL`.

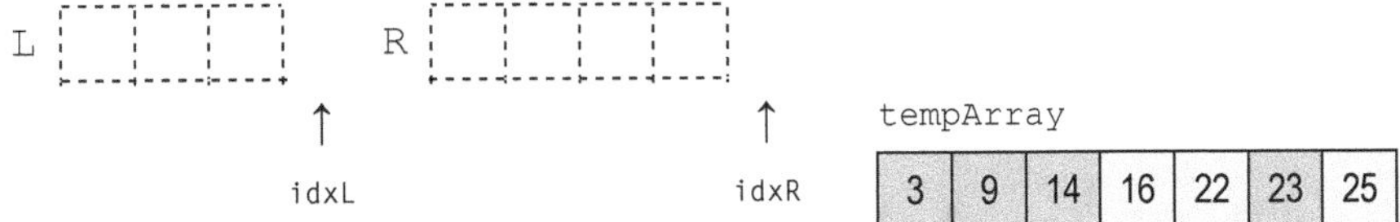

Now `idxL>length(L)` and `idxR>length(R)`, the condition for the while statement in line #16 is no longer met. The array saved in `tempArray` becomes the result of `MergeTwoArrays` module.

Merge sort algorithm is considered faster than selection, insertion and bubble sort, especially for arrays with large number of elements. However, note that this algorithm would still need to perform many calculations if the input array is already fully sorted.

Quick Sort

Quick sort algorithm is another sorting algorithm with recursion technique. This algorithm is considered as one of the best basic algorithms for sorting, capable of handling large amount of data.

The basic idea of quick sort algorithm is splitting input array into sub-arrays. It chooses a value from the input array to be treated as separating value (also known as *pivot point*). There are different versions on how to choose this pivot, which will greatly impact the performance of the algorithm. For simplicity, this book will start with using the first element of an input array as pivot point.

```
 1 module QuickSort(A)
 2   if length(A)>1 then
 3     select a pivot value from A
 4     arrLess=[]
 5     arrPivot=[]
 6     arrMore=[]
 7     for i=1 to length(A) do
 8       if A[i]=pivot then
 9         add A[i] to arrPivot
10       else if A[i]<pivot then
11         add A[i] to arrLess
12       else if A[i]>pivot then
13         add A[i] to arrMode
14       end if
15     end for
16     tempLess=QuickSort(arrLess)
17     tempMore=QuickSort(arrMore)
18     result=[tempLess,arrPivot,tempMore]
19   else
20     result=A
21   end if
22 end module
```

Algorithm 03-F Quick Sort Algorithm

The algorithm above is written in a generic way to accept different methods of selecting pivot point. After pivot selection, it goes on simple loop to check each element of the input array A and separate them into three sub-arrays. The pivot point itself becomes a sub-array with one element (`arrPivot`); another sub-array contains all values smaller than pivot point (`arrLess`); the last one contains all values greater than pivot point (`arrMore`).

Example:
Array A has 7 elements. The values of each element are shown below. Quick sort algorithm is used to sort the values in ascending order.

index	1	2	3	4	5	6	7
value	16	25	22	3	14	9	23

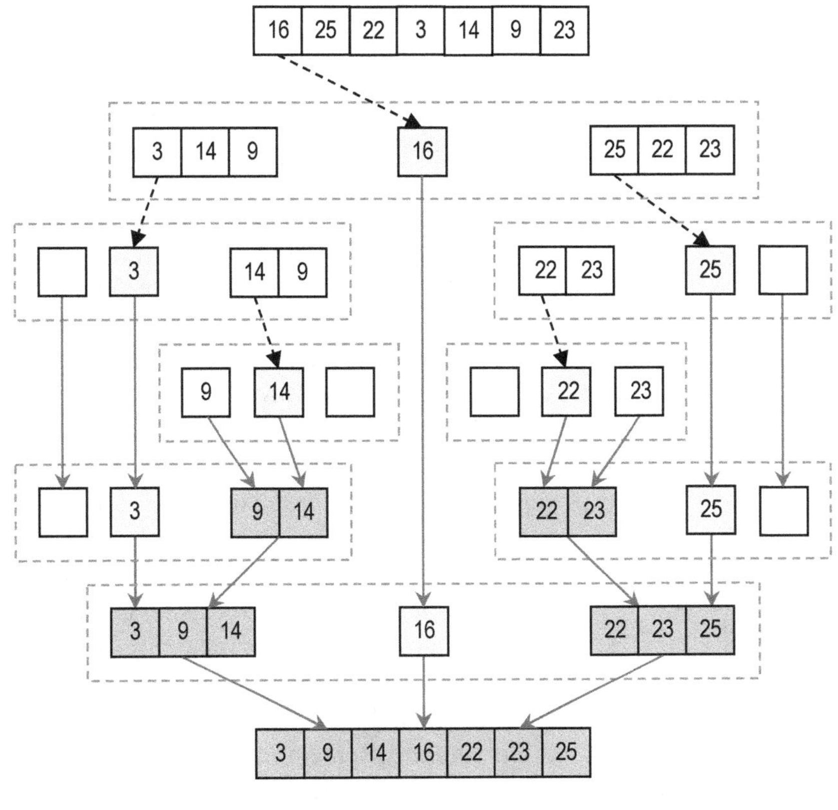

Following Algorithm 03-F, the algorithm takes array A and breaks it into 3 sub-arrays recursively:

- The first step is to decide on the first element of input array (16) as pivot point.
- Every element with value less than 16 goes to `arrLess`. These values are [3,14,9].
- Every element with value greater than 16 goes to `arrMore`. These values are [25,22,23].
- Module `MergeSort` is called again recursively to process `arrLess` [3,14,9] as input.
  - Value [3] becomes pivot point.
  - Every element with value less than 3 goes to `arrLess`. No value goes to `arrLess`.

- o Every element with value greater than 3 goes to `arrMore`. These values are [14,9].
- o Module `MergeSort` is called again recursively to process `arrLess` [] as input. Line #2 in algorithm evaluates as *false*, hence the recursion stops.
- o Module `MergeSort` is called again recursively to process `arrMore` [14,9] as input.
    - Value [14] becomes pivot point.
    - Every element with value less than 14 goes to `arrLess`. No value goes to `arrLess`.
    - Every element with value greater than 14 goes to `arrMore`. These values are [9].
    - Module `MergeSort` is called again recursively to process `arrLess` [] as input. Line #2 in algorithm evaluates as *false*, hence the recursion stops.
    - Module `MergeSort` is called again recursively to process `arrMore` [9] as input. Line #2 in algorithm evaluates as *false*, hence the recursion stops.
    - Result of calculation is constructed by connecting `arrLess` [], `arrPivot` [9], and `arrMore` [14]. The result is [9,14], this would become `arrMore` in for the caller from previous recursion.
- o Result of calculation is constructed by connecting `arrLess` [], `arrPivot` [3], and `arrMore` [9,14]. The result is [3,9,14], this would become `arrLess` in for the caller from previous recursion.
- Module `MergeSort` is called again recursively to process `arrMore` [25,22,23] as input.
  - o Value [25] becomes pivot point.
  - o Every element with value less than 25 goes to `arrLess`. These values are [22,23].
  - o Every element with value greater than 25 goes to `arrMore`. No value goes to `arrMore`.
  - o Module `MergeSort` is called again recursively to process `arrLess` [22,23] as input.
    - Value [22] becomes pivot point.
    - Every element with value less than 22 goes to `arrLess`. No value goes to `arrLess`.
    - Every element with value greater than 22 goes to `arrMore`. These values are [23].

- ▪ Module `MergeSort` is called again recursively to process `arrLess` [] as input. Line #2 in algorithm evaluates as *false*, hence the recursion stops.
- ▪ Module `MergeSort` is called again recursively to process `arrMore` [23] as input. Line #2 in algorithm evaluates as *false*, hence the recursion stops.
- ▪ Result of calculation is constructed by connecting `arrLess` [], `arrPivot` [22], and `arrMore` [23]. The result is [22,23], this would become `arrLess` in for the caller from previous recursion.
- o Module `MergeSort` is called again recursively to process `arrMore` [] as input. Line #2 in algorithm evaluates as *false*, hence the recursion stops.
- o Result of calculation is constructed by connecting `arrLess` [22,23], `arrPivot` [25], and `arrMore` []. The result is [22,23,25], this would become `arrMore` in for the caller from previous recursion.
- • Result of calculation is constructed by connecting `arrLess` [3,9,14], `arrPivot` [16], and `arrMore` [22,23,25]. The result is [3,9,14,16,22,23,25], this is the final result.

The whole calculation will be different if pivot value is chosen using different rule instead of always choosing the first element. Some possible alternatives are:

- • Choose the value of middle element as pivot value. For example: this means element #4 in an input array with 7 elements.
- • Choose the value of the last element as pivot value. For example: this means element #7 in an input array with 7 elements.
- • Compare the first, middle and last element and choose the middle value. For example: this will compare values of element #1, #4 and #7 and choose the middle value. In the array A from prior example, this means comparing values 16, 3 and 23. Value 16 is chosen because 3 < 16 < 23. For long arrays with many elements, this technique could sometimes bring faster result.
- • Choose a random value from input array as pivot value. This technique does not guarantee effective performance, but it does reduce the possibility of worst-case scenario.

Quick sort algorithm implements divide-and-conquer technique quite literally. It divides input array into smaller pieces, then resolve the smaller pieces recursively. In the end, it only needs to put the pieces back as the overall solution. Different from merge sort, the process of putting solved pieces back together does not need further processing, allowing quick sort to perform faster in many scenarios.

Binary Search

A user needs find out if value 22 exists in array [16,25,22,3,14,9,23]. While a human user can quickly look at the array and finds that value 22 can be found in element #3, computer algorithm needs specific steps to find the value. One of the most basic techniques to find a value is by comparing the searched value against each element in an array. This technique is called sequential search. As the name suggests, it searches the value in an array sequentially.

```
 1 module SeqSearch(ToFind,A)
 2   i=1
 3   while (i<=length(A)) and (A[i]<>ToFind) do
 4     i=i+1
 5   end while
 6   if A[i]=ToFind then
 7     result=i
 8   else
 9     result=-1
10   end if
11 end module
```

Algorithm 03-G Sequential Search Algorithm

Lines #3 to #5 from Algorithm 03-G would check every single value in array A until the value equal to ToFind variable is found, or until all elements in array A has been searched. Line #6 would check if the searching loop ended with the value found in array or not. If the value was found, module SeqSearch produces the location of the value within the array, otherwise it will produce special value -1. Note that if multiple values equal to ToFind variable are in array A, only the first occurrence will be detected because the algorithm will stop when the first equal value is found.

This simple technique can be used to search any value in an array, regardless of whether the values in such array are sorted or not. However, imagine if the algorithm needs to find a value from a complex data structure with more than a billion records. The searching process would take very significant amount of processing time, showing that the algorithm is far from being efficient.

One of searching techniques with better performance is binary search. This technique requires input array to be sorted before search processing can start. At the very basic level, binary search algorithm divides an array into 2 sub-arrays and focuses searching in just one of them, gradually narrowing down the search area, allowing faster processing for arrays with large amount of data.

```
 1 module BinarySearch(ToFind,A)
 2   idxLow=1
 3   idxHigh=length(A)
 4   idxFound=-1
 5   while (idxFound=-1) and (idxLow<=idxHigh) do
 6     idxM=(idxL+idxR) div 2
 7     if A[idxMid]=ToFind then
 8       idxFound=idxMid
 9     else if A[idxMid]>ToFind then
10       idxHigh=idxMid-1
11     else if A[idxMid]<ToFind then
12       idxLow=idxMid+1
13     end if
14   end while
15   result=idxFound
16 end module
```

Algorithm 03-H Binary Search Algorithm

idxLow and idxHigh variables are used to break array A into two parts. At the beginning, the algorithm needs to find ToFind value in the whole array A, hence idxLow is set to 1 and idxHigh is set to the last element of A, indicating that the search area is from the beginning to the end of array A.

In every iteration, the algorithm calculates idxMid as the middle location. This is treated as a temporary guess of the location of ToFind value. Finding that value in idxMid location is equal to ToFind value means the search process is successful and the algorithm can stop. If the value in idxMid location is greater than ToFind, it means the ToFind value is somewhere on the left side. Otherwise, if the value in idxMid location is less than ToFind, the algorithm needs to continue searching on the right side.

Example:
Array A has 7 elements sorted in ascending order. The values of each element are shown below. Use Binary Search algorithm to find value 14.

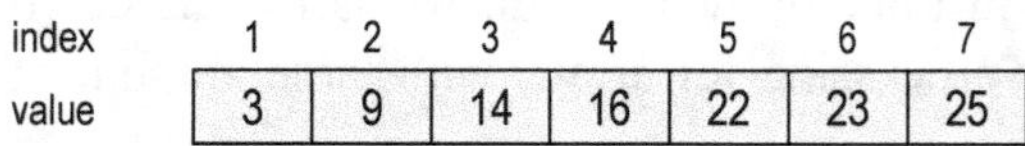

First, `idxLow` is set to 1 and `idxHigh` is set to 7.

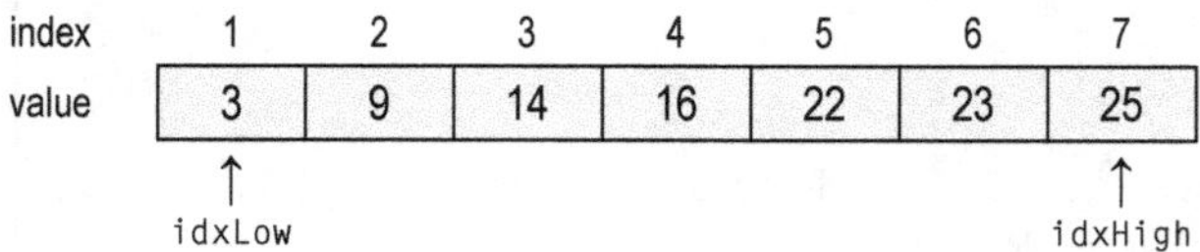

The position of `idxMid` is calculated using the formula in line #6. (1+7) div 2 is 4, hence the first value of `idxMid` is 4.

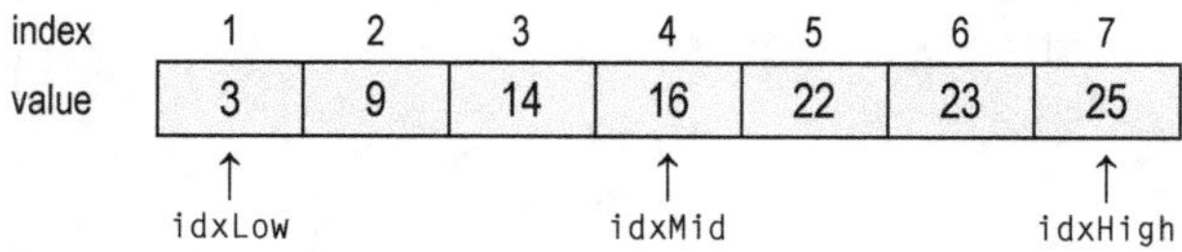

Compare A[4] with `ToFind`. 16 is not equal to 14. Since A[4]>ToFind, the searching process needs to focus on elements on the left side of `idxMid`. Therefore, `idxHigh` is set as `idxMid-1`.

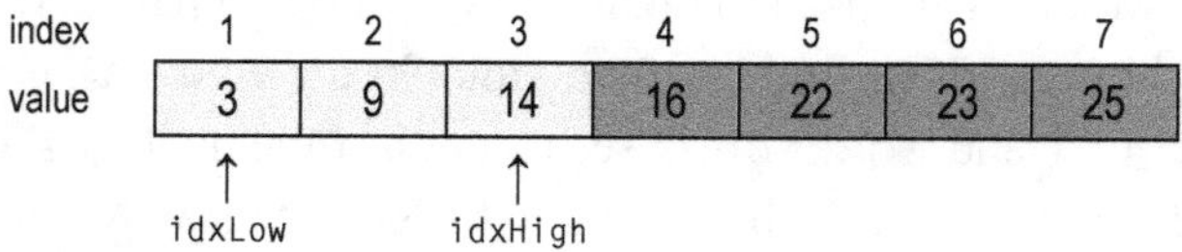

New position of `idxMid` is calculated using the formula in line #6. (1+3) div 2 is 2, hence the first value of `idxMid` is 2.

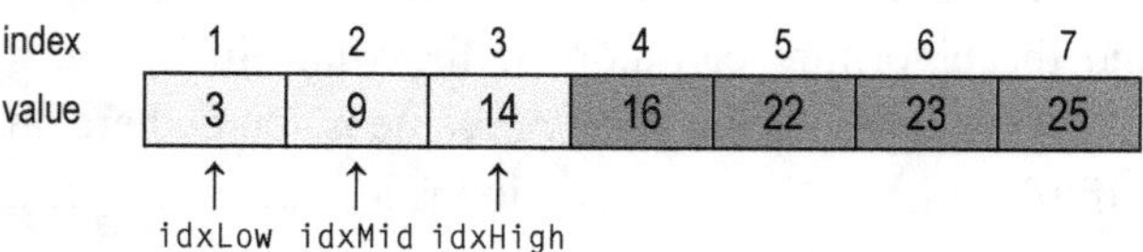

Compare A[2] with `ToFind`. 9 is not equal to 14. Since A[2]<ToFind, the searching process needs to focus on elements on the right side of `idxMid`.

Therefore, `idxLow` is set as `idxMid+1`.

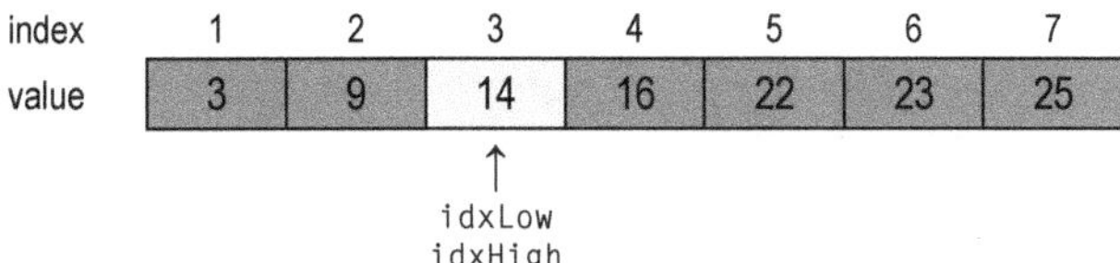

New position of `idxMid` is calculated using the formula in line #6. (3+3) div 2 is 3, hence the first value of `idxMid` is 3.

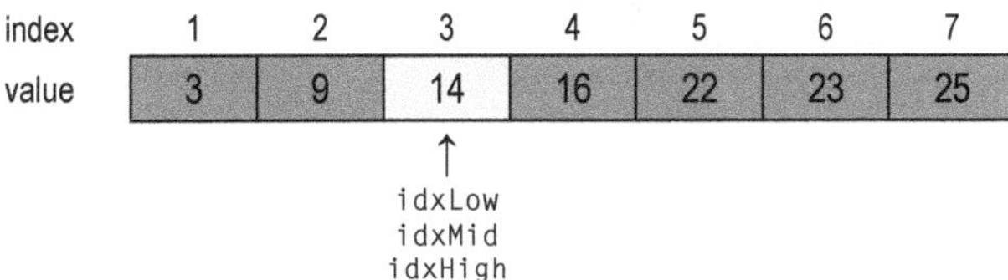

Compare `A[3]` with `ToFind`. 14 is equal to 14. The search value is located at element #3, `idxFound` is set to 3. The next evaluation of line #5 will evaluate to false because `idxFound` is not -1 anymore. This will stop the while loop and produce the result.

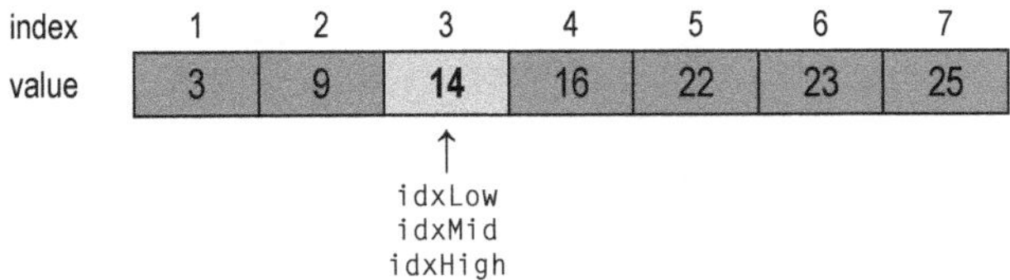

What will happen if `ToFind` value does not exist in array `A`? Binary Search algorithm will end with `idxLow>idxHigh` even though the value of `idxFound` is still -1 (not found). This will make line #5 evaluates to *false*.

Example:
Array `A` has 7 elements sorted in ascending order. The values of each element are shown below. Use Binary Search algorithm to find value 24.

index	1	2	3	4	5	6	7
value	3	9	14	16	22	23	25

Like the previous example, `idxLow` is set to 1 and `idxHigh` is set to 7.

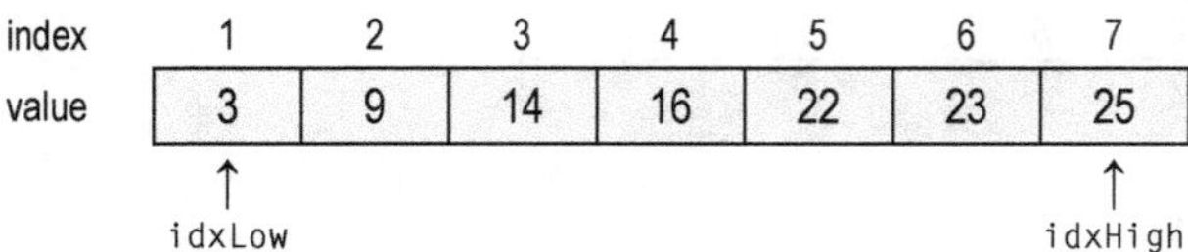

The position of `idxMid` is calculated using the formula in line #6. (1+7) div 2 is 4, hence the first value of `idxMid` is 4.

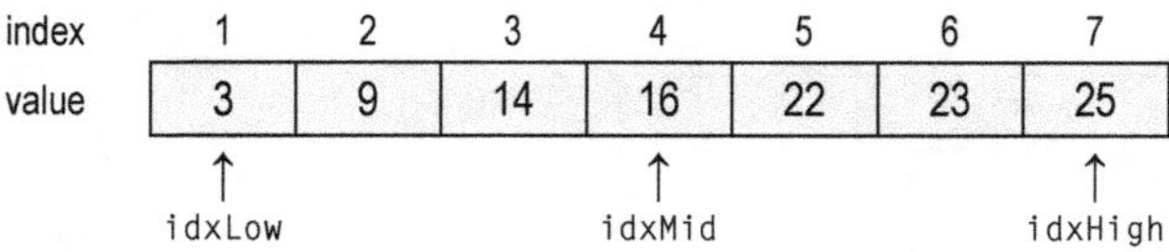

Compare `A[4]` with `ToFind`. 16 is not equal to 24. Since `A[4]<ToFind`, the searching process needs to focus on elements on the right side of `idxMid`. Therefore, `idxLow` is set as `idxMid+1`.

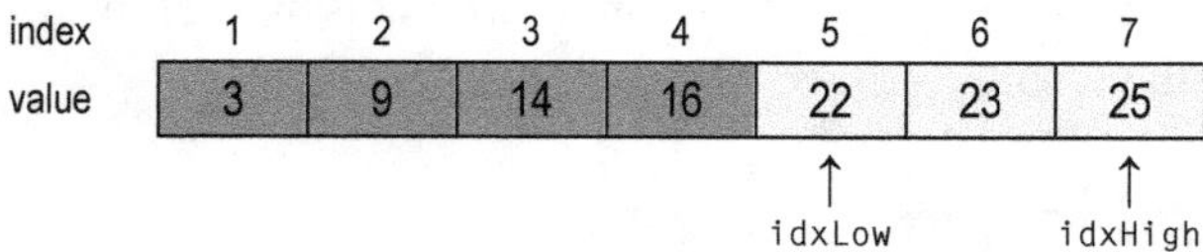

New position of `idxMid` is calculated using the formula in line #6. (5+7) div 2 is 6, hence the first value of `idxMid` is 6.

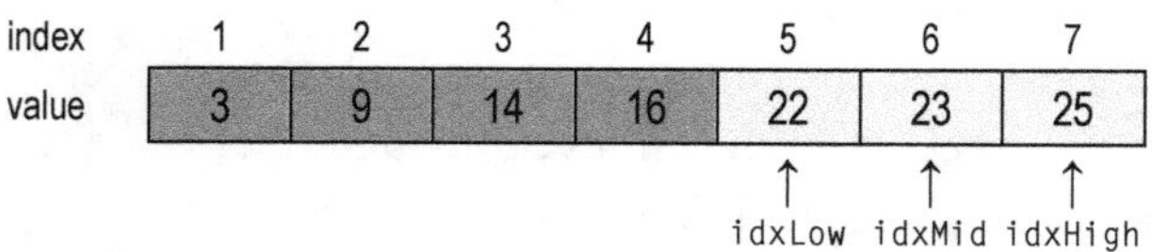

Compare `A[2]` with `ToFind`. 23 is not equal to 24. Since `A[6]<ToFind`, the searching process needs to focus on elements on the right side of `idxMid`. Therefore, `idxLow` is set as `idxMid+1`.

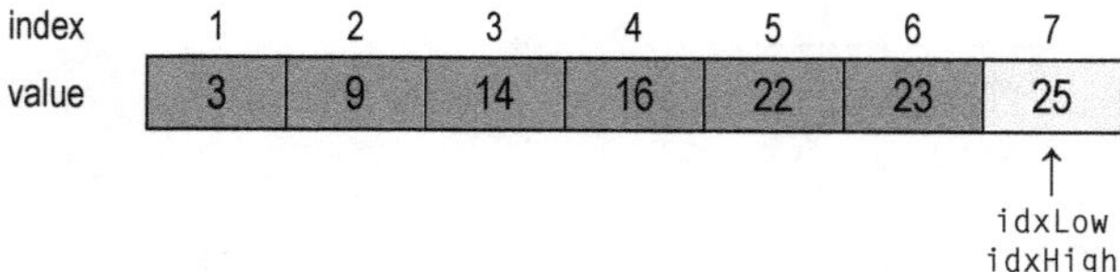

New position of `idxMid` is calculated using the formula in line #6. (7+7) div 2 is 7, hence the first value of `idxMid` is 7.

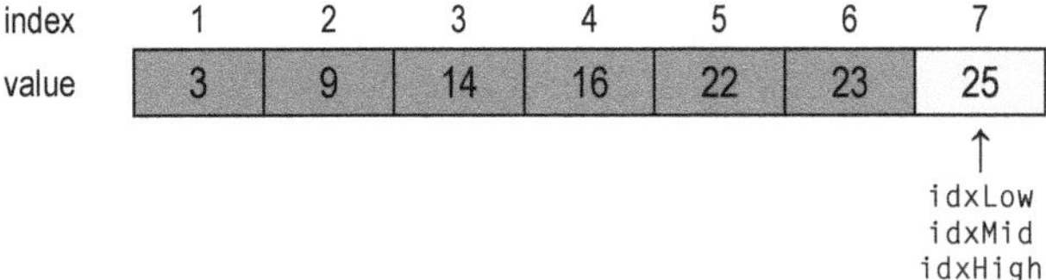

Compare `A[3]` with `ToFind`. 25 is not equal to 24. Since `A[7]>ToFind`, the searching process needs to focus on elements on the left side of `idxMid`. Therefore, `idxHigh` is set as `idxMid-1`.

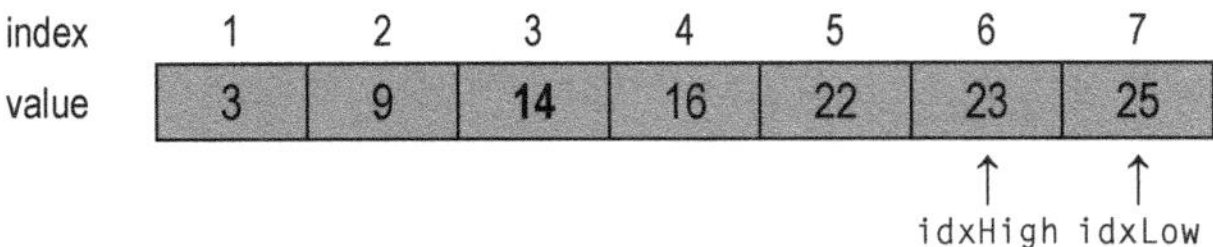

The next evaluation of line #5 will evaluate to *false* because `idxLow>idxHigh`, even though `idxFound` is still -1. This will stop the while loop and produce value -1 as the result, indicating that `ToFind` value is not located within array `A`.

There are further possible improvements of Binary search, such as calculating relative value between the first and last element of array `A`. If the first element of array `A` is 1 and the last element is 100, the search value (`ToFind`) is 80 and array `A` has 1000 elements. An algorithm can "guess" that value 80 is likely to be found around 800th element in the array instead of the middle element. Of course, the result of such technique depends on whether the value within array is distributed uniformly or not.

04. GREEDY ALGORITHMS

Some problem-solving algorithms produce a set of choices as part of their solutions. Ideally, a solution needs to be the best possible set of choices from all possible combinations. In reality, calculating all possible combinations is not always feasible when dealing with large amount of data or massive number of possible choices. This can get much worse in the case where the order of the choice matters (permutation instead of combination).

Greedy algorithms make one choice at a time and always choose the best immediate option for that choice without considering the combined impact with other choices. In other words, greedy algorithms always choose the *local optimal* choice during each stage of their journeys.

Since they do not consider the big picture, greedy algorithms are usually simpler to implement with processing time that does not exponentially increase with the addition of possibilities. They produce some results reasonably quickly, but the results could be less than optimal.

Consider this example. A person wants to eat something. Instead of planning the food properly, this person opens the cupboard and find two options: bacon and bread. He chooses bacon because he likes it better than bread. Next, he opens his fridge and find milk and yogurt. He likes yogurt better, so he takes it, mix it with the bacon he got earlier. Each of them was his choice, something he likes better than the other option of each step. Mixing them together might not be the best decision. Combination of bread and milk might taste better, but this person did not consider combination of choices in earlier decision making.

Greedy technique is not to be confused with divide-and-conquer technique, which focuses on breaking down calculations into smaller pieces. Greedy algorithms make choices, one at a time. They work by choosing what appears to be the best choice at a point, seeing the decision point as an isolated case, without considering the overall impact.

Knapsack Problem

Knapsack problem is a good example of optimising combination of choices. The order of which element gets chosen first does not matter, but the choice of each element is associated with cost and benefit. The goal of solving this problem is to achieve maximum profit while keeping the cost within the allowed limit.

Suppose we have a knapsack capable of holding maximum 20 kgs of items. There are 4 items available, let us call them A, B, C, D, and E.

- Item A weighs 7 kgs and is worth $2,975
- Item B weighs 3 kgs and is worth $1,230
- Item C weighs 9 kgs and is worth $3,870
- Item D weighs 2 kgs and is worth $840
- Item E weighs 5 kgs and is worth $2,250

Which items need to be carried in the knapsack to maximise the value worth?

Such problem is an example of knapsack problem. The name came from a fictional story of a burglar entering a house and find multiple valuable items, but the knapsack that he carries can only bring limited weight of items. The thief must make decision which items he chooses and which ones he should ignore to maximise his gain. This problem is a good abstraction of many real-life situations.

There are several variations of knapsack problem:

- *Fractional Knapsack Problem*
  We can choose to bring a fraction of an item. This variation makes sense for items such as flour, sugar, and so on.

- *0/1 Knapsack Problem*
  There is only one unit of each item. Take it or leave it.

- *Bounded Knapsack Problem*
  Items are available in limited quantities (n).

- *Unbounded Knapsack Problem*
  Items are available in unlimited quantities.

The simplest of the above variations is 0/1 knapsack problem. Since there is only 1 unit available for each item, full combination table to enumerate all possible solutions can be generated manually.

Items	Weight	Value
{}	0	$0
{A}	7	$2,975
{B}	3	$1,230
{C}	9	$3,870
{D}	2	$840
{E}	5	$2,250
{A,B}	10	$4,205
{A,C}	16	$6,845
{A,D}	9	$3,815
{A,E}	12	$5,225
{B,C}	12	$5,110
{B,D}	5	$2,070
{B,E}	8	$3,480
{C,D}	11	$4,710
{C,E}	14	$6,120
{D,E}	7	$3,090

Items	Weight	Value
{A,B,C}	19	$8,085
{A,B,D}	12	$5,045
{A,B,E}	15	$6,455
{A,C,D}	18	$7,685
~~{A,C,E}~~	~~21~~	~~$9,095~~
{A,D,E}	14	$6,065
{B,C,D}	14	$5,940
{B,C,E}	17	$7,350
{B,D,E}	10	$4,320
{C,D,E}	16	$6,960
~~{A,B,C,D}~~	~~21~~	~~$8,915~~
~~{A,B,C,E}~~	~~24~~	~~$10,325~~
{A,B,D,E}	17	$7,295
~~{A,C,D,E}~~	~~23~~	~~$9,935~~
{B,C,D,E}	19	$8,190
~~{A,B,C,D,E}~~	~~27~~	~~$11,165~~

As shown in the above table, there are 32 possible combinations of solutions. Not all of them are valid. Combinations of {A,C,E}, {A,B,C,D}, {A,B,C,E}, and {A,B,C,D,E} are not valid because they weight more than 20 kgs, hence they need to be eliminated from the list of possible solutions.

All possible combinations of items that weigh 20 kgs or less are considered as valid solution. Some valid solutions are better than others. For example, taking just item A in the knapsack is not against the problem rule because there is no minimum weight. However, choosing both A and B is also valid, and would produce higher value. Therefore, {A,B} is a better solution than {A}.

Comparing all valid solutions is an easy way to find optimal solution. In this case, choosing {B,C,D,E} is a feasible solution with the highest value. This is the optimal solution.

Problem solving by exploring all possible combination will always guarantee the best possible outcome. However, it is not always feasible when there are many parameters to consider. Greedy algorithm can be used to calculate solution when exploring all possible combination is considered not feasible.

Greedy technique to solve knapsack problem can be summarised as follow:
- Calculate value per kg.
- Find item with highest value per kg.
- Choose item with highest value per kg, as many as possible.
- If there is some weight capacity left, choose item with the next highest value per kg that will not violate the maximum weight limitation.
- Repeat until no additional item can be chosen.

Using the same example, it can be observed that items A, B, C, D and E have different values and different weights. To find which item has the highest value per kg:
- Item A weighs 7 kgs and is worth $2,975; value per kg is $425.
- Item B weighs 3 kgs and is worth $1,230; value per kg is $410.
- Item C weighs 9 kgs and is worth $3,870; value per kg is $430.
- Item D weighs 2 kgs and is worth $840; value per kg is $420.
- Item E weighs 5 kgs and is worth $2,250; value per kg is $450.

Item E with the highest value per kg should get the highest priority to be chosen, followed by item C, then then A, then item D, and the lowest value per kg is item B.

For 0/N unbounded knapsack problem, greedy algorithm would simply take 4 units of item E and obtain total value of $9,000. The total weight is already 20kgs, so there is no need to consider additional item.

Now, consider slight change in the knapsack problem rule. If the maximum weight that can be carried by knapsack is 23 kgs, then we still have 3 kgs capacity after choosing 4 units of item E.
- Item with second highest value per kg (item C) weighs more than 3 kgs, so it cannot be selected.
- Item with third highest value per kg (item A) also weighs more than 3 kgs, so it cannot be selected.
- Item with fourth highest value per kg (item D) weighs 2 kgs. This is a valid option. Therefore, greedy algorithm will choose this. Maximum number of item D that can be added is 1.

With 4 units of item E and 1 unit of item D already selected, the total weight is 22 kgs with total value of $9,420. There is 1 kg remaining weight capacity. Item with fifth highest value per kg (item B) weighs more than 1 kg, so it cannot be selected.

No item weighs 1 kg or less. Therefore, greedy algorithm will stop with {D,E,E,E,E} as the solution.

Is {D,E,E,E,E} really the optimal (best possible) solution? Not really. Another feasible solution with 1 unit of item B and 4 units of item E weighs 23 kgs and has $10,320 value. Greedy algorithm achieves a solution that is good enough, but not always the actual best solution because every decision made is a local optimal (highest value per kg).

On the other hand, if the knapsack problem becomes fractional unbounded knapsack problem, greedy algorithm would be able to calculate best solution.

Suppose we have a knapsack capable of holding maximum 23 kgs of items. There are 4 items available, let us call them A, B, C, D, and E. All items are in the form of powder. Therefore, we can choose to take fractions of it with unlimited availability.
- Item A weighs 7 kgs and is worth $2,975.
- Item B weighs 3 kgs and is worth $1,230.
- Item C weighs 9 kgs and is worth $3,870.
- Item D weighs 2 kgs and is worth $840.
- Item E weighs 5 kgs and is worth $2,250.

Using the same steps of greedy algorithm:
- Calculate value per kg.
- Item E has the highest value per kg.
- Choose item E.
- Since we can choose fractional amount of item E, we can simply take 23 kgs of item E. This means 4.6 units of item E with value $4.6 \times \$2,250 = \$10,350$.

This time, choosing 4.6 units of item E is the best possible solution.

Simple Job Scheduling

Job scheduling with single deadline constraint is one of the simplest forms of scheduling problem. In this problem, we are given a list of jobs, each will give different profits. Each job has a simple deadline: it can only be taken as the first x jobs in a sequence. The solution is a sequence of jobs to take to gain maximum profit.

Example 1:

There are 4 jobs available.

- Job A will give $110k profit if taken no later than second sequence.
- Job B will give $47k profit if taken no later than first sequence.
- Job C will give $25k profit if taken no later than second sequence.
- Job D will give $20k profit if taken no later than first sequence.

This example can be expressed using the following input data:

```
n=4;  (pA,pB,pC,pD)=(110k,47k,25k,20k);

(dA,dB,dC,dD)=(2,1,2,1)
```

with n is the number of available jobs, p is the profit of each job, and d is the jobs' deadlines.

Example 1 only have small number of possibilities. Therefore, it is feasible to list all possible valid solutions:

Sequence	Profit
A	$110k
B	$47k
C	$25k
D	$20k

Sequence	Profit
A,C	$135k
B,A	$157k
B,C	$72k

Sequence	Profit
C,A	$135k
D,A	$130k
D,C	$45k

All 4 jobs can be taken as the first job in the sequence. Hence {A}, {B}, {C} and {D} are all valid solutions. Next, {A,B} is not valid because job B cannot be taken as second job in the sequence. {A,C} is valid because both jobs A and C can be taken as either first or second job in sequence. {A,D} is not valid because job D has to be taken as first job in the sequence. Using the same process, the table above presents all valid sequences with the corresponding profits. Taking job B then job A is the sequence with highest profit of $157k.

Greedy algorithm can be used to solve example 1:

- Find the job with highest profit: job A.
- Job A can be taken as the first job. Candidate is valid. Choose job A as the first job in sequence.
- Current job sequence is {A}.
- Find the job with second highest profit: job B.
- Job B cannot be taken as the second job. Candidate is rejected.
- Current job sequence is still {A}.
- Find the job with third highest profit: job C.
- Job C can be taken as the second job. Candidate is valid. Choose job C and add to job sequence.

- Current job sequence is {A,C}.
- Find the job with fourth highest profit: job D.
- Job C cannot be taken as the second job. Candidate is rejected.
- Current job sequence is still {A,C}.
- No further candidate. Greedy algorithm stops with {A,C} as the solution, achieving profit of #135k.

The steps above can be represented in table form:

Candidate	Analysis	Sequence
Job A	Deadline is 2. Can be assigned to [1,2]. Accept candidate.	{A}
Job B	Deadline is 1. Can be assigned to [1]. Reject candidate.	{A}
Job C	Deadline is 2. Can be assigned to [1,2]. Accept candidate.	{A,C}
Job D	Deadline is 1. Can be assigned to [1]. Reject candidate.	{A,C}

Evidently, greedy algorithm manages to calculate a feasible solution that is "good enough" with profit $135k. However, it is not the best possible solution because choosing job sequence {B,A} will enable $157k profit.

Example 2:
There are 6 jobs available with the following profits and deadlines.

```
n=6;

(pA,pB,pC,pD,pE,pF)=(65k,45k,75k,30k,35k,70k);

(dA,dB,dC,dD,dE,dF)=(2,1,2,2,3,1)
```

The steps to solve example 2 using greedy algorithm:

Candidate	Analysis	Sequence
Job C	Deadline is 2. Can be assigned to [1,2]. Accept candidate.	{C}
Job F	Deadline is 1. Can be assigned to [1]. Reject candidate.	{C}
Job A	Deadline is 2. Can be assigned to [1,2]. Accept candidate.	{C,A}
Job B	Deadline is 1. Can be assigned to [1]. Reject candidate.	{C,A}
Job E	Deadline is 3. Can be assigned to [1,2,3]. Accept candidate.	{C,A,E}
Job D	Deadline is 2. Can be assigned to [1,2]. Reject candidate.	{C,A,E}

The solution calculated by greedy algorithm is to take jobs {C,A,E} with profit of $175k. Is this really the best possible solution? Sequence {F,C,E} is another valid solution with 180k profit. This is the actual best possible solution, but it was not detected by greedy algorithm because greedy algorithm only calculates local optimal, choosing valid jobs with highest profit, one at a time.

Shortest Path

Shortest path problem attempts to find the shortest possible route in a weighted graph from a start node to end node. The length of a route is calculated from all the weight of edges within a path.

Greedy algorithm tries to solve shortest path problem by looking at an edge with smallest weight within each step. There is no consideration how choice of edge from one step will impact the others. At every step, local optimal is calculated, hoping to get reasonably good solution in the end.

Example:
Available routes between cities A, B, C, D, E and F can be simplified into a weighted graph. A salesman wants to travel from city A to city F. What is the route that he needs to take to get the shortest possible path?

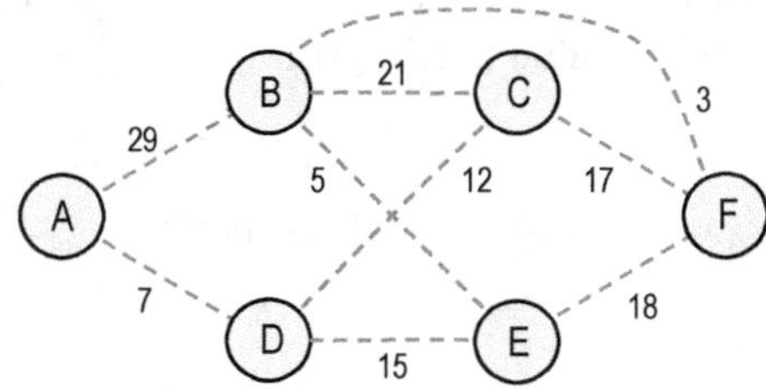

Start node A is selected as the first active node.

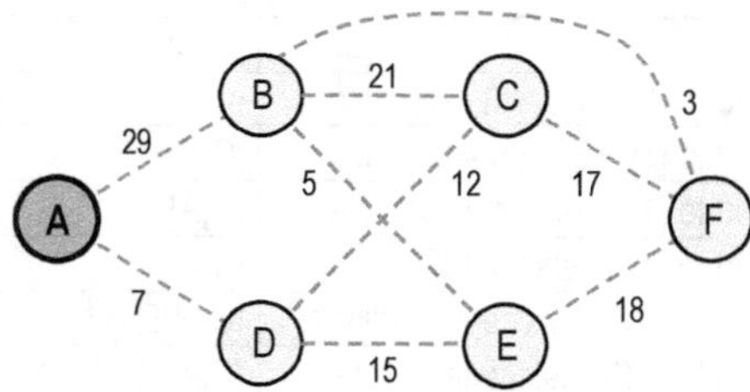

From A, there are 2 edges available: AB and AD. AD is selected because it has smaller weight. Node D becomes the new active node.

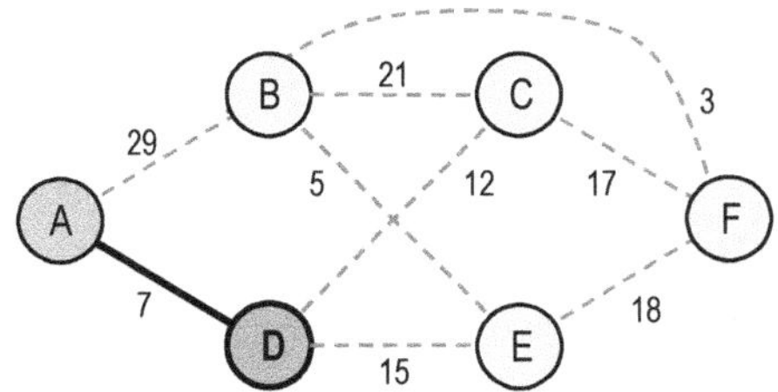

From D, there are 2 edges available: DC and DE. DC is selected because it has smaller weight. Node C becomes the new active node.

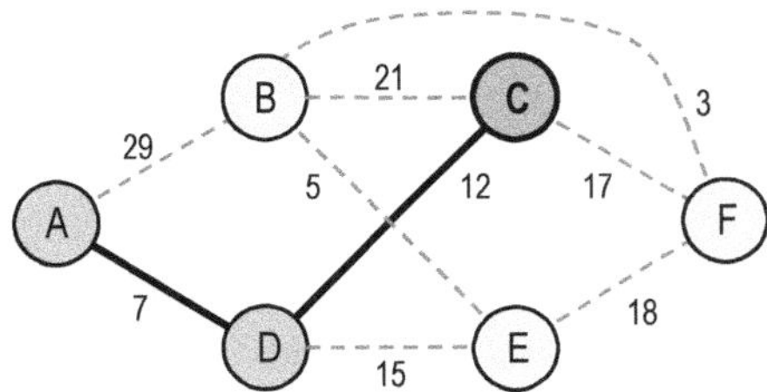

From C, there are 2 edges available: CB and CF. CF is selected because it has smaller weight. Node F becomes the new active node. This is already the end node. It means the solution (A-D-C-F) has been found.

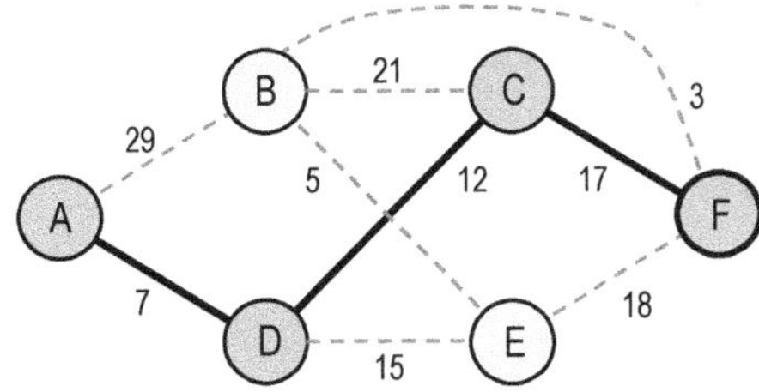

The solution found by greedy algorithm has total path distance of 36. Is this really the shortest path? No. The actual shortest path is A-D-E-B-F with total distance 30.

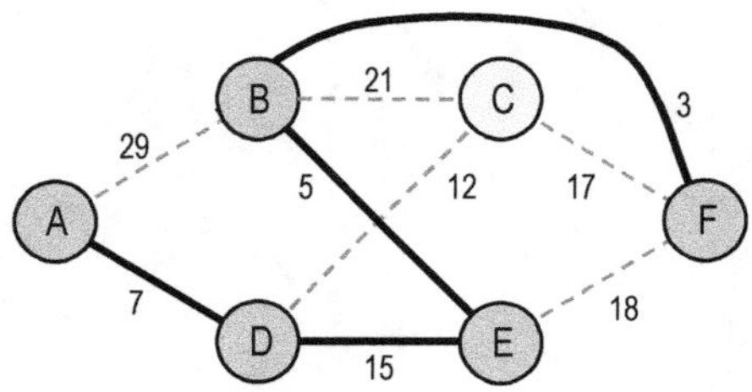

The greedy algorithm failed to see that choosing DE instead of DC will lead to shorter path because it simply compares weight 12 and 15. Then it chooses 12 as local optimal.

Minimum Spanning Tree

A graph is an abstract data type with a number of nodes connected by edges. Any node can be connected to any number of other nodes through edges. A tree is a special type of graph with each node only have one parent node but can still have any number child nodes. Please review chapter 02 for refresher.

Minimum spanning tree problem aims to convert a weighted graph into a tree by keeping all nodes but removing some edges to meet the criteria of a tree. This can be achieved by removing edges that would form a loop. Since each edge has assigned weight, the goal of minimum spanning tree problem is to choose which edges to keep so that the total weight is minimum.

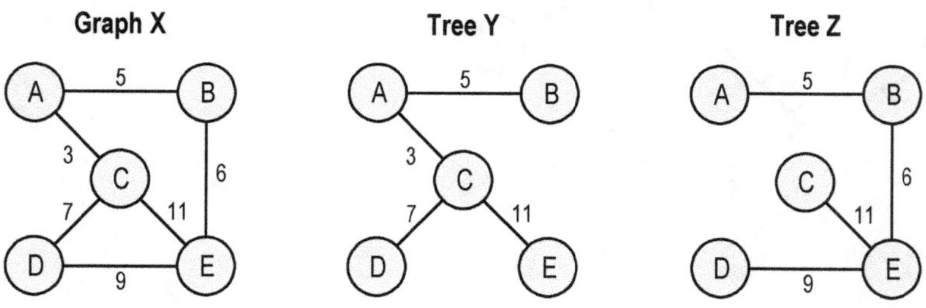

Weighted graph X is not a tree because it contains loops (for example: A-B-E-C-A). Tree Y is a tree created by removing edges BE and DE. Tree Z is another possibility to turn graph X into a tree by removing edges AC and CD.

Total weight of tree Y is (5+3+7+11) = 26. Total weight of tree Z is (5+6+11+9) = 31. In minimum spanning tree problem, tree Y is considered a better solution than tree Z.

Prim-Dijkstra Algorithm

Prim-Dijkstra algorithm uses the following steps to solve minimum spanning tree problem using greedy technique. This algorithm was developed by Robert Prim and Edsger Dijkstra. Some other materials might refer this as Prim's algorithm or DJP algorithm.

The basic steps of Prim-Dijkstra algorithm:
1. Choose starting node, declare it as part of the tree.
2. From all edges connected to the tree, find an edge with the smallest weight. Choose that edge to join the tree.
3. Find all nodes connected by all edges in the tree, add those nodes into the tree.
4. Check all the other edges that have not joined the tree, if both nodes connected by an edge is already part of the tree, mark the edge so that it will not be selected to join the tree.
5. Repeat from step #2 until all nodes are part of the tree.

Example:
An Prim-Dijkstra algorithm needs to convert weighted graph with 8 nodes [A,B,C,D,E,F,G,H] into a minimum spanning tree. Which edges need to be removed?

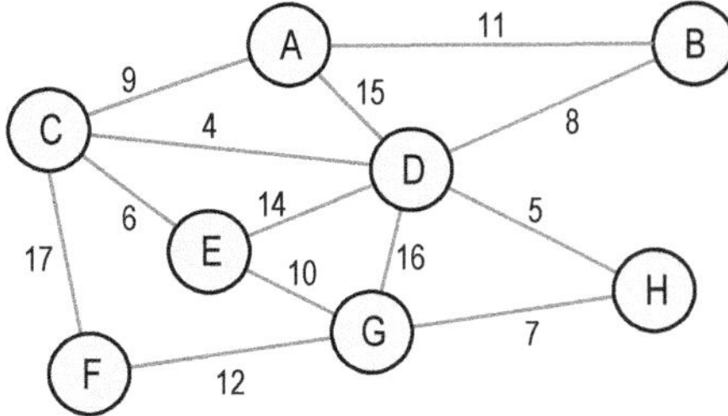

First, starting node A is chosen as starting point. There are 3 edges connected to A: AB, AC and AD. Edge AC has the smallest weight (9). AC is chosen as part of the tree. Node C is added into the tree.

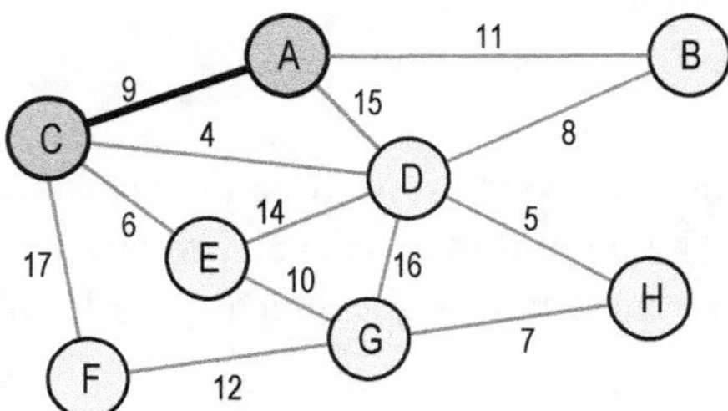

Next, compare all edges connected to the tree so far. There are 5 edges connected to the tree: AB, AD, CD, CD, CF. Edge CD has the smallest weight (4). CD is chosen as part of the tree. Node D is added into the tree.

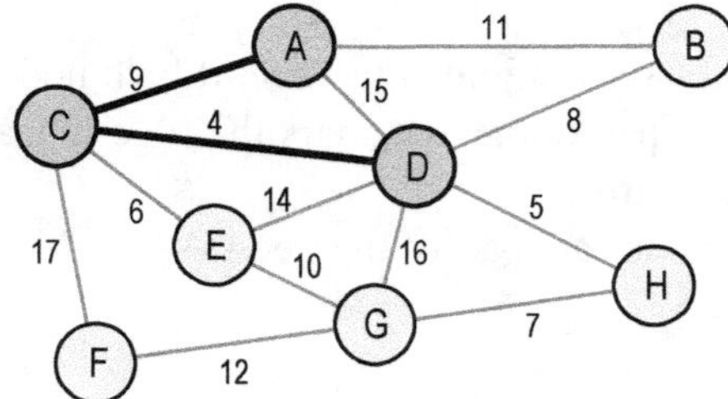

Edge AD connects nodes A and D. Both nodes are already part of the tree, mark edge AD so that it will not be selected to join minimum spanning tree.

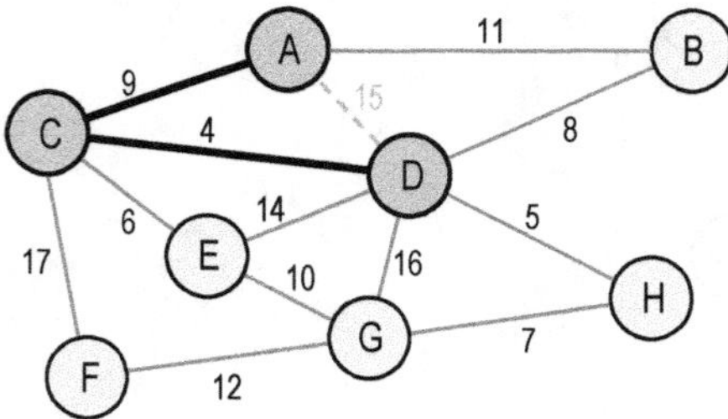

Next, compare all edges connected to the tree so far. There are 7 edges connected to the tree: AB, DB, DH, DG, DE, CE, and CF. Edge DH has the smallest weight (5). DH is chosen as part of the tree. Node H is added into the tree.

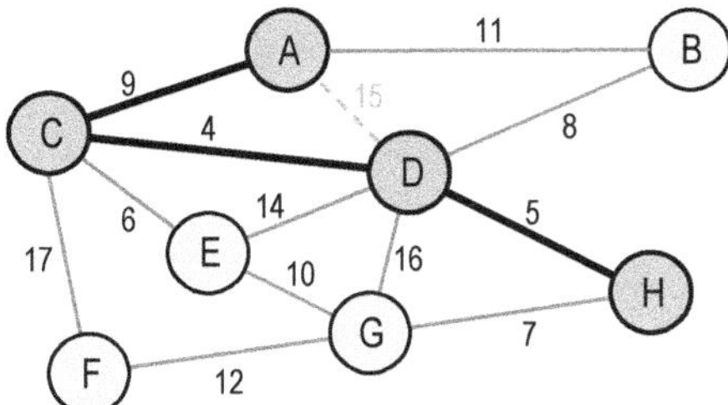

Compare all edges connected to the tree so far. There are 7 edges connected to the tree: AB, DB, HG, DG, DE, CE, and CF. Edge CE has the smallest weight (6). CE is chosen as part of the tree. Node E is added into the tree.

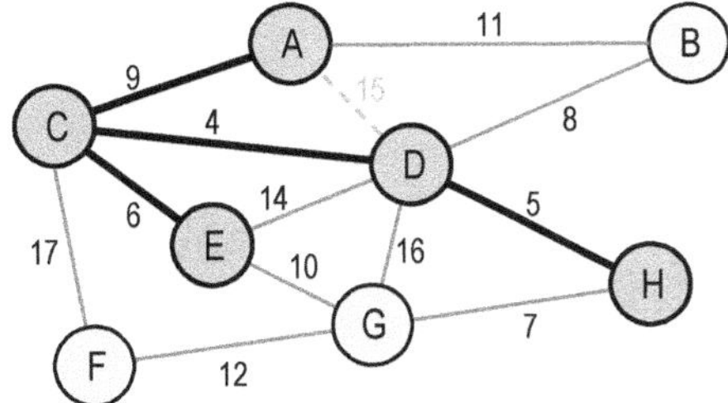

Edge DE connects nodes D and E. Both nodes are already part of the tree, mark edge DE so that it will not be selected to join minimum spanning tree.

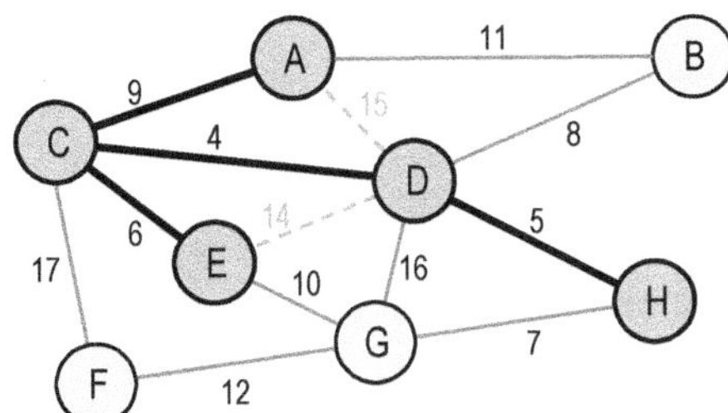

Next, compare all edges connected to the tree so far. There are 6 edges connected to the tree: AB, DB, DG, HG, EG, and CF. Edge HG has the smallest weight (7). HG is chosen as part of the tree. Node G is added into the tree.

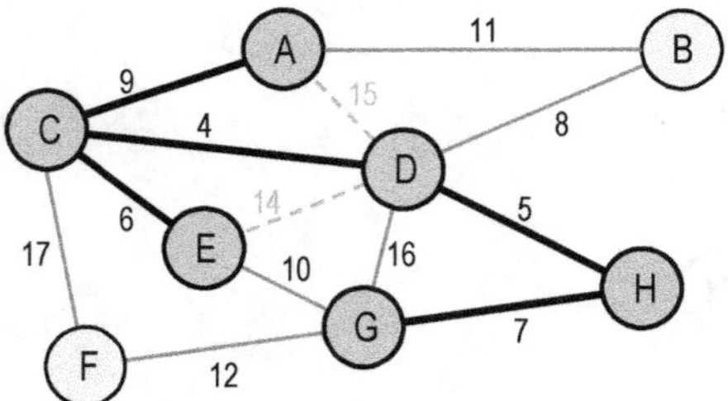

Edge EG connects nodes E and G. Both nodes are already part of the tree, mark edge EG so that it will not be selected to join minimum spanning tree. Do the same for edge DG.

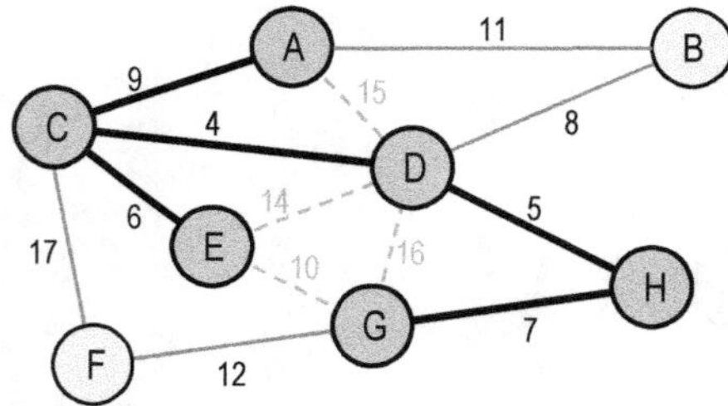

Compare all edges connected to the tree so far. There are 4 edges connected to the tree: AB, DB, CF, and GF. Edge DB has the smallest weight (8). DB is chosen as part of the tree. Node B is added into the tree.

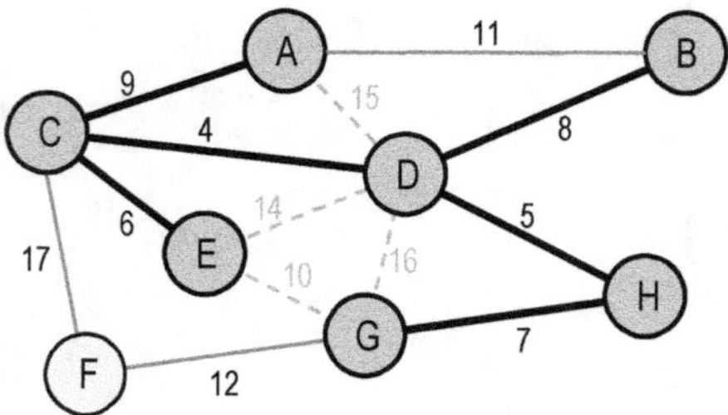

Edge AB connects nodes A and B. Both nodes are already part of the tree, mark edge AB so that it will not be selected to join minimum spanning tree.

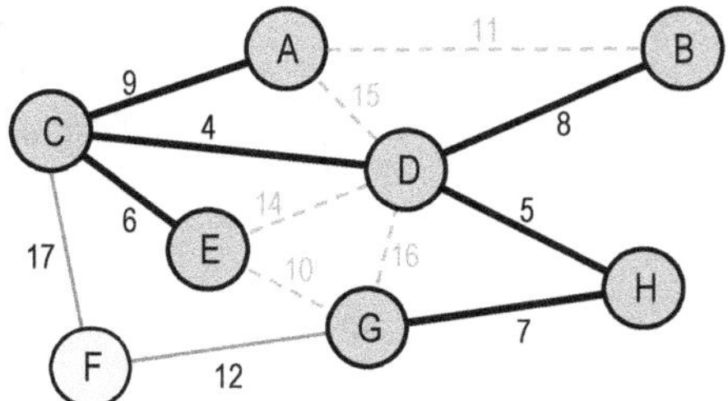

Next, compare all edges connected to the tree so far. There are 2 edges connected to the tree: CF and GF. Edge GF has the smallest weight (12). GF is chosen as part of the tree. Node F is added into the tree.

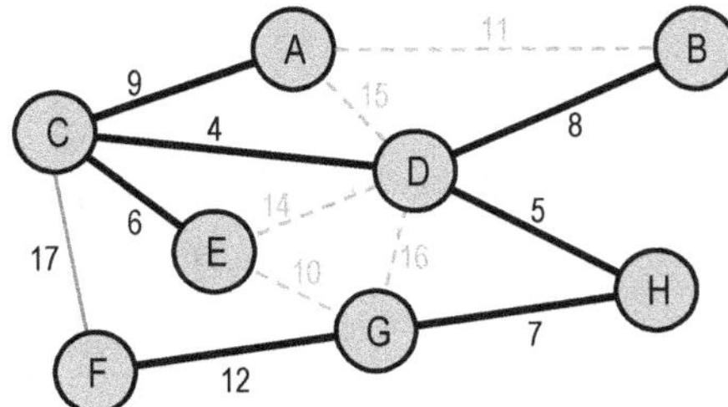

Edge CF connects nodes C and F. Both nodes are already part of the tree, mark edge CF so that it will not be selected to join minimum spanning tree.

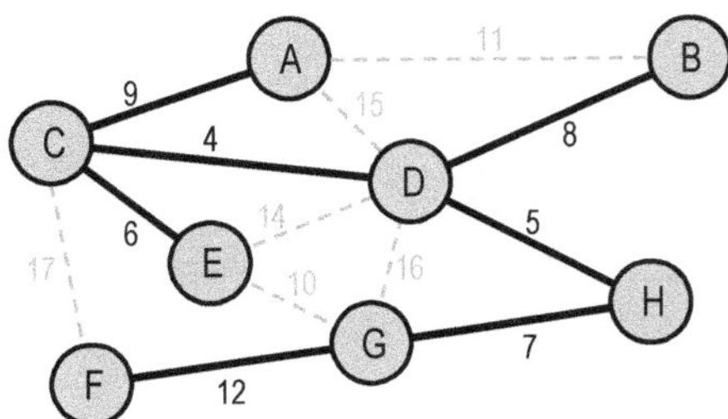

All nodes are already part of the tree. The above solution is the minimum spanning tree.

Kruskal Algorithm

Kruskal algorithm takes different approach to solve minimum spanning tree problem using greedy technique. Instead of starting with a node, Kruskal algorithm chooses valid edge with smallest weight during every step, then eliminates invalid edges. This algorithm was developed by Joseph Kruskal.

The basic steps of Kruskal algorithm:
1. All edges are considered valid.
2. From all valid edges connected to the tree, find an edge with the smallest weight. Choose that edge to join the tree.
3. Find all nodes connected by all edges in the tree, add those nodes into the tree.
4. Check all the other edges that have not joined the tree, if both nodes connected by an edge is already part of the tree, mark the edge as invalid.
5. Repeat from step #2 until all nodes are part of the tree.

Example:
An Kruskal algorithm needs to convert weighted graph with 8 nodes [A,B,C,D,E,F,G,H] into a minimum spanning tree. Which edges need to be removed?

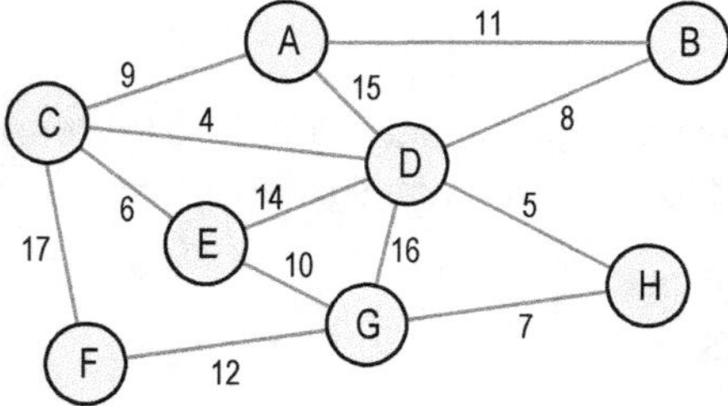

First, all edges are considered valid. Edge CD has the smallest weight (4). CD is chosen as part of the tree. Nodes C and D are added into the tree.

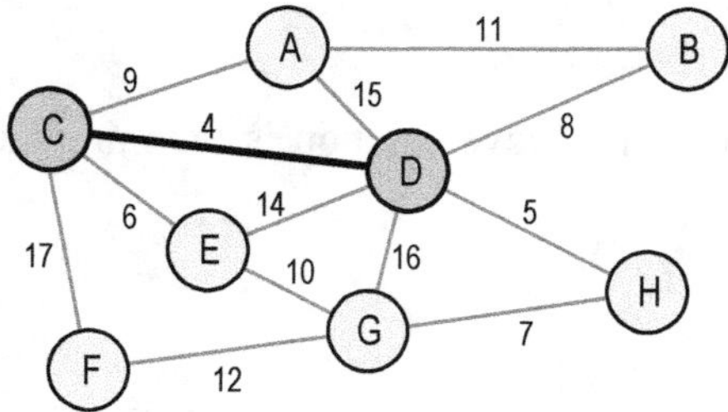

Edge DH has the smallest weight (5). DH is chosen as part of the tree. Node H is added into the tree.

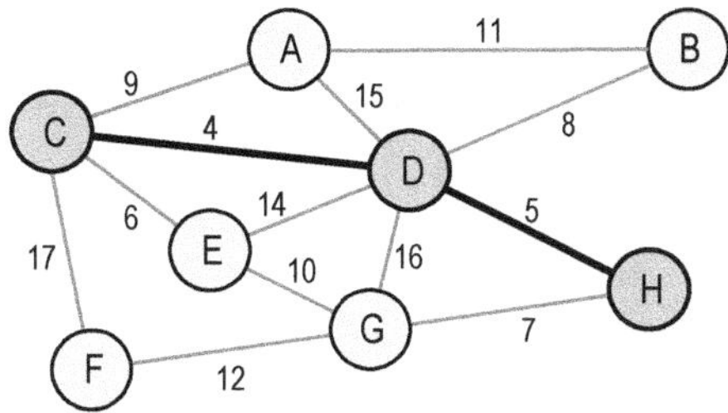

Edge CE has the smallest weight (6). CE is chosen as part of the tree. Node E is added into the tree.

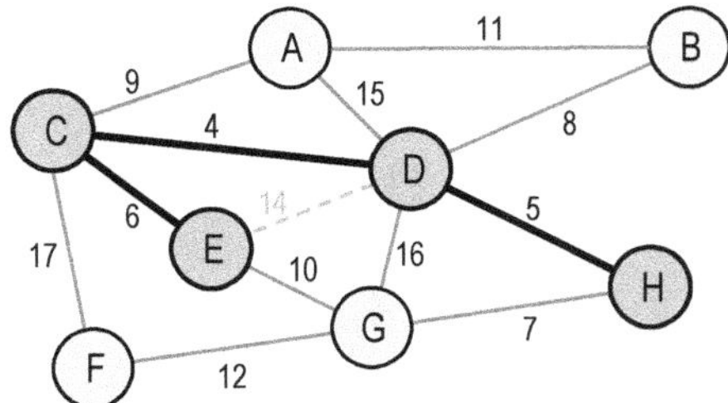

Edge ED connects nodes E and D. Both nodes are already part of the tree, mark edge ED as invalid.

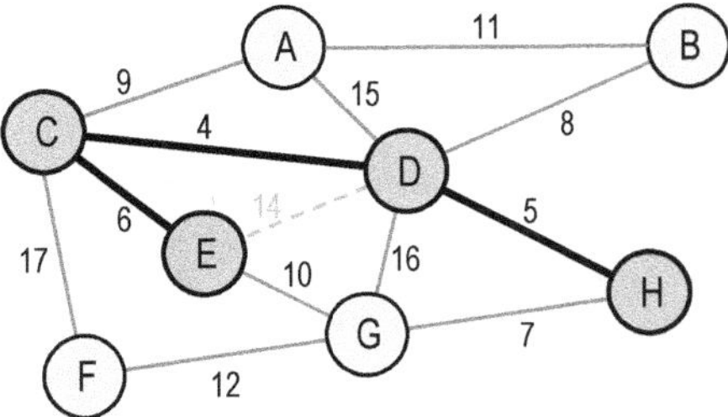

Edge GH has the smallest weight (7). GH is chosen as part of the tree. Node G is added into the tree.

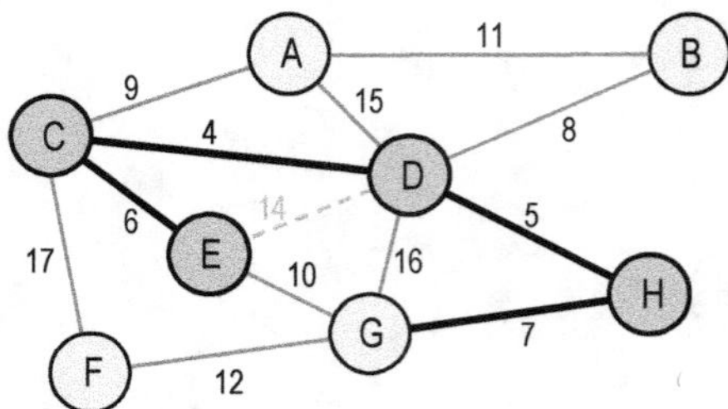

Edge EG connects nodes E and G. Both nodes are already part of the tree, mark edge EG as invalid. Do the same for edge DG.

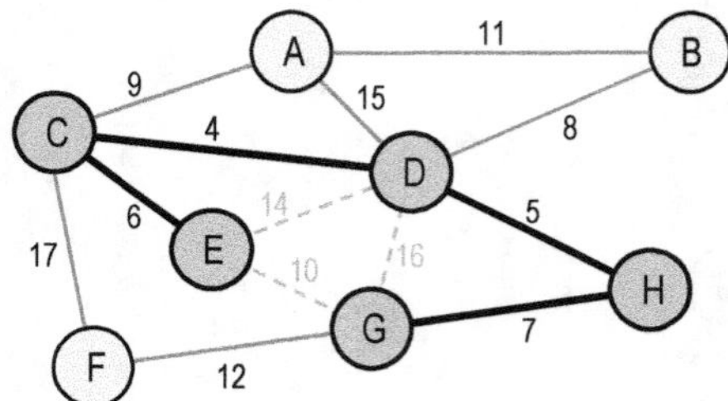

Edge DB has the smallest weight (8). DB is chosen as part of the tree. Node B is added into the tree.

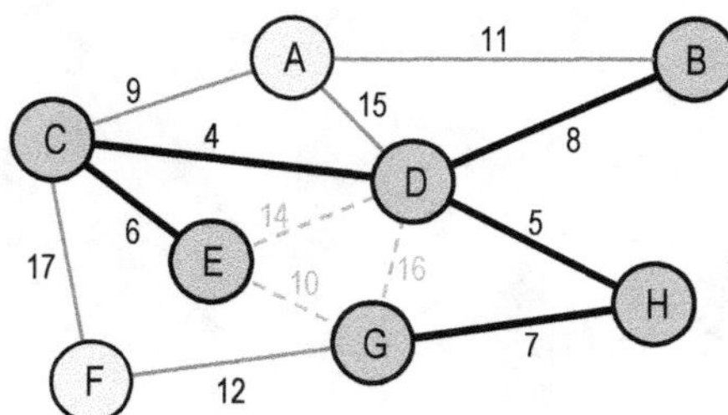

Edge CA has the smallest weight (9). CA is chosen as part of the tree. Node A is added into the tree.

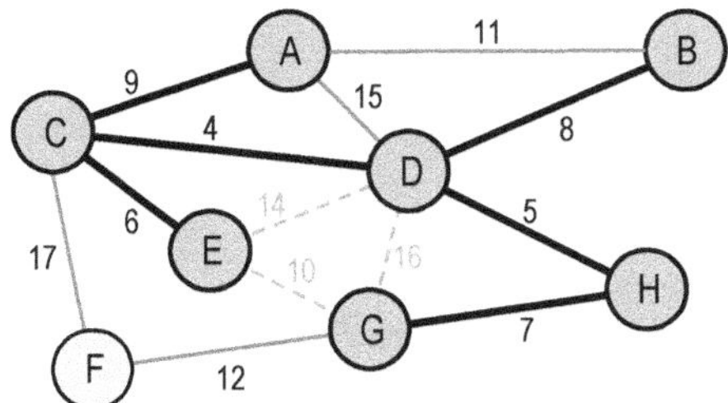

Edge AD connects nodes A and D. Both nodes are already part of the tree, mark edge AD as invalid. Do the same for edge AB.

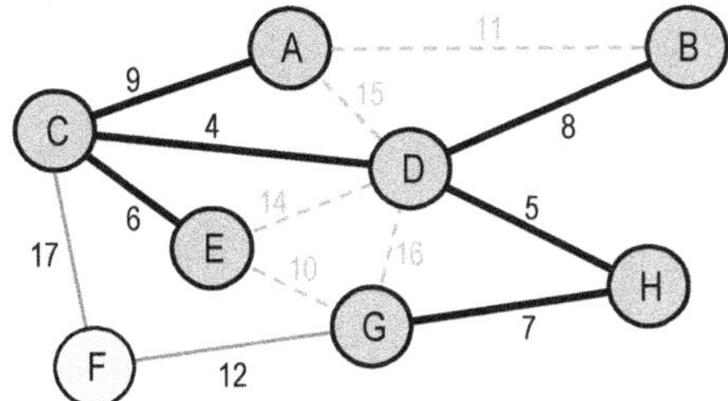

Edge GF has the smallest weight (12). GF is chosen as part of the tree. Node F is added into the tree.

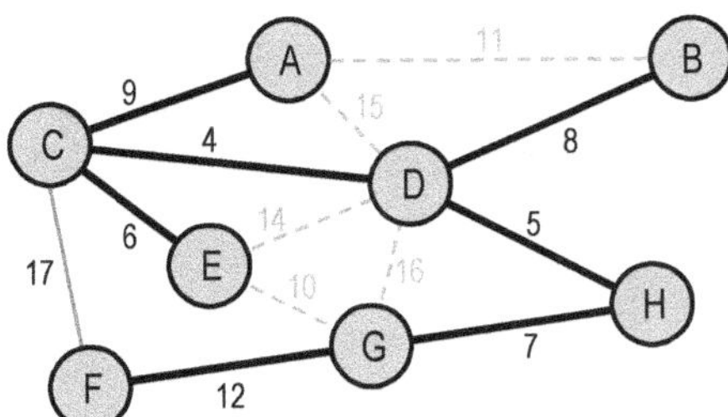

Edge CF connects nodes C and F. Both nodes are already part of the tree, mark edge CF as invalid.

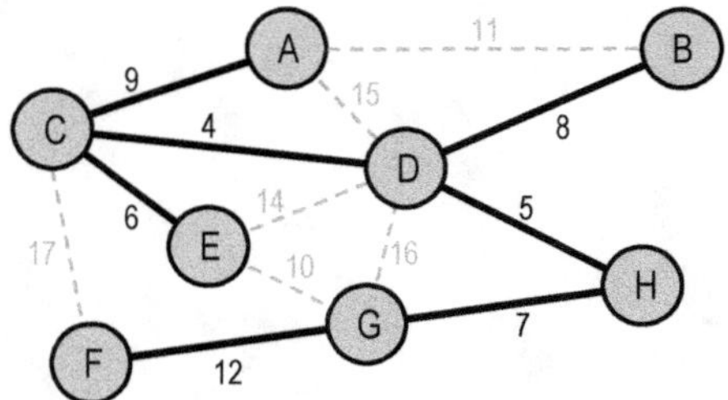

All nodes are already part of the tree. The above solution is the minimum spanning tree. Note that the minimum spanning tree calculated by Kruskal algorithm is identical to the solution calculated by Prim-Dijkstra algorithm. This will be the case for most weighted graphs with some exceptions where many edges have the same weight.

Graph and Map Colouring

Graph colouring is a classic algorithm problem to assign colours to nodes in a graph in such a way that two nodes connected through an edge cannot be assigned the same colour. The challenge of this algorithm is to achieve the colouring using minimum number of colour possible.

In the graph below, every node is assigned a colour of red (R) or blue (B) or yellow (Y) in such a way that no 2 nodes connected through a node have the same colour. The number of required colours is three (red, blue, and yellow). This minimum number of required colours is known as *chromatic number*.

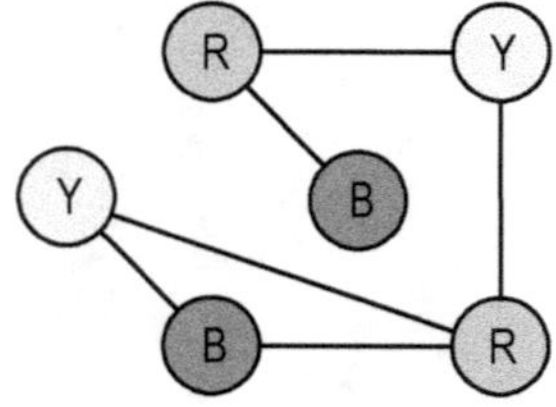

Edge colouring problem is a variation of graph colouring problem. Colours are assigned to edges instead to nodes. Edges that meet on the same node cannot be assigned the same colour.

Region colouring problem assigns colours to sub-regions in such a way that regions that are connected to a shared border cannot have the same colour. This problem is also known as *map colouring*. Decades ago, back in the time when digital maps with location detection was not the norm, maps were printed on paper. The world map, for example, will be printed with different colour to show the areas of different countries. To save printing cost, map publishers were trying to use minimum colour possible.

Map colouring problem can be solved in the same way as graph colouring problem. In the case of colouring countries in world map, for example, each country can be represented by a node and each border between countries is represented by edge.

Please observe the below map of South America:

This book chooses the map of South America because it has unique border structure to show the complexity of map colouring. To assign colours to each country area, a process of converting areas into nodes are needed.

- Venezuela is represented by node A.
- Guyana is represented by node B.
- Suriname is represented by node C.

- French Guiana is represented by node D.
- Colombia is represented by node E.
- Ecuador is represented by node F.
- Peru is represented by node G.
- Brazil is represented by node H.
- Bolivia is represented by node I.
- Paraguay is represented by node J.
- Chile is represented by node K.
- Argentina is represented by node L.
- Uruguay is represented by node M.

Venezuela shares borders with Colombia, Guyana, and Brazil. Therefore, node A has edges to nodes E, B and H. There is no border between Venezuela and Suriname. There should be no edge connecting nodes A and C. Using the same principle, the map of South America can be represented by the graph below.

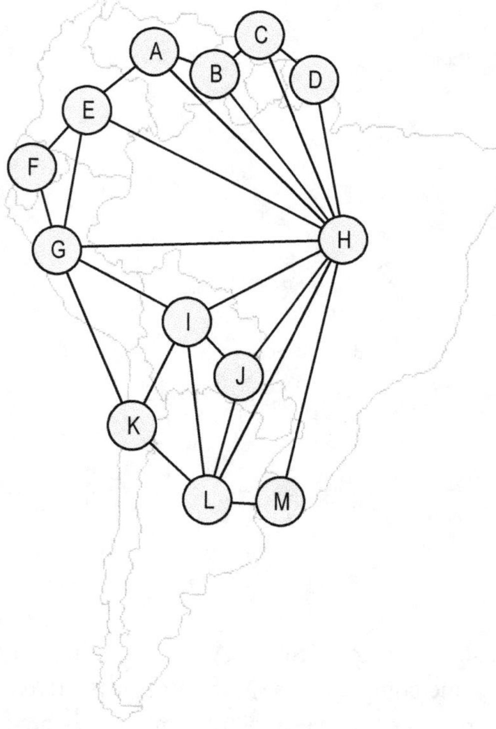

The simplest technique to solve graph colouring problem is **Welsh and Powell algorithm**. This technique implements greedy approach using the following steps:

1. For each node, count how many edges are connected to that node.
2. Sort nodes from the ones with highest number of connected edges (descending order). Choose the first active colour.
3. Assign the first colour to a node with highest number of connected edges.
4. Choose the next node with highest number of connected edges with no colour assignment.
5. If the node is not connected to any other nodes with active colour, assign active colour to the node.
6. Repeat from step #4 until all nodes have been evaluated.
7. After all nodes have been evaluated, change the active colour, go back from the beginning of node list, and repeat from step #3. Do this until all nodes are assigned with colours.

Using the steps above, the graph of South American countries can be coloured with the below steps:

- Steps 1 and 2: Count the number of edges connected to each node. Then sort the nodes in descending order. The results are H(10), G(5), I(5), L(5), E(4), A(3), B(3), C(3), J(3), K(3), D(2), F(2), and M(2). Choose red as active colour.
- Step 3: Assign first colour (red) to node H.
- Steps 4 and 5: Check nodes G, I, and L as unassigned nodes with next highest number of edges. All three of them are connected to a node with red colour (node H). Therefore, these nodes cannot be assigned red.
- Steps 4 and 5: Check node E as the unassigned node with next highest number of edges. Node E is connected to a node with red colour (node H). Therefore, this node cannot be assigned red.
- Steps 4 and 5: Check nodes A, B, C, J, and K.
  - Nodes A, B, C, and J are connected to red node (H), so it cannot be assigned red.
  - Node K is not connected to any red nodes. Therefore, red is assigned to node K.
- Steps 4 and 5: Check nodes D, F and M.
  - Node D is connected to a red node (H), so it cannot be assigned red.
  - Node F is not connected to any red nodes. Therefore, red is assigned to node F.

- o Node M is connected to a red node (H), so it cannot be assigned red.
- Step 6: All nodes have been evaluated for this iteration. The newly coloured nodes are H, K and F. Red nodes are shown as rhombus-shaped nodes in the graph below.

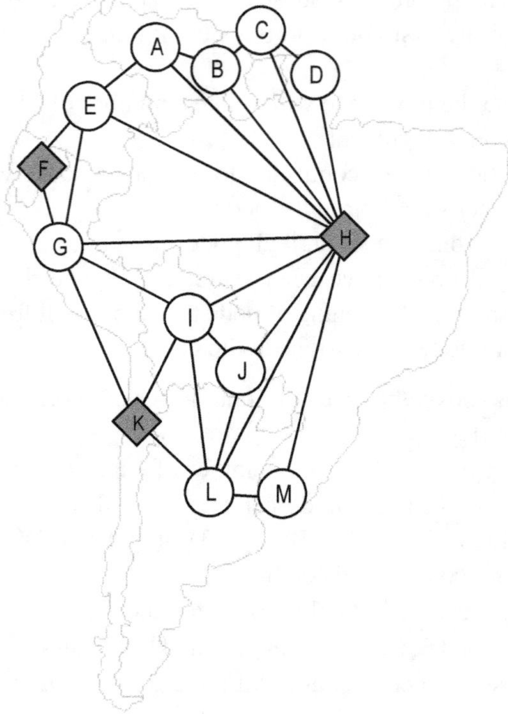

- Step 7: Change active colour from red to yellow. Then go back to the beginning of node list and repeat from step #3.
- Steps 3: Second iteration with new active colour (yellow). Choose node G as the next node with highest number of connected edges with no colour assignment. Assign yellow to node G.
- Steps 4 and 5: Check nodes I and L as unassigned nodes with next highest number of edges.
    - o Node I is connected to a yellow node (G), so it cannot be assigned yellow.
    - o Node L is not connected to any yellow nodes. Therefore, yellow is assigned to node L.
- Steps 4 and 5: Check node E as the unassigned node with next highest number of edges. Node E is connected to a node with yellow colour (node G). Therefore, this node cannot be assigned yellow.

- Steps 4 and 5: Check nodes A, B, C, and J.
    - o Node A is not connected to any yellow nodes. Therefore, yellow is assigned to node A.
    - o Node B is now connected to a yellow node (A), so it cannot be assigned yellow.
    - o Node C is not connected to any yellow nodes. Therefore, yellow is assigned to node C.
    - o Node J is connected to a yellow node (L), so it cannot be assigned yellow.
- Steps 4 and 5: Check nodes D and M. Both nodes are connected to nodes with yellow colour (nodes C and L). Therefore, these nodes cannot be assigned yellow.
- Step 6: All nodes have been evaluated for this iteration. The newly coloured nodes are G, L, A, and C. Yellow nodes are shown as pentagon-shaped nodes in the graph below.

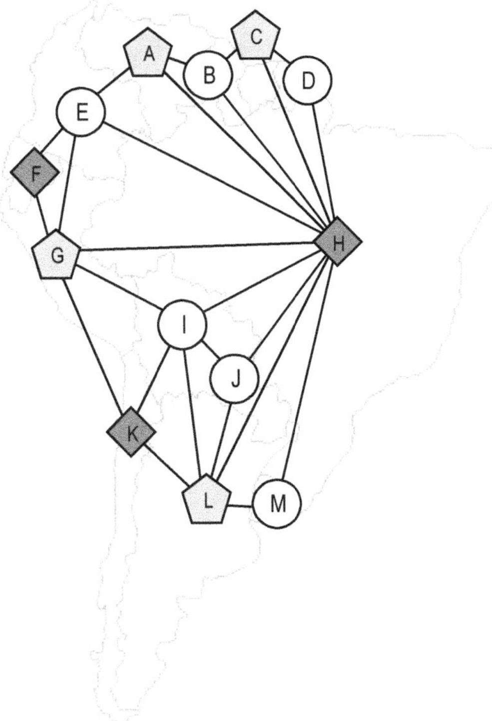

- Step 7: Change active colour from yellow to green. Then go back to the beginning of node list and repeat from step #3.

- Steps 3: Third iteration with new active colour (green). Choose node I as the next node with highest number of connected edges with no colour assignment. Assign green to node I.
- Steps 4 and 5: Check node E as the unassigned node with next highest number of edges. Node E is not connected to any green nodes. Therefore, green is assigned to node E.
- Steps 4 and 5: Check nodes B and J.
  - Node B is not connected to any green nodes. Therefore, green is assigned to node B.
  - Node J is connected to a green node (I), so it cannot be assigned green.
- Steps 4 and 5: Check nodes D and M. Both nodes are not connected to any green nodes. Therefore, green is assigned to nodes D and M.
- Step 6: All nodes have been evaluated for this iteration. The newly coloured nodes are I, E, B, D, and M. Green nodes are shown as hexagon-shaped nodes in the graph below.

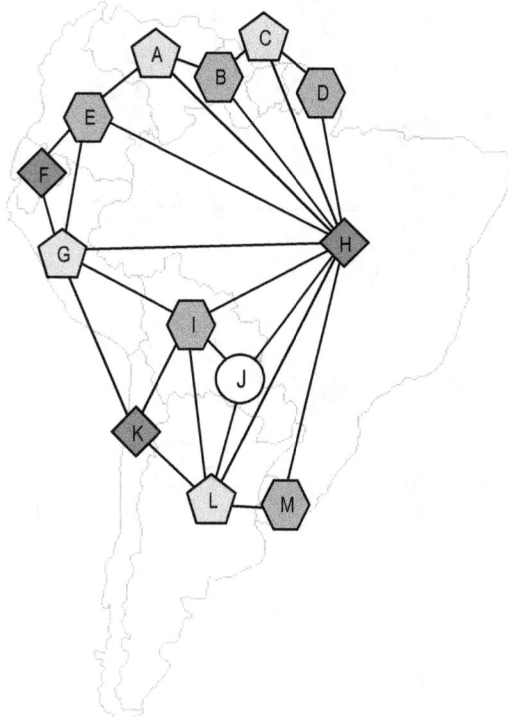

- Step 7: Change active colour from green to blue. Then go back to the beginning of node list and repeat from step #3.

- Steps 3: Fourth iteration with new active colour (blue). Choose node J as the next unassigned node with highest number of connected edges. Assign blue to node J.
- Step 7: Colours have been assigned to all nodes. The newly coloured node is J. Blue nodes are shown as square-shaped nodes in the graph below.

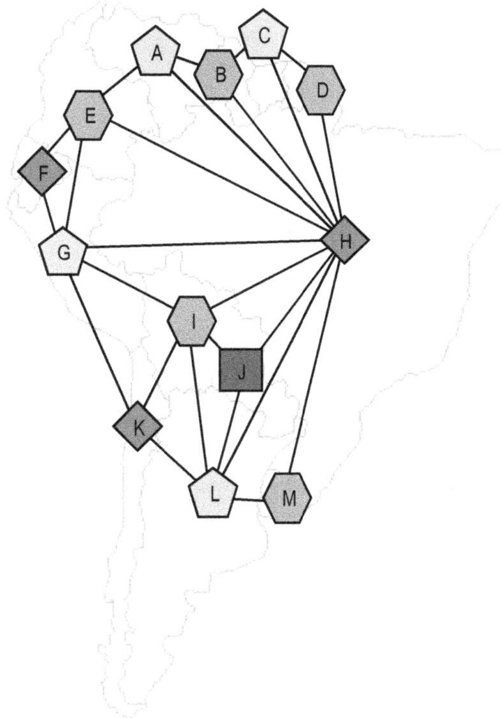

Welsh and Powell algorithm solves the graph colouring problem above using four colours (red, yellow, green, and blue). The colours of each node can be mapped into the country areas in the original map.

Note that solving map colouring problem with greedy algorithm does not guarantee perfect solution. However, Welsh and Powell algorithm is capable of producing good results for most simple maps. Full calculation of graph colouring problem is an NP-Complete problem (non-deterministic polynomial time) and will not be discussed in this book. According to *four colour theorem*, any map can be coloured with four colours or less regardless of the shapes of regions within a map.

05. DYNAMIC PROGRAMMING

Similar to greedy algorithm from the previous chapter, dynamic programming is a different technique to solve problems that contain a sequence of decisions. Contrary to greedy algorithm's one-decision-at-a-time approach, dynamic programming splits a problem into multiple overlapping sub-problems. By evaluating overlapping sub-problems, dynamic programming takes some impacts of one decision to other decisions, making it better than greedy algorithm which completely ignore any other steps when choosing a decision.

Dynamic programming considers more possible solutions than greedy algorithm without exploring all possible solutions. Execution time is considerably faster than calculating all possibilities, especially when a problem has very large number of feasible solutions.

Fibonacci Sequence Problem

Fibonacci sequence is a series of numbers starting from 0 and 1, then each number in the sequence is the sum of two previous numbers: 0, 1, 1, 2, 3, 5, 8, 13, 21, 34, 55, ... This chapter will compare different ways to write an algorithm to display the first 100 numbers in Fibonacci sequence.

```
1 module Fibo(n)
2   if (n=1) or (n=2) then
3     result=n-1
4   else if (n>2) then
5     result=Fibo(n-1)+Fibo(n-2)
6   end if
7 end module
8
9 for i=1 to 50 do
10   display Fibo(i)," "
11 end for
```

Algorithm 05-A   Fibonacci Sequence Algorithm – Naïve Version

The naïve version of Fibonacci algorithm takes n as input and will calculate the nth number in Fibonacci sequence. It uses recursion to calculate the previous two numbers and simply adds them up. Sounds correct and it is indeed a correct algorithm. However, being correct does not always mean that an algorithm follows best practices with regards to performance.

To calculate the first or second element in Fibonacci sequence, Fibo function is called once. To calculate the sixth element, the same function needs to be multiple times because it needs to call the same function with different parameters (5 and 4) recursively.

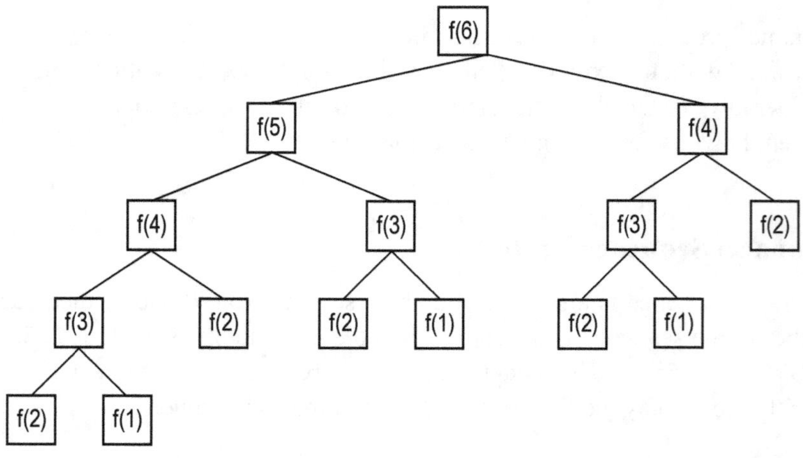

Each box in the illustration above represents one call of Fibo function. This means, to calculate the sixth element in Fibonacci sequence, Algorithm 05-A needs to be called 15 times. Using the same recursion, calculating the 20th element would require 13,529 calls and calculating the 50th element would need massive number of 25,172,538,049 calls.

Element #n	How many calls of `Fibo` function?
1	1
2	1
3	3
4	5
5	9
6	15
7	25
8	41
...	...
20	13,529
...	...
50	25,172,538,049

In real world math, one rarely need just one element of Fibonacci sequence. Instead, the normal use is to calculate and display the first x numbers in Fibonacci sequence. Executing line #9, #10 and #11 from Algorithm 05-A would require even higher number of function calls.

#n	Calls to calculate element #n	Calls to calculate element #1 to #n
1	1	1
2	1	2
3	3	5
4	5	10
5	9	19
6	15	34
7	25	59
8	41	100
...	...	...
20	13,529	35,400
...	...	...
50	25,172,538,049	69,902,560,146

Calculating and displaying the first 50 numbers in Fibonacci sequence would require over 69 billion times of function calls. No matter how fast a machine can perform calculation, calling the same function 69 billion times to calculate the first 50 numbers in Fibonacci sequence is not a good practice because within the calculation of each iteration, massive number of calculations are redundant.

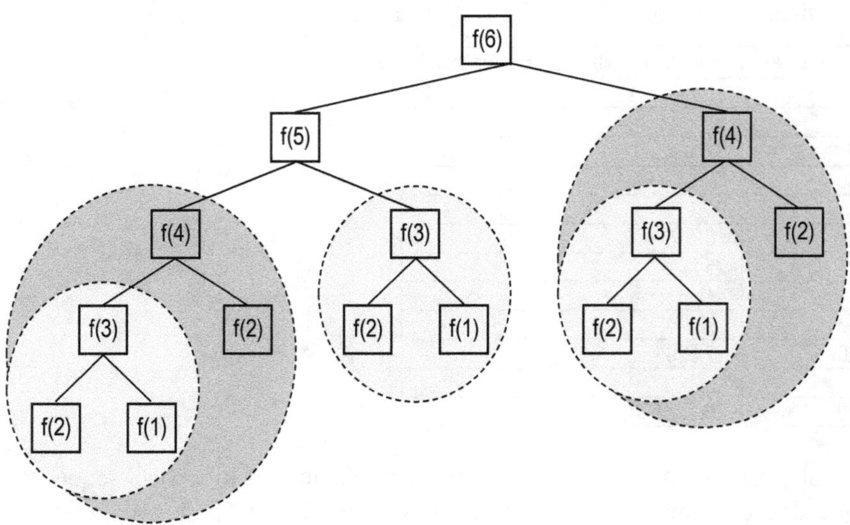

Back to the first example of calculating the sixth element in Fibonacci sequence. Remember that recursion tree is explored with depth-first method, meaning if a node has sub-nodes, all the sub-nodes must be resolved first, starting from left to right. On calculating `Fibo(5)`, the algorithm needs to calculate `Fibo(4)` and `Fibo(3)`. To calculate `Fibo(4)`, the algorithm needs to calculate `Fibo(3)` and `Fibo(2)`. Once `Fibo(3)` and `Fibo(2)` are resolved, the algorithm now have the value of `Fibo(4)`. However, to calculate `Fibo(5)`, it will calculate `Fibo(3)` once again. Later on, to calculate `Fibo(6)`, the algorithm will repeat the calculation of `Fibo(4)` and then `Fibo(3)`.

Memoisation technique can be used to significantly improve the efficiency of Fibonacci algorithm by writing memos to remember the results of previous calculations so that the algorithm would not need to perform redundant function calls.

```
 1 module Fibo(n)
 2   if (n=1) or (n=2) then
 3     result=n-1
 4   else if (n>2) then
 5     if F[n-1]=0 then F[n-1]=Fibo(n-1)
 6     if F[n-2]=0 then F[n-2]=Fibo(n-2)
 7     F[n]=F[n-1]+F[n-2]
 8     result=F[n]
 9   end if
10 end module
11
12 for i=1 to 50 do F[i]=0
13
14 for i=1 to 50 do
15   display Fibo(i)," "
16 end for
```

Algorithm 05-B   Fibonacci Algorithm with Memoisation

Line #12 from Algorithm 05-B creates array F as the memo, making sure the elements in the array are set to zero. Line #14, #15 and #16 displays the first 50 elements in Fibonacci sequence by calling Fibo function. The function itself has been modified to record memo of past Fibonacci sequence into array F. Instead of calling the function recursively, line #7 simply gets the values of previous Fibonacci numbers from F.

If known that Fibo function will only be used to display the first x elements of Fibonacci sequence, line #5 and #6 can be safely removed because by the time Fibo function is called with parameter n, it is known that F[n-1] and F[n-2] should already been calculated before. However, Fibo function can be called independently. Another module might call Fibo(27) without previously call Fibo(25) and Fibo(26), for example. It is generally a good practice to ensure that a function has independent characteristics that will work regardless of how it will be called.

With memoisation, displaying the first 50 elements of Fibonacci sequence would require 50 calls of Fibo function instead of 69,902,560,146 times. Note that displaying just the 50th elements (instead of the first 50 elements) would still require 50 calls because the memo is empty when the function is called for the first time.

There are two possible scenarios of memoisation. In *top-down* calculation, result is achieved by breaking down a problem into smaller components. This technique is commonly used in algorithms with recursion. Memoisation in top-down scenario remembers the result of smaller components and use it to construct the result.

In *bottom-up* calculation, result is calculated by building up from a starting point towards the solution, usually in an iterative algorithm. Memoisation would remember the results of earlier calculations to be used during further iterations.

```
1 F[1]=1
2 F[2]=1
3 display F[1]," ",F[2]," "
4 for i=3 to 50 do
5   F[i]=F[i-1]+F[i-2]
6   display F[i]," "
7 end for
```

Algorithm 05-C Fibonacci Algorithm with Bottom-Up Memoisation

In Algorithm 05-C, there is no function to be called because the whole calculation happens in one simple loop. The algorithm starts by assigning initial values to the first 2 elements of array F, then continues with filling up the array, one step at a time. Line #6 display each newly calculated element as part of the final solution.

It is worth to note that memoisation strategy basically exchange calculation count with memory space. More things to be remembered would require larger memory capacity to store.

Storing array F with 50 elements is not a big problem for modern computing. However, more complex problem would require exponentially larger memory to store the memo and further optimisation could be required.

```
1 f1=1
2 f2=1
3 display f1," ",f2," "
4 for i=3 to 50 do
5   iFibo=f1+f2
6   display iFibo," "
7   f2=f1
8   f1=iFibo
9 end for
```

Algorithm 05-D Fibonacci Algorithm with Improved Memoisation

Instead of using array F to store each element of Fibonacci elements, Algorithm 05-D uses two simple numeric variables. The previous/last element is stored in `f1` and the second last element is stored in `f2`. During each iteration, the algorithm in line #5 would calculate the new Fibonacci element from the two previous results. After calculating new element and displaying the result, the algorithm discards the second last element and moves the last element into second last element (line #7). Then, the new element becomes the last element for the next iteration (line #8).

This tweak is only made possible because Fibonacci sequence only need to calculate the last 2 elements. The need to remember all elements calculated so far is replaced by remembering only the last two elements. Other kinds of problems might require an algorithm to remember more for memoisation strategy.

Coin Change Problem

Back on the days when people still use physical money in stores, often some coins are given as change when a buyer does not have the exact amount of money. For example, when buying an item that costs $47, a buyer gives $50 note to the cashier and receives $3 change in the form of one $2 coin and one $1 coin.

Sometimes, some change values cannot be achieved using the available coins. In 2023, Australia has coins of $2, $1, 50c, 20c, 10c and 5c. This means, a cashier will not be able to give someone a change money of $3.21 because there is no coin worth 1 cent.

Coin change problem tries to calculate change money of a specific value using the available coins. This is a popular math problem to teach the basic principles of dynamic programming. Originally introduced by German mathematician Ferdinand Georg Frobenius, coin change problem is also known in some other books as *Frobenius Problem*.

Example:
Country Z has coins in three values: $3, $5 and $12.
- Can someone give change of $23 using those coins?
- How many coins minimum is needed to make $23?

Can we give change of $23 using $3, $5 and $12 coins?

Using human logic, we know that we can give $6 change using 2 coins of $3. $8 change can be given using 1 coin of $3 and 1 coin of $5. However, $7 could not be given using any combination of $3, $5 and $12 coins. How can an algorithm solve this?

Analysis for this question starts with listing the most basic values that can be given using the available coins:

- $3 can be given using 1 coin of $3.
- $5 can be given using 1 coin of $5.
- $12 can be given using 1 coin of $12.

Mathematically, the above points can be written as:

- `f(3)  = true`
- `f(5)  = true`
- `f(12) = true`
- `f(x)  = false for x < 0`
- `f(n)  = f(n-3) OR f(n-5) OR f(n-12)`

There are two possible algorithms to implement the above rules. The first algorithm uses *pull* technique; the status of a value is decided by evaluating prior values. The second algorithm uses *push* technique, where current iteration for a particular value would impact the statuses of upcoming relevant values.

Algorithm with *pull technique*:

- To find out whether $23 can be given, algorithm needs to find out whether $20, $18 or $11 can be given.
- As generalisation: <u>to find out whether x can be given, algorithm needs to find out whether (x-3) or (x-5) or (x-12) can be given</u>.
- To find out whether (x-3) can be given, algorithm needs to find out whether (x-3)-3 or (x-3)-5 or (x-3)-12 can be given.
    - To find out whether (x-3-3) can be given, algorithm needs to find out whether (x-3-3)-3 or (x-3-3)-5 or (x-3-3)-12 can be given.
    - And so on.
- To find out whether (x-5) can be given, algorithm needs to find out whether (x-5)-3 or (x-5)-5 or (x-5)-12 can be given.
- To find out whether (x-12) can be given, algorithm needs to find out whether (x-12)-3 or (x-12)-5 or (x-12)-12 can be given.
- And so on.

Algorithm with *push technique*:

- If $3 change can be given, then $6, $8 or $15 can be given.
- As generalisation: <u>if x change can be given, then (x+3) and (x+5) and (x+12) can be given.</u>
- If (x+3) change can be given, then (x+3)+3 and (x+3)+5 and (x+3)+12 can be given.
  - o If (x+3+3) change can be given, then (x+3+3)+3 and (x+3+3)+5 and (x+3+3)+12 can be given.
  - o And so on.
- If (x+5) change can be given, then (x+5)+3 and (x+5)+5 and (x+5)+12 can be given.
- If (x+12) change can be given, then (x+12)+3 and (x+12)+5 and (x+12)+12 can be given.
- And so on.

Either pull or push technique can be used to implement dynamic algorithm to solve this coin change problem. Pull technique is arguably more popular for new learners because the concept is easier to understand.

Algorithm 05-E uses array `arrC` to store flags representing whether a particular value can be given using the available coins. The size of array is defined as 25 only for the purpose of this example. It is sufficient because this algorithm only needs to calculate whether $23 can be given or not. Changing the value of `iArraySize` variable will adjust the size of `arrC`.

```
 1 iArraySize=25
 2 iNumOfCoins=3
 3 coin[1]=3
 4 coin[2]=5
 5 coin[3]=12
 6 for i=1 to iArraySize do
 7   arrC[i]="N"
 8 end for
 9 for i=1 to iNumOfCoins do
10   arrC[coin[i]]="Y"
11 end for
12 for x=1 to iArraySize do
13   for j=1 to iNumOfCoins do
14     if (x-coin[j])>=1 then
15       if arrC[x-coin[j]]="Y" then
16         arrC[i]="Y"
17       end if
18     end if
19   end for
20 end for
21 if arrC[23]="Y" then
22   display "Value 23 can be given."
23 else
24   display "Value 23 cannot be given."
25 end if
```

Algorithm 05-E Pull Technique for "can x be given?"

Lines #2 to #5 defines the values of available coins. Simple loop in lines #6 to #8 sets initial values of arrC, marking every value with N (no) flag/status. It means, every value is initially assumed to be not possible until algorithm finds otherwise. Furthermore, lines #9 to #11 mark values 3, 5 and 12 in arrC (or whatever values are defined as available coins) as Y (yes) because those values can be given using just 1 of the possible coins.

The next part of the algorithm is quite straightforward. A big loop (lines #12 to #20) is executed for every element of arrC to find whether the value can be given. For each value of x, if any of (x-3) or (x-5) or (x-12) are marked as Y, the pull algorithm will mark x element in arrC as Y.

Step 1. At the beginning, each element of arrC is marked as N.

1	2	3	4	5	6	7	8	9	10	11	12	13	14	15	16	17	18	19	20	21	22	23	24	25
N	N	N	N	N	N	N	N	N	N	N	N	N	N	N	N	N	N	N	N	N	N	N	N	N

Step 2. Elements 3, 5 and 12 are set to Y (lines #9 to #11).

1	2	3	4	5	6	7	8	9	10	11	12	13	14	15	16	17	18	19	20	21	22	23	24	25
N	N	Y	N	Y	N	N	N	N	N	N	Y	N	N	N	N	N	N	N	N	N	N	N	N	N

Step 3. Start the big loop (lines #12 to #20). When x is 1, 2 and 3 (the first three iterations), the values of (x-3), (x-5) and (x-12) are all negative values and can be ignored (see line #14).

1	2	3	4	5	6	7	8	9	10	11	12	13	14	15	16	17	18	19	20	21	22	23	24	25
N	N	Y	N	Y	N	N	N	N	N	N	Y	N	N	N	N	N	N	N	N	N	N	N	N	N

When x=4, the value of (x-3)=1 is a positive number, so it needs to be evaluated. If the flag in arrC[1] is Y, then arrC[4] needs to be updated to Y. However, since arrC[1] is flagged as N, no change is made to arrC[4].

1	2	3	4	5	6	7	8	9	10	11	12	13	14	15	16	17	18	19	20	21	22	23	24	25
N	N	Y	N	Y	N	N	N	N	N	N	Y	N	N	N	N	N	N	N	N	N	N	N	N	N

When x=5, the value of (x-3)=2 is a positive number. If the flag in arrC[2] is Y, then arrC[5] needs to be updated to Y. However, since arrC[2] is flagged as N, no change is made to arrC[5].

1	2	3	4	5	6	7	8	9	10	11	12	13	14	15	16	17	18	19	20	21	22	23	24	25
N	N	Y	N	Y	N	N	N	N	N	N	Y	N	N	N	N	N	N	N	N	N	N	N	N	N

When x=6, the values of (x-3)=3 and (x-5)=1 are positive numbers. If the flag in arrC[1] or arrC[3] is Y, then arrC[6] needs to be updated. In this case, arrC[3] is Y. Therefore, arrC[6] is updated to Y.

1	2	3	4	5	6	7	8	9	10	11	12	13	14	15	16	17	18	19	20	21	22	23	24	25
N	N	Y	N	Y	Y	N	N	N	N	N	Y	N	N	N	N	N	N	N	N	N	N	N	N	N

When x=7, the values of (x-3)=4 and (x-5)=2 are positive numbers. If the flag in arrC[2] or arrC[4] is Y, then arrC[7] needs to be updated. In this case, neither of them has Y flag. Therefore, no change is made to arrC[7].

1	2	3	4	5	6	7	8	9	10	11	12	13	14	15	16	17	18	19	20	21	22	23	24	25
N	N	Y	N	Y	Y	N	N	N	N	N	Y	N	N	N	N	N	N	N	N	N	N	N	N	N

When x=8, the values of (x-3)=5 and (x-5)=3 are positive numbers. If the flag in arrC[3] or arrC[5] is Y, then arrC[8] needs to be updated. In this case, both have Y flag. Therefore, arrC[8] is updated to Y.

1	2	3	4	5	6	7	8	9	10	11	12	13	14	15	16	17	18	19	20	21	22	23	24	25
N	N	Y	N	Y	Y	N	Y	N	N	N	Y	N	N	N	N	N	N	N	N	N	N	N	N	N

When x=9, the values of $(x-3)=6$ and $(x-5)=4$ are positive numbers. If the flag in `arrC[4]` or `arrC[6]` is Y, then `arrC[9]` needs to be updated. In this case, `arrC[6]` has Y flag. Therefore, `arrC[9]` is updated to Y.

1	2	3	4	5	6	7	8	9	10	11	12	13	14	15	16	17	18	19	20	21	22	23	24	25
N	N	Y	N	Y	Y	N	Y	Y	N	N	Y	N	N	N	N	N	N	N	N	N	N	N	N	N

When x=10, the values of $(x-3)=7$ and $(x-5)=5$ are positive numbers. If the flag in `arrC[5]` or `arrC[7]` is Y, then `arrC[10]` needs to be updated. In this case, `arrC[5]` has Y flag. Therefore, `arrC[10]` is updated to Y.

1	2	3	4	5	6	7	8	9	10	11	12	13	14	15	16	17	18	19	20	21	22	23	24	25
N	N	Y	N	Y	Y	N	Y	Y	Y	N	Y	N	N	N	N	N	N	N	N	N	N	N	N	N

When x=15, the values of $(x-3)=12$ and $(x-5)=10$ and $(x-12)=3$ are positive numbers. If the flag in `arrC[3]` or `arrC[10]` or `arrC[12]` is Y, then `arrC[15]` needs to be updated. In this case, all of them have Y flag. Therefore, `arrC[15]` is updated to Y.

1	2	3	4	5	6	7	8	9	10	11	12	13	14	15	16	17	18	19	20	21	22	23	24	25
N	N	Y	N	Y	Y	N	Y	Y	Y	Y	Y	Y	Y	Y	N	N	N	N	N	N	N	N	N	N

When x=23, the values of $(x-3)=20$ and $(x-5)=18$ and $(x-12)=11$ are positive numbers. If the flag in `arrC[11]` or `arrC[18]` or `arrC[20]` is Y, then `arrC[23]` needs to be updated. In this case, all of them have Y flag. Therefore, `arrC[23]` is updated to Y.

1	2	3	4	5	6	7	8	9	10	11	12	13	14	15	16	17	18	19	20	21	22	23	24	25
N	N	Y	N	Y	Y	N	Y	Y	Y	Y	Y	Y	Y	Y	Y	Y	Y	Y	Y	Y	Y	Y	N	N

When x=24, the values of $(x-3)=21$ and $(x-5)=19$ and $(x-12)=12$ are positive numbers. If the flag in `arrC[12]` or `arrC[19]` or `arrC[21]` is Y, then `arrC[24]` needs to be updated. In this case, all of them have Y flag. Therefore, `arrC[24]` is updated to Y.

1	2	3	4	5	6	7	8	9	10	11	12	13	14	15	16	17	18	19	20	21	22	23	24	25
N	N	Y	N	Y	Y	N	Y	Y	Y	Y	Y	Y	Y	Y	Y	Y	Y	Y	Y	Y	Y	Y	Y	N

When x=25, the values of $(x-3)=22$ and $(x-5)=20$ and $(x-12)=13$ are positive numbers. If the flag in `arrC[13]` or `arrC[20]` or `arrC[22]` is Y, then `arrC[25]` needs to be updated. In this case, all of them have Y flag. Therefore, `arrC[25]` is updated to Y.

1	2	3	4	5	6	7	8	9	10	11	12	13	14	15	16	17	18	19	20	21	22	23	24	25
N	N	Y	N	Y	Y	N	Y	Y	Y	Y	Y	Y	Y	Y	Y	Y	Y	Y	Y	Y	Y	Y	Y	Y

To answer the question from example, the 23rd element of `arrC` is marked as Y. It means that $23 change can be given from a combination of #3, #5 and $12 coins. From the same array, the algorithm calculated that $1, $2, $4 and $7 cannot be given using any combination of available coins.

For each value of x, the flag of whether value x can be given is *pulled* from 3 other flags prior to that value. Note that this algorithm only checks one step backward. There is no need to check the flag of `arrC[(x-3)-3]`, or even `arrC[((x-3)-3)-3]`, for example, because those would have been covered from previous iterations. This illustrates the implementation of dynamic programming.

```
 1 iArraySize=25
 2 iNumOfCoins=3
 3 coin[1]=3
 4 coin[2]=5
 5 coin[3]=12
 6 for i=1 to iArraySize do
 7   arrC[i]="N"
 8 end for
 9 for i=1 to iNumOfCoins do
10   arrC[coin[i]]="Y"
11 end for
12 for x=1 to iArraySize do
13   if arrC[x]="Y" then
14     for j=1 to iNumOfCoins do
15       if (x+coin[j])<=iArraySize then
16         if arrC[x+coin[j]]="N" then
17           arrC[x+coin[j]]="Y"
18         end if
19       end if
20     end for
21   end if
22 end for
23 if arrC[23]="Y" then
24   display "Value 23 can be given."
25 else
26   display "Value 23 cannot be given."
27 end if
```

Algorithm 05-F Push Technique for "can x be given?"

Algorithm 05-FAlgorithm 05-E uses array `arrC` to store flags representing whether a particular value can be given using the available coins, just like Algorithm 05-E. Note that lines #12 to #22 are the only difference between the two algorithms.

In push technique, each iteration has the potential of updating multiple flags of larger elements in `arrC`. If the flag of a particular x value is Y, then the flags of `(x+3)`, `(x+5)` and `(x+12)` need to be updated to Y.

Step 1. At the beginning, each element of `arrC` is marked as N.

1	2	3	4	5	6	7	8	9	10	11	12	13	14	15	16	17	18	19	20	21	22	23	24	25
N	N	N	N	N	N	N	N	N	N	N	N	N	N	N	N	N	N	N	N	N	N	N	N	N

Step 2. Elements 3, 5 and 12 are set to Y (lines #9 to #11).

1	2	3	4	5	6	7	8	9	10	11	12	13	14	15	16	17	18	19	20	21	22	23	24	25
N	N	Y	N	Y	N	N	N	N	N	N	Y	N	N	N	N	N	N	N	N	N	N	N	N	N

Step 3. Start the big loop (lines #12 to #22). When x is 1 and 2 (the first two iterations), the flag of x is N. Therefore, no update is needed.

1	2	3	4	5	6	7	8	9	10	11	12	13	14	15	16	17	18	19	20	21	22	23	24	25
N	N	Y	N	Y	N	N	N	N	N	N	Y	N	N	N	N	N	N	N	N	N	N	N	N	N

When x=3, the flag in `arrC[3]` is Y. Therefore, elements `(x+3)`, `(x+5)` and `(x+12)` need to be updated. This iteration updates `arrC[6]`, `arrC[8]` and `arrC[15]` to Y.

1	2	3	4	5	6	7	8	9	10	11	12	13	14	15	16	17	18	19	20	21	22	23	24	25
N	N	Y	N	Y	Y	N	Y	N	N	N	Y	N	N	Y	N	N	N	N	N	N	N	N	N	N

When x=4, the flag in `arrC[4]` is N. Therefore, no change is required for elements `(x+3)`, `(x+5)` and `(x+12)`.

1	2	3	4	5	6	7	8	9	10	11	12	13	14	15	16	17	18	19	20	21	22	23	24	25
N	N	Y	N	Y	Y	N	Y	N	N	N	Y	N	N	Y	N	N	N	N	N	N	N	N	N	N

When x=5, the flag in `arrC[5]` is Y. Therefore, elements `(x+3)`, `(x+5)` and `(x+12)` might need to be updated. Note that the flag in `arrC[8]` is already Y (see line #16). This iteration updates `arrC[10]` and `arrC[17]` to Y.

1	2	3	4	5	6	7	8	9	10	11	12	13	14	15	16	17	18	19	20	21	22	23	24	25
N	N	Y	N	Y	Y	N	Y	N	Y	N	Y	N	N	Y	N	Y	N	N	N	N	N	N	N	N

When x=6, the flag in `arrC[6]` is Y. Therefore, elements `(x+3)`, `(x+5)` and `(x+12)` need to be updated. This iteration updates `arrC[9]`, `arrC[11]` and `arrC[18]` to Y.

1	2	3	4	5	6	7	8	9	10	11	12	13	14	15	16	17	18	19	20	21	22	23	24	25
N	N	Y	N	Y	Y	N	Y	Y	Y	Y	Y	N	N	Y	N	Y	Y	N	N	N	N	N	N	N

When x=7, the flag in arrC[7] is N. Therefore, no change is required for elements (x+3), (x+5) and (x+12).

1	2	3	4	5	6	7	8	9	10	11	12	13	14	15	16	17	18	19	20	21	22	23	24	25
N	N	Y	N	Y	Y	N	Y	Y	Y	Y	Y	N	N	Y	N	Y	Y	N	N	N	N	N	N	N

When x=8, the flag in arrC[8] is Y. Therefore, elements (x+3), (x+5) and (x+12) might need to be updated. Note that the flag in arrC[11] is already Y. This iteration updates arrC[13] and arrC[20] to Y.

1	2	3	4	5	6	7	8	9	10	11	12	13	14	15	16	17	18	19	20	21	22	23	24	25
N	N	Y	N	Y	Y	N	Y	Y	Y	Y	Y	Y	N	Y	N	Y	Y	N	Y	N	N	N	N	N

When x=9, the flag in arrC[9] is Y. Therefore, elements (x+3), (x+5) and (x+12) might need to be updated. Note that the flag in arrC[12] is already Y. This iteration updates arrC[14] and arrC[21] to Y.

1	2	3	4	5	6	7	8	9	10	11	12	13	14	15	16	17	18	19	20	21	22	23	24	25
N	N	Y	N	Y	Y	N	Y	Y	Y	Y	Y	Y	Y	Y	N	Y	Y	N	Y	Y	N	N	N	N

When x=10, the flag in arrC[10] is Y. Therefore, elements (x+3), (x+5) and (x+12) might need to be updated. Note that the flags in arrC[13] and arrC[15] are already Y. This iteration updates arrC[22] to Y.

1	2	3	4	5	6	7	8	9	10	11	12	13	14	15	16	17	18	19	20	21	22	23	24	25
N	N	Y	N	Y	Y	N	Y	Y	Y	Y	Y	Y	Y	Y	N	Y	Y	N	Y	Y	Y	N	N	N

When x=14, the flag in arrC[14] is Y. Therefore, elements (x+3), (x+5) and (x+12) might need to be updated. Element (x+12)=26 is greater than the maximum element in arrC (see line #15). The flag in arrC[17] is already Y. This iteration updates arrC[19] to Y.

1	2	3	4	5	6	7	8	9	10	11	12	13	14	15	16	17	18	19	20	21	22	23	24	25
N	N	Y	N	Y	Y	N	Y	Y	Y	Y	Y	Y	Y	Y	Y	Y	Y	Y	Y	Y	Y	N	N	N

When x=22, the flag in arrC[22] is Y. Therefore, elements (x+3), (x+5) and (x+12) might need to be updated. Elements (x+5)=27 and (x+12)=34 are greater than the maximum element in arrC. The flag in arrC[25] is already Y. This iteration does not update any element.

1	2	3	4	5	6	7	8	9	10	11	12	13	14	15	16	17	18	19	20	21	22	23	24	25
N	N	Y	N	Y	Y	N	Y	Y	Y	Y	Y	Y	Y	Y	Y	Y	Y	Y	Y	Y	Y	Y	Y	Y

When $x=25$, the flag in `arrC[25]` is Y. Elements $(x+3)=28$, $(x+5)=30$ and $(x+12)=37$ are greater than the maximum element in `arrC`. This iteration does not update any element.

1	2	3	4	5	6	7	8	9	10	11	12	13	14	15	16	17	18	19	20	21	22	23	24	25
N	N	Y	N	Y	Y	N	Y	Y	Y	Y	Y	Y	Y	Y	Y	Y	Y	Y	Y	Y	Y	Y	Y	Y

To answer the question from example, the 23rd element of `arrC` is marked as Y. It means that $23 change can be given from a combination of #3, #5 and $12 coins. From the same array, the algorithm calculated that $1, $2, $4 and $7 cannot be given using any combination of available coins. Algorithm 05-E and Algorithm 05-F produce identical `arrC` flags.

For each value of x, the flags Y are *pushed* to 3 other flags in the locations of $(x+3)$, $(x+5)$ and $(x+12)$. Note that this algorithm only pushes one step forward. When processing x, there is no need to change the flags in `arrC[(x+3)+3]`, or even `arrC[((x+3)+3)+3]`, for example, because those will be covered in later iterations. This illustrates the implementation of dynamic programming.

How many coins minimum is needed to make $23?

Using human logic, we know that we can give $23 change using 6 coins of $3 and 1 coin of $5 (making 7 coins in total). However, we can also give $23 change using 4 coins of $5 and 1 coin of $3 (making 5 coins in total). Is 5 coins really the minimum number of coins to make $23? How can an algorithm solve this?

The minimum number of coins to make x can be calculated by comparing the minimum numbers of coins to make $(x-3)$, $(x-5)$ and $(x-12)$.

- If the minimum number of coins to make $(x-3)$ is n1, then x can be made using n1+1 coins.
- If the minimum number of coins to make $(x-5)$ is n2, then x can be made using n2+1 coins.
- If the minimum number of coins to make $(x-12)$ is n3, then x can be made using n3+1 coins.
- The minimum number of coins to make x is the smallest number from (n1+1), (n2+1) or (n3+1).

Mathematically, the above points can be written as:

- `f(23) = min[f(20),f(18),f(11)]+1`
- `f(n)  = min[f(n-3),f(n-5),f(n-12)]+1`

Algorithm with *pull technique*:

- To find out the minimum number of coins to make $23, algorithm needs to calculate the minimum number of coins to make $20, $18 and $11, choose the smallest number and add 1.
- As generalisation: <u>to find out the minimum number of coins to make x, algorithm needs to calculate the minimum number of coins to make (x-3), (x-5) and (x-12), choose the smallest number and add 1.</u>
- To find out the minimum number of coins to make (x-3), algorithm needs to calculate the minimum number of coins to make (x-3)-3, (x-3)-5 and (x-3)-12, choose the smallest number and add 1.
    - To find out the minimum number of coins to make (x-3-3), algorithm needs to calculate the minimum number of coins to make (x-3-3)-3, (x-3-3)-5 and (x-3-3)-12, choose the smallest number and add 1.
    - And so on.
- To find out the minimum number of coins to make (x-5), algorithm needs to calculate the minimum number of coins to make (x-5)-3, (x-5)-5 and (x-5)-12, choose the smallest number and add 1.
- To find out the minimum number of coins to make (x-12), algorithm needs to calculate the minimum number of coins to make (x-12)-3, (x-12)-5 and (x-12)-12, choose the smallest number and add 1.
- And so on.

Algorithm with *push technique*:

- If $3 change can be given using 1 coin, then $6, $8 or $15 can be given using 2 coins.
- As generalisation: <u>if x change can be given using n coins, then (x+3) and (x+5) and (x+12) can be given using n+1 coins, update the minimum number of coins for those values if n+1 is less than their current minimum.</u>
- If (x+3) change can be given using n coins, then (x+3)+3 and (x+3)+5 and (x+3)+12 can be given using n+1 coins.
    - If (x+3+3) change can be given using n coins, then (x+3+3)+3 and (x+3+3)+5 and (x+3+3)+12 can be given using n+1 coins.
    - And so on.
- If (x+5) change can be given using n coins, then (x+5)+3 and (x+5)+5 and (x+5)+12 can be given using n+1 coins.

- If $(x+12)$ change can be given using n coins, then $(x+12)+3$ and $(x+12)+5$ and $(x+12)+12$ can be given using n+1 coins.
- And so on.

Either pull or push technique can be used to implement dynamic algorithm to solve this coin change problem. Instead of flagging each element in array arrC with Y or N, the algorithm stores minimum number of coins to make certain value.

```
 1 iArraySize=25
 2 iNumOfCoins=3
 3 coin[1]=3
 4 coin[2]=5
 5 coin[3]=12
 6 for i=1 to iArraySize do
 7   arrC[i]=0
 8 end for
 9 for i=1 to iNumOfCoins do
10   arrC[coin[i]]=1
11 end for
12 for x=1 to iArraySize do
13   for j=1 to iNumOfCoins do
14     idx=x-coin[j]
15     if (idx>=1) and (arrC[idx]>0) then
16       if (arrC[x]=0) or (arrC[x]>arrC[idx]+1) then
17         arrC[x]=arrC[idx]+1
18       end if
19     end if
20   end for
21 end for
22 display "Min coins to make 23: ",arrC[23]
```

Algorithm 05-G Pull Technique for "minimum number of coins to make x"

Algorithm 05-G uses array arrC to store counters representing the number of coins to make a value. Every time a smaller number is found, this number is updated. At the end of calculation, the counters stored in each element of the array will represent the minimum number of coins to make those values. The size of array is defined as 25 only for the purpose of this example. It is sufficient because this algorithm only needs to calculate minimum number of coins to make $23. Changing the value of iArraySize variable will adjust the size of arrC.

For each iteration of x, this algorithm looks at three prior values of $(x-3)$, $(x-5)$ and $(x-12)$. If a prior value has 0 counter, it means the value cannot be made using the available coins. If the prior value has greater-than-zero counter, the algorithm compares the counter in x against the counter in prior value plus one. The smaller value will be updated as new counter in x.

Step 1. At the beginning, each element of `arrC` is set to have counter value of zero (lines #6 to #8).

1	2	3	4	5	6	7	8	9	10	11	12	13	14	15	16	17	18	19	20	21	22	23	24	25
0	0	0	0	0	0	0	0	0	0	0	0	0	0	0	0	0	0	0	0	0	0	0	0	0

Step 2. Counters in elements 3, 5 and 12 are set to 1 (lines #9 to #11).

1	2	3	4	5	6	7	8	9	10	11	12	13	14	15	16	17	18	19	20	21	22	23	24	25
0	0	1	0	1	0	0	0	0	0	0	1	0	0	0	0	0	0	0	0	0	0	0	0	0

Step 3. Start the big loop (lines #12 to #21). When x is 1, 2 and 3 (the first three iterations), the values of `(x-3)`, `(x-5)` and `(x-12)` are all negative values and can be ignored (see line #15).

1	2	3	4	5	6	7	8	9	10	11	12	13	14	15	16	17	18	19	20	21	22	23	24	25
0	0	1	0	1	0	0	0	0	0	0	1	0	0	0	0	0	0	0	0	0	0	0	0	0

When x=4, the value of `(x-3)=1` is a positive number, so it needs to be evaluated. The counter in `arrC[1]` is zero. Therefore, no change is made (see line #15).

1	2	3	4	5	6	7	8	9	10	11	12	13	14	15	16	17	18	19	20	21	22	23	24	25
0	0	1	0	1	0	0	0	0	0	0	1	0	0	0	0	0	0	0	0	0	0	0	0	0

When x=5, the value of `(x-3)=2` is a positive number. The counter in `arrC[2]` is zero. Therefore, no change is made.

1	2	3	4	5	6	7	8	9	10	11	12	13	14	15	16	17	18	19	20	21	22	23	24	25
0	0	1	0	1	0	0	0	0	0	0	1	0	0	0	0	0	0	0	0	0	0	0	0	0

When x=6, the values of `(x-3)=3` and `(x-5)=1` are positive numbers.

- The counter in `arrC[3]` is not zero and the counter in `arrC[x]` is zero. Counter in `arrC[6]` is updated with the counter in `arrC[3]` plus one.
- The counter in `arrC[1]` is zero, no change is made.

1	2	3	4	5	6	7	8	9	10	11	12	13	14	15	16	17	18	19	20	21	22	23	24	25
0	0	1	0	1	2	0	0	0	0	0	1	0	0	0	0	0	0	0	0	0	0	0	0	0

When x=7, the values of `(x-3)`=4 and `(x-5)`=2 are positive numbers.

- The counter in `arrC[4]` is zero, no change is made.
- The counter in `arrC[2]` is zero, no change is made.

1	2	3	4	5	6	7	8	9	10	11	12	13	14	15	16	17	18	19	20	21	22	23	24	25
0	0	1	0	1	2	0	0	0	0	0	1	0	0	0	0	0	0	0	0	0	0	0	0	0

When x=8, the values of `(x-3)`=5 and `(x-5)`=3 are positive numbers.

- The counter in `arrC[5]` is not zero and the counter in `arrC[x]` is zero. Counter in `arrC[6]` is updated with the counter in `arrC[5]` plus one.
- The counter in `arrC[3]` is not zero. The counter in `arrC[x]` is neither zero or larger than `arrC[3]` plus one, no change is made.

1	2	3	4	5	6	7	8	9	10	11	12	13	14	15	16	17	18	19	20	21	22	23	24	25
0	0	1	0	1	2	0	2	0	0	0	1	0	0	0	0	0	0	0	0	0	0	0	0	0

When x=9, the values of `(x-3)`=6 and `(x-5)`=4 are positive numbers.

- The counter in `arrC[6]` is not zero and the counter in `arrC[x]` is zero. Counter in `arrC[9]` is updated with the counter in `arrC[6]` plus one.
- The counter in `arrC[4]` is zero, no change is made.

1	2	3	4	5	6	7	8	9	10	11	12	13	14	15	16	17	18	19	20	21	22	23	24	25
0	0	1	0	1	2	0	2	3	0	0	1	0	0	0	0	0	0	0	0	0	0	0	0	0

When x=10, the values of `(x-3)`=7 and `(x-5)`=5 are positive numbers.

- The counter in `arrC[7]` is zero, no change is made.
- The counter in `arrC[5]` is not zero and the counter in `arrC[x]` is zero. Counter in `arrC[10]` is updated with the counter in `arrC[5]` plus one.

1	2	3	4	5	6	7	8	9	10	11	12	13	14	15	16	17	18	19	20	21	22	23	24	25
0	0	1	0	1	2	0	2	3	2	0	1	0	0	0	0	0	0	0	0	0	0	0	0	0

When x=15, the values of `(x-3)`=12 and `(x-5)`=10 and `(x-12)`=3 are positive numbers.

- The counter in `arrC[12]` is not zero and the counter in `arrC[x]` is zero. Counter in `arrC[15]` is updated with the counter in `arrC[12]` plus one.

- The counter in `arrC[10]` is not zero. The counter in `arrC[x]` is neither zero or larger than `arrC[10]` plus one, no change is made.
- The counter in `arrC[3]` is not zero. The counter in `arrC[x]` is neither zero or larger than `arrC[3]` plus one, no change is made.

1	2	3	4	5	6	7	8	9	10	11	12	13	14	15	16	17	18	19	20	21	22	23	24	25
0	0	1	0	1	2	0	2	3	2	3	1	3	4	2	0	0	0	0	0	0	0	0	0	0

When x=25, the values of (x-3)=22 and (x-5)=20 and (x-12)=13 are positive numbers.

- The counter in `arrC[22]` is not zero and the counter in `arrC[x]` is zero. Counter in `arrC[25]` is updated with the counter in `arrC[22]` plus one.
- The counter in `arrC[20]` is not zero. The counter in `arrC[x]` is neither zero or larger than `arrC[20]` plus one, no change is made.
- The counter in `arrC[13]` is not zero. The counter in `arrC[x]` is neither zero or larger than `arrC[13]` plus one, no change is made.

1	2	3	4	5	6	7	8	9	10	11	12	13	14	15	16	17	18	19	20	21	22	23	24	25
0	0	1	0	1	2	0	2	3	2	3	1	3	4	2	4	2	3	5	3	4	3	4	2	4

To answer the question from example, minimum 4 coins are needed to make $23. This can be observed from the counter in 23rd element of `arrC`. From the same array, the algorithm calculated that minimum 5 coins are needed to give $19 change.

For each value of x, the counter of minimum coins to make x is *pulled* from 3 other counters prior to that value. Note that there is no need to update the counters in `arrC[(x-3)-3]`, or even `arrC[((x-3)-3)-3]` because those would have been covered from previous iterations.

For reference, the below table shows the counters stored in `arrC` during each iteration of `x` using pull technique:

1	2	3	4	5	6	7	8	9	10	11	12	13	14	15	16	17	18	19	20	21	22	23	24	25
0	0	1	0	1	0	0	0	0	0	0	1	0	0	0	0	0	0	0	0	0	0	0	0	0
0	0	1	0	1	0	0	0	0	0	0	1	0	0	0	0	0	0	0	0	0	0	0	0	0
0	0	1	0	1	0	0	0	0	0	0	1	0	0	0	0	0	0	0	0	0	0	0	0	0
0	0	1	0	1	0	0	0	0	0	0	1	0	0	0	0	0	0	0	0	0	0	0	0	0
0	0	1	0	1	0	0	0	0	0	0	1	0	0	0	0	0	0	0	0	0	0	0	0	0
0	0	1	0	1	2	0	0	0	0	0	1	0	0	0	0	0	0	0	0	0	0	0	0	0
0	0	1	0	1	2	0	0	0	0	0	1	0	0	0	0	0	0	0	0	0	0	0	0	0
0	0	1	0	1	2	0	2	0	0	0	1	0	0	0	0	0	0	0	0	0	0	0	0	0
0	0	1	0	1	2	0	2	3	0	0	1	0	0	0	0	0	0	0	0	0	0	0	0	0
0	0	1	0	1	2	0	2	3	2	0	1	0	0	0	0	0	0	0	0	0	0	0	0	0
0	0	1	0	1	2	0	2	3	2	3	1	0	0	0	0	0	0	0	0	0	0	0	0	0
0	0	1	0	1	2	0	2	3	2	3	1	0	0	0	0	0	0	0	0	0	0	0	0	0
0	0	1	0	1	2	0	2	3	2	3	1	3	0	0	0	0	0	0	0	0	0	0	0	0
0	0	1	0	1	2	0	2	3	2	3	1	3	4	0	0	0	0	0	0	0	0	0	0	0
0	0	1	0	1	2	0	2	3	2	3	1	3	4	2	0	0	0	0	0	0	0	0	0	0
0	0	1	0	1	2	0	2	3	2	3	1	3	4	2	4	0	0	0	0	0	0	0	0	0
0	0	1	0	1	2	0	2	3	2	3	1	3	4	2	4	2	0	0	0	0	0	0	0	0
0	0	1	0	1	2	0	2	3	2	3	1	3	4	2	4	2	3	0	0	0	0	0	0	0
0	0	1	0	1	2	0	2	3	2	3	1	3	4	2	4	2	3	5	0	0	0	0	0	0
0	0	1	0	1	2	0	2	3	2	3	1	3	4	2	4	2	3	5	3	0	0	0	0	0
0	0	1	0	1	2	0	2	3	2	3	1	3	4	2	4	2	3	5	3	4	0	0	0	0
0	0	1	0	1	2	0	2	3	2	3	1	3	4	2	4	2	3	5	3	4	3	0	0	0
0	0	1	0	1	2	0	2	3	2	3	1	3	4	2	4	2	3	5	3	4	3	4	0	0
0	0	1	0	1	2	0	2	3	2	3	1	3	4	2	4	2	3	5	3	4	3	4	2	0
0	0	1	0	1	2	0	2	3	2	3	1	3	4	2	4	2	3	5	3	4	3	4	2	4

```
 1 iArraySize=25
 2 iNumOfCoins=3
 3 coin[1]=3
 4 coin[2]=5
 5 coin[3]=12
 6 for i=1 to iArraySize do
 7   arrC[i]=0
 8 end for
 9 for i=1 to iNumOfCoins do
10   arrC[coin[i]]=1
11 end for
12 for x=1 to iArraySize do
13   for j=1 to iNumOfCoins do
14     idx=x+coin[j]
15     if (idx<=iArraySize) and (arrC[x]>0) then
16       if (arrC[idx]=0) or (arrC[idx]>arrC[x]+1) then
17         arrC[idx]=arrC[x]+1
18       end if
19     end if
20   end for
21 end for
22 display "Min coins to make 23: ",arrC[23]
```

Algorithm 05-H Push Technique for "minimum number of coins to make x"

Algorithm 05-H is very similar to Algorithm 05-G, only lines #14 to #17 are different. Instead of looking into previous elements, push technique uses the counter in element currently observed as x and use it to update counters in elements (x+3), (x+5) and (x+12).

Step 1. At the beginning, each element of arrC is set to have counter value of zero (lines #6 to #8).

1	2	3	4	5	6	7	8	9	10	11	12	13	14	15	16	17	18	19	20	21	22	23	24	25
0	0	0	0	0	0	0	0	0	0	0	0	0	0	0	0	0	0	0	0	0	0	0	0	0

Step 2. Counters in elements 3, 5 and 12 are set to 1 (lines #9 to #11).

1	2	3	4	5	6	7	8	9	10	11	12	13	14	15	16	17	18	19	20	21	22	23	24	25
0	0	1	0	1	0	0	0	0	0	0	1	0	0	0	0	0	0	0	0	0	0	0	0	0

Step 3. Start the big loop (lines #12 to #21). When x is 1 and 2 (the first two iterations), the counter of x is 0. Therefore, no update is needed.

1	2	3	4	5	6	7	8	9	10	11	12	13	14	15	16	17	18	19	20	21	22	23	24	25
0	0	1	0	1	0	0	0	0	0	0	1	0	0	0	0	0	0	0	0	0	0	0	0	0

When $x=3$, the counter in `arrC[3]` is not zero. Therefore, elements $(x+3)$, $(x+5)$ and $(x+12)$ need to be evaluated.

- Counter in `arrC[6]` is zero, it is updated with counter in `arrC[3]` plus one.
- Counter in `arrC[8]` is zero, it is updated with counter in `arrC[3]` plus one.
- Counter in `arrC[15]` is zero, it is updated with counter in `arrC[3]` plus one.

1	2	3	4	5	6	7	8	9	10	11	12	13	14	15	16	17	18	19	20	21	22	23	24	25
0	0	1	0	1	2	0	2	0	0	0	0	1	0	0	2	0	0	0	0	0	0	0	0	0

When $x=4$, the counter in `arrC[x]` is zero. Therefore, no change is required for elements $(x+3)$, $(x+5)$ and $(x+12)$.

1	2	3	4	5	6	7	8	9	10	11	12	13	14	15	16	17	18	19	20	21	22	23	24	25
0	0	1	0	1	2	0	2	0	0	0	0	1	0	0	2	0	0	0	0	0	0	0	0	0

When $x=5$, the counter in `arrC[5]` is not zero. Therefore, elements $(x+3)$, $(x+5)$ and $(x+12)$ need to be evaluated.

- Counter in `arrC[8]` is neither zero or larger than `arrC[5]` plus one, no change is made.
- Counter in `arrC[10]` is zero, it is updated with counter in `arrC[5]` plus one.
- Counter in `arrC[17]` is zero, it is updated with counter in `arrC[5]` plus one.

1	2	3	4	5	6	7	8	9	10	11	12	13	14	15	16	17	18	19	20	21	22	23	24	25
0	0	1	0	1	2	0	2	0	2	0	1	0	0	2	0	2	0	0	0	0	0	0	0	0

When $x=6$, the counter in `arrC[6]` is not zero. Therefore, elements $(x+3)$, $(x+5)$ and $(x+12)$ need to be evaluated.

- Counter in `arrC[9]` is zero, it is updated with counter in `arrC[6]` plus one.
- Counter in `arrC[11]` is zero, it is updated with counter in `arrC[6]` plus one.
- Counter in `arrC[18]` is zero, it is updated with counter in `arrC[6]` plus one.

1	2	3	4	5	6	7	8	9	10	11	12	13	14	15	16	17	18	19	20	21	22	23	24	25
0	0	1	0	1	2	0	2	3	2	3	1	0	0	2	0	2	3	0	0	0	0	0	0	0

When $x=7$, the counter in `arrC[x]` is zero. Therefore, no change is required for elements `(x+3)`, `(x+5)` and `(x+12)`.

1	2	3	4	5	6	7	8	9	10	11	12	13	14	15	16	17	18	19	20	21	22	23	24	25
0	0	1	0	1	2	0	2	3	2	3	1	0	0	2	0	2	3	0	0	0	0	0	0	0

When $x=8$, the counter in `arrC[8]` is not zero. Therefore, elements `(x+3)`, `(x+5)` and `(x+12)` need to be evaluated.

- Counter in `arrC[11]` is neither zero or larger than `arrC[8]` plus one, no change is made.
- Counter in `arrC[13]` is zero, it is updated with counter in `arrC[8]` plus one.
- Counter in `arrC[20]` is zero, it is updated with counter in `arrC[8]` plus one.

1	2	3	4	5	6	7	8	9	10	11	12	13	14	15	16	17	18	19	20	21	22	23	24	25
0	0	1	0	1	2	0	2	3	2	3	1	3	0	2	0	2	3	0	3	0	0	0	0	0

When $x=9$, the counter in `arrC[9]` is not zero. Therefore, elements `(x+3)`, `(x+5)` and `(x+12)` need to be evaluated.

- Counter in `arrC[12]` is neither zero or larger than `arrC[9]` plus one, no change is made.
- Counter in `arrC[14]` is zero, it is updated with counter in `arrC[9]` plus one.
- Counter in `arrC[21]` is zero, it is updated with counter in `arrC[9]` plus one.

1	2	3	4	5	6	7	8	9	10	11	12	13	14	15	16	17	18	19	20	21	22	23	24	25
0	0	1	0	1	2	0	2	3	2	3	1	3	4	2	0	2	3	0	3	4	0	0	0	0

When $x=14$, the counter in `arrC[14]` is not zero. Therefore, elements `(x+3)`, `(x+5)` and `(x+12)` need to be evaluated.

- Counter in `arrC[17]` is neither zero or larger than `arrC[14]` plus one, no change is made.
- Counter in `arrC[19]` is zero, it is updated with counter in `arrC[14]` plus one.
- Element 26 is not a valid element in `arrC` because it is larger than `iArraySize`, no change is made.

1	2	3	4	5	6	7	8	9	10	11	12	13	14	15	16	17	18	19	20	21	22	23	24	25
0	0	1	0	1	2	0	2	3	2	3	1	3	4	2	4	2	3	5	3	4	3	4	2	4

When $x=25$, the counter in `arrC[14]` is not zero. Elements `(x+3)=28`, `(x+5)=30` and `(x+12)=37` are greater than the maximum element in `arrC`.

This iteration does not update any element.

1	2	3	4	5	6	7	8	9	10	11	12	13	14	15	16	17	18	19	20	21	22	23	24	25
0	0	1	0	1	2	0	2	3	2	3	1	3	4	2	4	2	3	**5**	3	4	3	4	2	4

To answer the question from example, minimum 4 coins are needed to make $23 change. This can be observed from the counter in 23rd element of arrC. Note that the final result recorded in arrC is identical from the result of pull technique.

For each value of x, the counter of minimum coins to make x is *pushed* to 3 other counters after to that value. There is no need to update the counters of arrC[(x+3)+3], or even arrC[((x+3)+3)+3] because those will be covered in later iterations.

For reference, the below table shows the counters stored in arrC during each iteration of x using push technique:

1	2	3	4	5	6	7	8	9	10	11	12	13	14	15	16	17	18	19	20	21	22	23	24	25
0	0	1	0	1	0	0	0	0	0	0	1	0	0	0	0	0	0	0	0	0	0	0	0	0
0	0	1	0	1	0	0	0	0	0	0	1	0	0	0	0	0	0	0	0	0	0	0	0	0
0	0	1	0	1	2	0	2	0	0	0	1	0	0	2	0	0	0	0	0	0	0	0	0	0
0	0	1	0	1	2	0	2	0	0	0	1	0	0	2	0	0	0	0	0	0	0	0	0	0
0	0	1	0	1	2	0	2	0	2	0	1	0	0	2	0	2	0	0	0	0	0	0	0	0
0	0	1	0	1	2	0	2	3	2	3	1	0	0	2	0	2	3	0	0	0	0	0	0	0
0	0	1	0	1	2	0	2	3	2	3	1	0	0	2	0	2	3	0	0	0	0	0	0	0
0	0	1	0	1	2	0	2	3	2	3	1	3	0	2	0	2	3	0	3	0	0	0	0	0
0	0	1	0	1	2	0	2	3	2	3	1	3	4	2	0	2	3	0	3	4	0	0	0	0
0	0	1	0	1	2	0	2	3	2	3	1	3	4	2	0	2	3	0	3	4	3	0	0	0
0	0	1	0	1	2	0	2	3	2	3	1	3	4	2	4	2	3	0	3	4	3	4	0	0
0	0	1	0	1	2	0	2	3	2	3	1	3	4	2	4	2	3	0	3	4	3	4	2	0
0	0	1	0	1	2	0	2	3	2	3	1	3	4	2	4	2	3	0	3	4	3	4	2	4
0	0	1	0	1	2	0	2	3	2	3	1	3	4	2	4	2	3	5	3	4	3	4	2	4
0	0	1	0	1	2	0	2	3	2	3	1	3	4	2	4	2	3	5	3	4	3	4	2	4
0	0	1	0	1	2	0	2	3	2	3	1	3	4	2	4	2	3	5	3	4	3	4	2	4
0	0	1	0	1	2	0	2	3	2	3	1	3	4	2	4	2	3	5	3	4	3	4	2	4
0	0	1	0	1	2	0	2	3	2	3	1	3	4	2	4	2	3	5	3	4	3	4	2	4
0	0	1	0	1	2	0	2	3	2	3	1	3	4	2	4	2	3	5	3	4	3	4	2	4
0	0	1	0	1	2	0	2	3	2	3	1	3	4	2	4	2	3	5	3	4	3	4	2	4
0	0	1	0	1	2	0	2	3	2	3	1	3	4	2	4	2	3	5	3	4	3	4	2	4
0	0	1	0	1	2	0	2	3	2	3	1	3	4	2	4	2	3	5	3	4	3	4	2	4
0	0	1	0	1	2	0	2	3	2	3	1	3	4	2	4	2	3	5	3	4	3	4	2	4
0	0	1	0	1	2	0	2	3	2	3	1	3	4	2	4	2	3	5	3	4	3	4	2	4
0	0	1	0	1	2	0	2	3	2	3	1	3	4	2	4	2	3	5	3	4	3	4	2	4

Multistage Graph Problem

A multistage graph is a graph that meets the following criteria:

- Each of its edges has direction (directed graph).
- Each of its edges has weight (weighted graph).
- It has exactly 1 *source* node (all edges connected to it are outgoing). Source node is referred to as s.
- It has exactly 1 *sink* node (all edges connected to it are incoming). Sink node is referred to as t.
- Paths from source to sink have multiple stages, called V_1 to V_k.
- Each edge connects a node in V_i to a node in V_{i+1} where $1 \le i \le k$.
- It has 2 or more stages ($k \ge 2$).
- Each path from s to t is a consequence of $k-1$ choices.

Multistage graph can be used as a model of decision-making process in real world scenarios. Source node represents current situation and sink node represents goal to be achieved. Each edge brings moves a situation closer to the goal, but different edges from a node represents different choices available, each carrying different levels of cost or difficulty (edge weight).

As the name suggests, *multistage graph problem* is a classic problem to find the shortest possible path (smallest possible sum of edge weights) from source to sink. This is another excellent example to illustrate an application of dynamic programming.

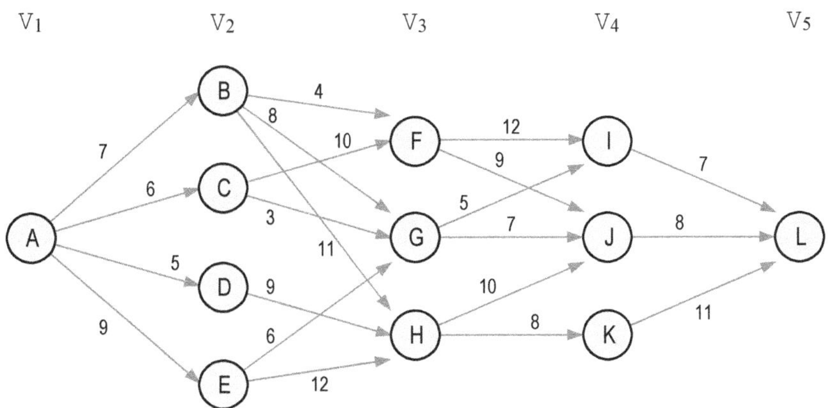

An example of Multistage Graph with 12 nodes is presented above. Nodes are grouped into 5 stages from V_1 to V_5. The first stage (V_1) contains source node A. Sink node L is in the final stage (V_5). All edges have direction and weight.

Note that each edge connects a node from a stage to another node from the next stage. There is no edge connecting a node to another node from previous or same stage.

Dynamic programming algorithm to find the shortest path from A to L can be calculated using two different techniques: forward and backward. In forward technique, shortest path is analysed by calculating forward paths from several nodes to *sink*. Backward technique calculates paths from *source* to several nodes.

Steps of *forward technique*:
- Main formula:
  `cost(x,i)=min{edge(x,y)+cost(y,i+1)}`
- `cost(x,i)` is the shortest path length from node x in stage V_i to sink (`t`).
- `edge(x,y)` is the weight of edge connecting nodes x and y.
- Calculation starts from nodes in stage `k-2`.

Using the same example of multistage graph above, dynamic programming calculates shortest path using the following steps:
1. Shortest paths from nodes in stage 4 can be obtained from direct observation: cost(I,4)=7, cost(J,4)=8 and cost(K,4)=11.
2. Calculation starts from nodes in stage 3 because `k-2=3`.
   Nodes in stage 3 are F, G and H.

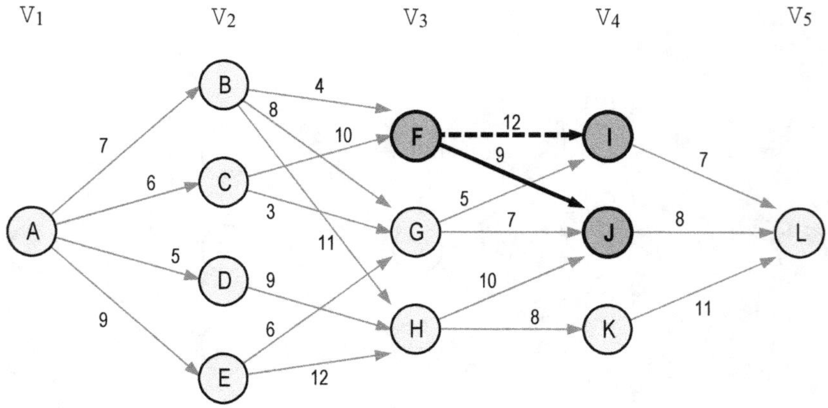

3. `cost(F,3)` is the length of shortest path from node F to sink.
   ```
   cost(F,3)=min{edge(F,I)+cost(I,4)|
                 edge(F,J)+cost(J,4)}
   cost(F,3)=min{12+7|9+8}=17
   ```

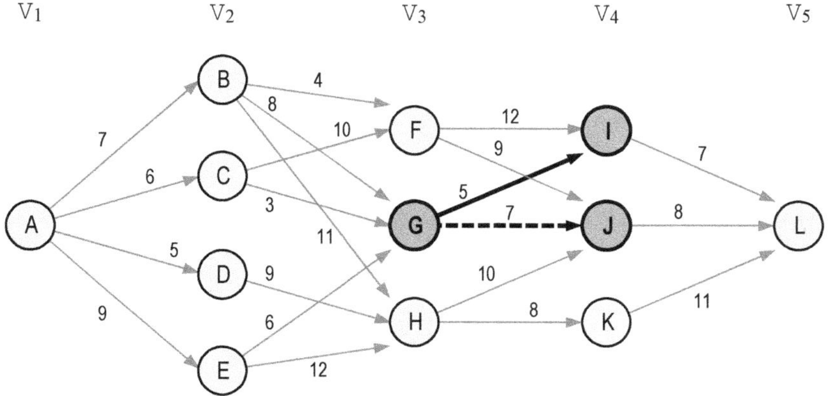

4. `cost(G,3)` is the length of shortest path from node G to sink.
```
cost(G,3)=min{edge(G,I)+cost(I,4)|
              edge(G,J)+cost(J,4)}
cost(G,3)=min{5+7|7+8}=12
```

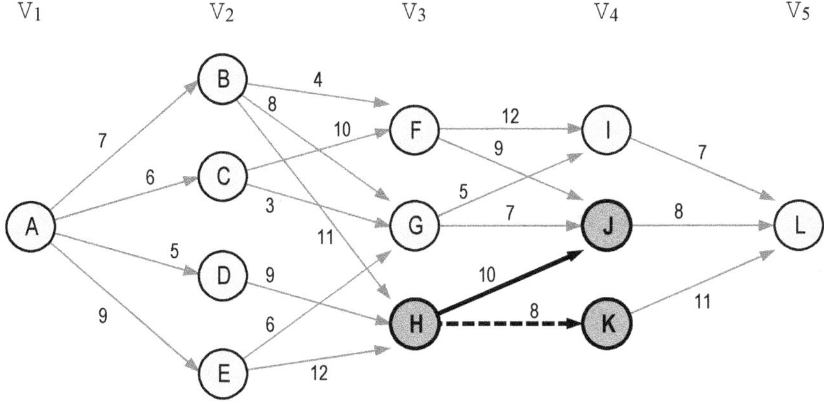

5. `cost(H,3)` is the length of shortest path from node H to sink.
```
cost(H,3)=min{edge(H,J)+cost(J,4)|
              edge(H,K)+cost(K,4)}
cost(H,3)=min{10+8|8+11}=18
```

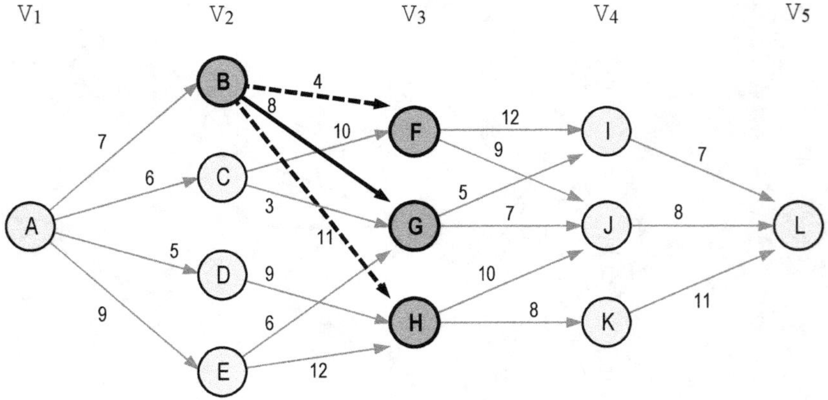

6. `cost(B,2)` is the length of shortest path from node B to sink.
    ```
    cost(B,2)=min{edge(B,F)+cost(F,3)|
                  edge(B,G)+cost(G,3)|
                  edge(B,H)+cost(H,3)}
    cost(B,2)=min{4+17|8+12|11+18}=20
    ```

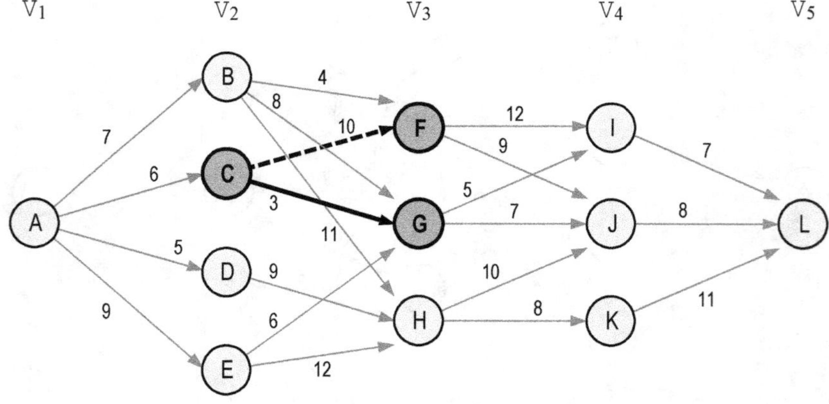

7. `cost(C,2)` is the length of shortest path from node C to sink.
    ```
    cost(C,2)=min{edge(C,F)+cost(F,3)|
                  edge(C,G)+cost(G,3)}
    cost(C,2)=min{10+17|3+12}=15
    ```

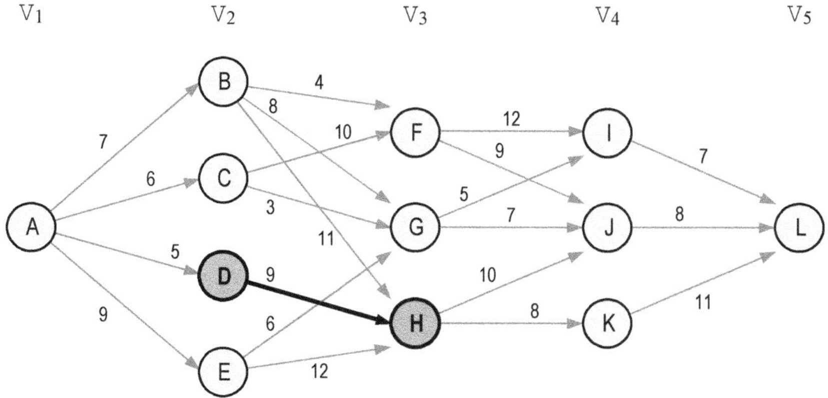

8. `cost(D,2)` is the length of shortest path from node D to sink.
   `cost(D,2)=min{edge(D,H)+cost(H,3)}`
   `cost(D,2)=min{9+18}=27`

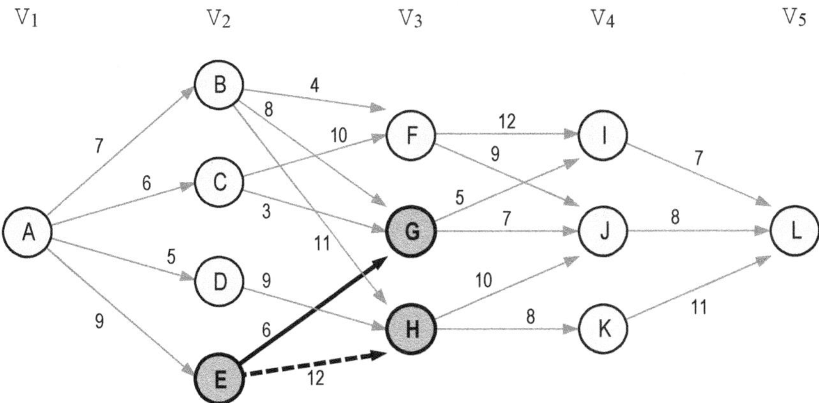

9. `cost(E,2)` is the length of shortest path from node E to sink.
   `cost(E,2)=min{edge(E,G)+cost(G,3)|`
   `            edge(E,H)+cost(H,3)}`
   `cost(E,2)=min{6+12|12+18}=18`

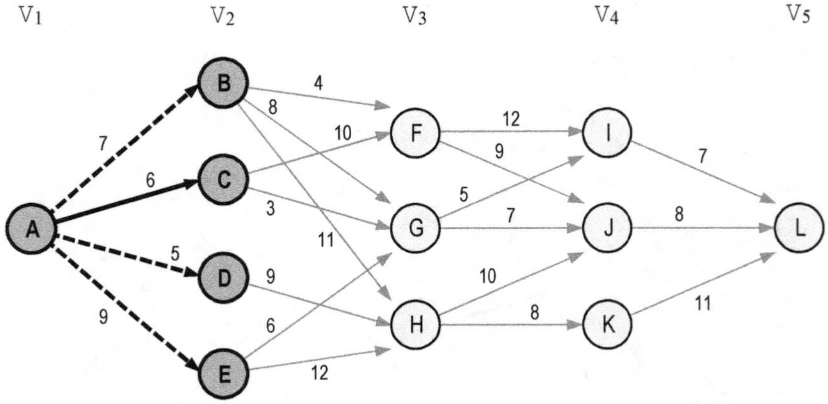

10. `cost(A,1)` is the length of shortest path from node A to sink.
    ```
    cost(A,1)=min{edge(A,B)+cost(B,2)|
                  edge(A,C)+cost(C,2)|
                  edge(A,D)+cost(D,2)|
                  edge(A,E)+cost(E,2)}
    cost(A,1)=min{7+20|6+15|5+27|9+18}=21
    ```
11. Dynamic programming calculates 21 as the shortest distance from A to L. Shortest path can be obtained by tracing back earlier choices.
12. The shortest distance from A to L is obtained from
    `edge(A,C)+cost(C,2)=21`.
    Therefore, AC is part of the shortest path.

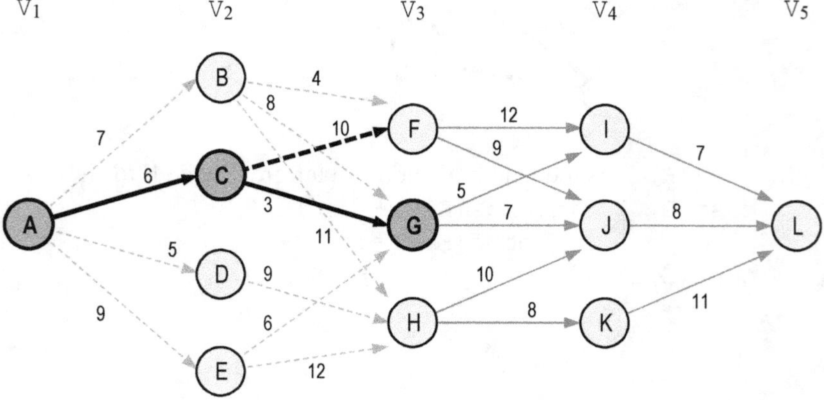

13. The shortest distance from C to L is obtained from
    `edge(C,G)+cost(G,3)=15`.

Therefore, CG is part of the shortest path.

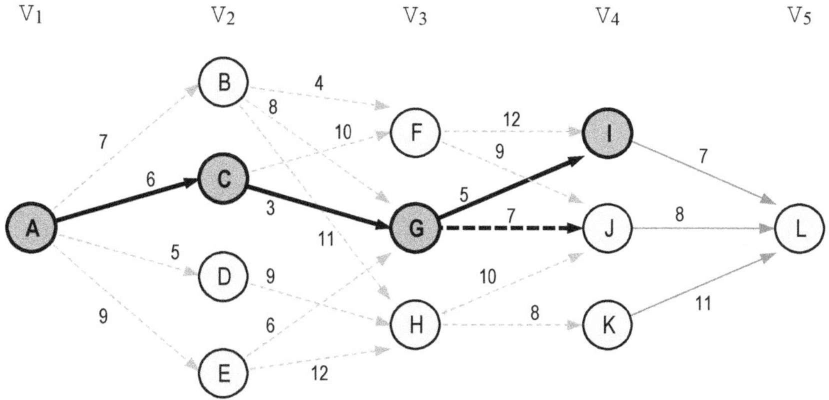

14. The shortest distance from G to L is obtained from
    `edge(G,I)+cost(I,4)=12.`
    Therefore, GI is part of the shortest path.

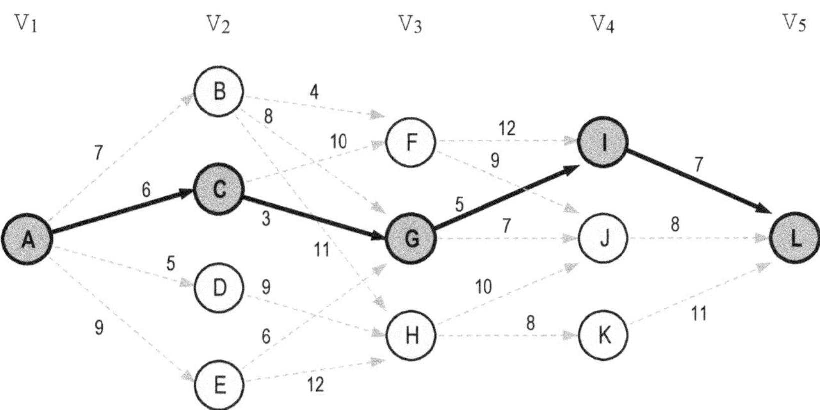

15. There is only one path from I to L. The shortest path is A-C-G-I-L.

Steps of *backward technique*:
- Main formula:
  `bcost(x,i)=min{bcost(y,i-1)+edge(y,x)}`
- `bcost(x,i)` is the shortest path length from source s to node x in stage V_i.
- `edge(y,x)` is the weight of edge connecting nodes y and x.

Using the same example of multistage graph above, dynamic programming calculates shortest path using the following steps:

1. Shortest paths from nodes in stage 2 can be obtained from direct observation: `cost(B,2)=7`, `cost(C,2)=6`, `cost(D,2)=5` and `cost(E,2)=9`.

2. Nodes in stage 3 are F, G and H.

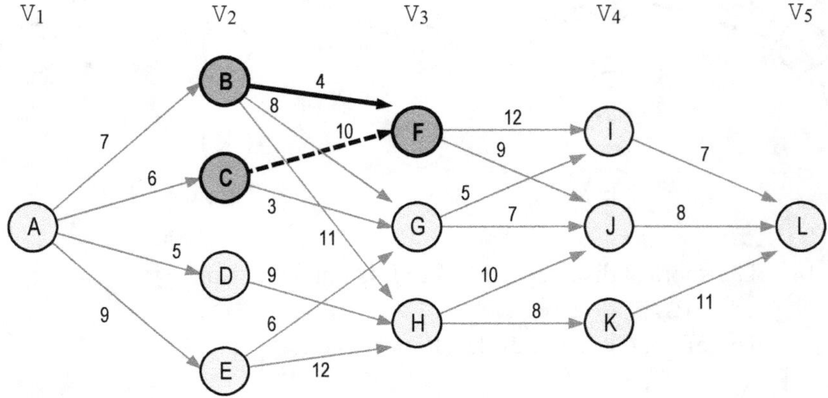

3. `bcost(F,3)` is the length of shortest path from source to node F.
```
bcost(F,3)=min{bcost(B,2)+edge(B,F)|
              bcost(C,2)+edge(C,F)}
bcost(F,3)=min{7+4|6+10}=11
```

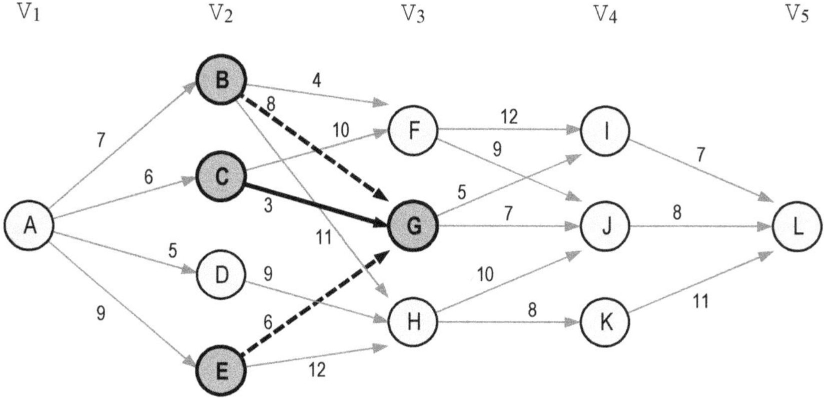

4. `bcost(G,3)` is the length of shortest path from source to node G.
```
bcost(G,3)=min{bcost(B,2)+edge(B,G)|
              bcost(C,2)+edge(C,G)|
              bcost(E,2)+edge(E,G)}
bcost(G,3)=min{7+8|6+3|9+6}=9
```

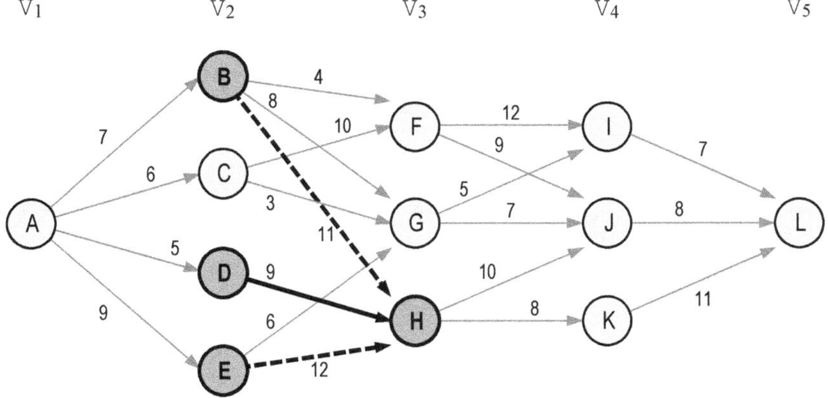

5. `bcost(H,3)` is the length of shortest path from source to node H.
```
bcost(H,3)=min{bcost(B,2)+edge(B,H)|
              bcost(D,2)+edge(D,H)|
              bcost(E,2)+edge(E,H)}
bcost(H,3)=min{7+11|5+9|9+12}=14
```

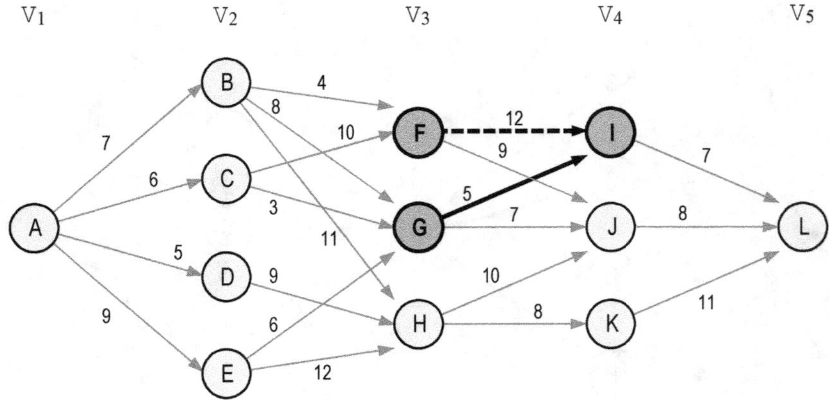

6. `bcost(I,4)` is the length of shortest path from source to node I.
    ```
    bcost(I,4)=min{bcost(F,3)+edge(F,I)|
                   bcost(G,3)+edge(G,I)}
    bcost(I,4)=min{11+12|9+5}=14
    ```

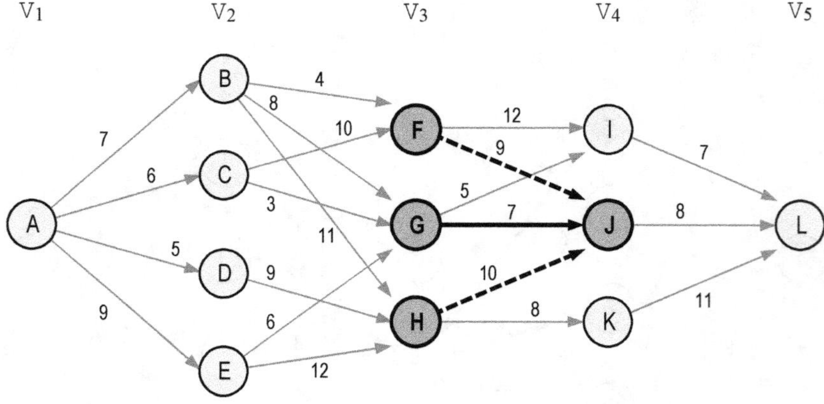

7. `bcost(J,4)` is the length of shortest path from source to node J.
    ```
    bcost(J,4)=min{bcost(F,3)+edge(F,J)|
                   bcost(G,3)+edge(G,J)|
                   bcost(H,3)+edge(H,J)}
    bcost(J,4)=min{11+9|9+7|14+10}=16
    ```

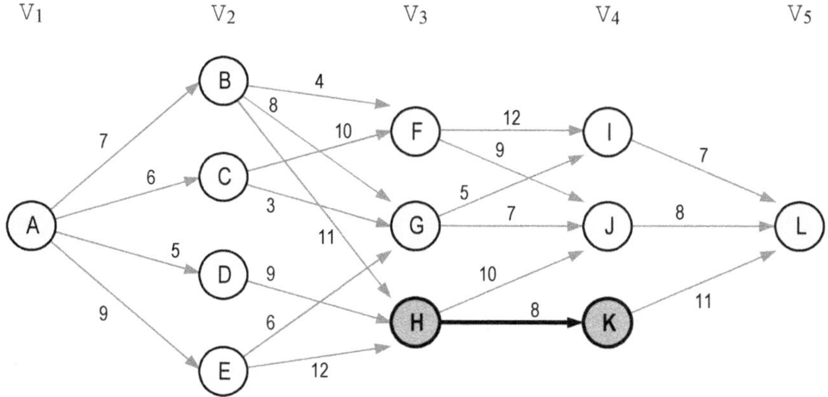

8. `bcost(J,4)` is the length of shortest path from source to node K.
`bcost(K,4)=min{bcost(H,3)+edge(H,K)}`
`bcost(K,4)=min{14+8}=22`

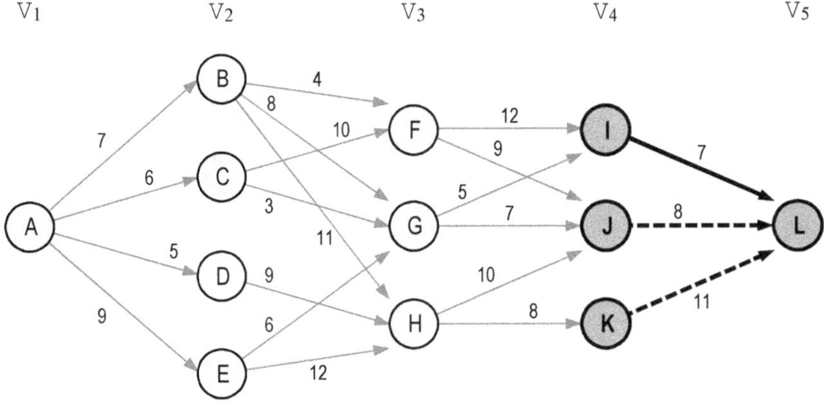

9. `bcost(L,5)` is the length of shortest path from source to node L.
`bcost(L,5)=min{bcost(I,4)+edge(I,L)|`
`bcost(J,4)+edge(J,L)|`
`bcost(K,4)+edge(K,L)}`
`bcost(L,5)=min{14+7|16+8|22+11}=21`

10. Dynamic programming calculates 21 as the shortest distance from A to L. Shortest path can be obtained by tracing back earlier choices.

11. The shortest distance from A to L is obtained from
`bcost(I,4)+edge(I,L).`
Therefore, IL is part of the shortest path.

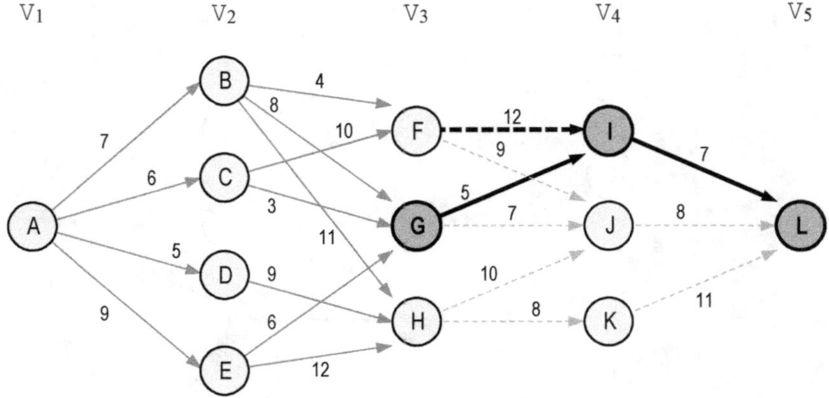

12. The shortest distance from A to I is obtained from
`bcost(G,3)+edge(G,I).`
Therefore, GI is part of the shortest path.

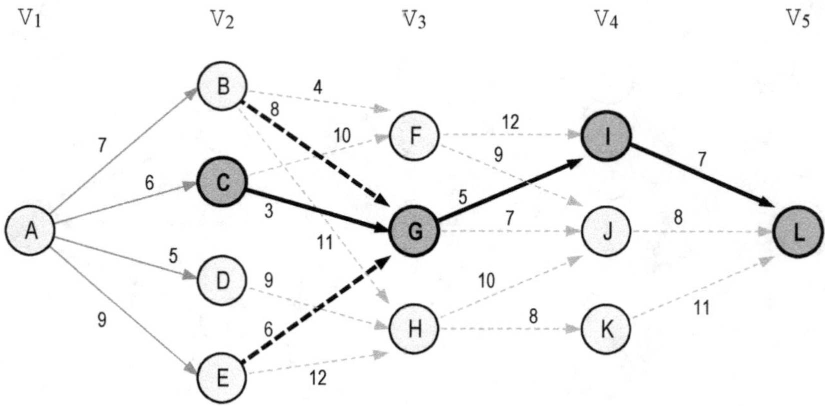

13. The shortest distance from A to G is obtained from
`bcost(C,2)+edge(C,G).`
Therefore, CG is part of the shortest path.

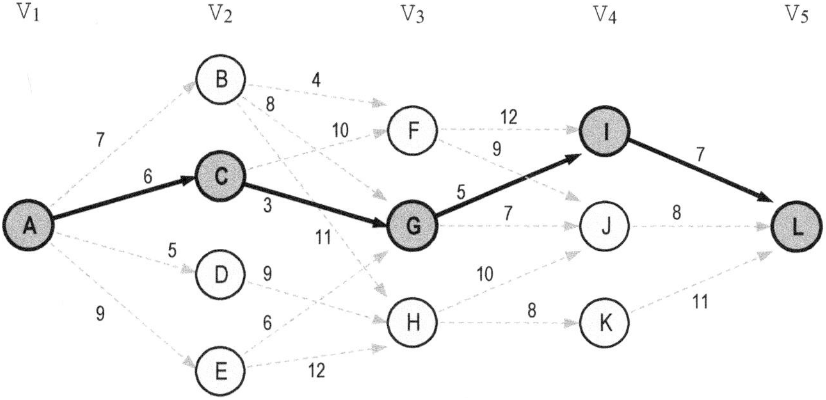

14. There is only one path from A to C. The shortest path is A-C-G-I-L.

0/1 Knapsack Problem

Suppose we have a knapsack capable of holding maximum 6 kgs of items. There are 4 items available, let us call them A, B, C, D, and E.

*   Item A weighs 3 kgs and is worth $6, only 1 item is available.
*   Item B weighs 2 kgs and is worth $5, only 1 item is available.
*   Item C weighs 5 kgs and is worth $9, only 1 item is available.
*   Item D weighs 4 kgs and is worth $8, only 1 item is available.

Which items need to be carried in the knapsack to maximise the value worth?

Such problem is an example of 0/1 knapsack problem. Only 1 unit is available for each item. The choice is either to put the item into the knapsack or leave it out. Please refer to chapter 04 for more explanation on different types of knapsack problem.

The example above can be easily solved using full combination table to enumerate all possible solutions.

Items	Weight	Value
{ }	0	$0
{A}	3	$6
{B}	2	$5
{C}	5	$9
{D}	4	$8
{A,B}	5	$11
{A,C}	8	$15
{A,D}	7	$14

Items	Weight	Value
{B,C}	7	$14
{B,D}	6	$13
{C,D}	9	$17
{A,B,C}	10	$20
{A,B,D}	9	$19
{A,C,D}	12	$23
{B,C,D}	11	$22
{A,B,C,D}	14	$28

As shown in the above table, there are 16 possible combinations of solutions. Not all of them are valid. Combinations of {A,C}, {B,C}, {C,D}, {A,B,C}, {A,B,D}, {A,C,D}, {B,C,D} and {A,B,C,D,E} are not valid because they weight more than 6 kgs, hence they need to be eliminated from the list of possible solutions.

All possible combinations of items that weigh 6 kgs or less are considered as valid solution. Some valid solutions are better than others. For example, taking just item A in the knapsack is not against the problem rule because there is no minimum weight. However, choosing both A and B is also valid, and would produce higher value. Therefore, {A,B} is a better solution than {A}.

Comparing all valid solutions is an easy way to find optimal solution. In this case, choosing {B,D} is a feasible solution with the highest value. This is the optimal solution.

Problem solving by exploring all possible combination will always guarantee the best possible outcome. This technique is easy to understand and practical when the number of items and the maximum weight are small. However, the number of feasible solutions will increase exponentially with larger number of items. Dynamic programming can be used to solve 0/1 knapsack problem with many items.

The example above can be represented as:

```
n = 4
Wmax = 6
(v1, v2, v3, v4) = (6, 5, 9, 8)
(w1, w2, w3, w4) = (3, 2, 5, 4)
```

n is the total number of items available. Wmax is the maximum weight of knapsack. v[i] is the value of item #i. w[i] is the weight of item #i.

```
 1 for i=1 to n do
 2   K[i,0]=0
 3 end for
 4 for j=0 to Wmax do
 5   K[0,j]=0
 6 end for
 7 for i=1 to n do
 8   for j=1 to Wmax do
 9     if w[i]<=j then
10       if v[i]+K[i-1,j-w[i]]>K[i-1,j] then
11         K[i,j]=v[i]+K[i-1,j-w[i]]
12       else
13         K[i,j]=K[i-1,j]
14       end if
15     else
16       K[i,j]=K[i-1,j]
17     end if
18   end for
19 end for
20 while K[i,j]>0 do
21   if K[i,j]>K[i-1,j] then
22     add item #i to knapsack
23     j=j-w[i]
24   end if
25   i=i-1
26 end while
```

Algorithm 05-I Solving 0/1 Knapsack Problem with Dynamic Programming

Algorithm 05-I is one of possible techniques to solve 0/1 knapsack problem using dynamic programming. Two-dimensional array of K[i,j] is used to help with calculating solution using dynamic programming. The rows of array K represents available items from item #1 to #n. Row #0 is needed because this algorithm needs to compare values from the previous row. Columns of array K represents weight from 0 to Wmax.

i\j	0	1	2	3	4	5	6
0	0	0	0	0	0	0	0
1	0						
2	0						
3	0						
4	0						

Lines #1 to #6 from Algorithm 05-I prepares array `K` by filling row #0 and column #0 with zeroes. These values represent the initial situation of empty knapsack before selecting any item.

Calculating row #1:

$i=1$ $\qquad$ $v[1]=6$ $\qquad$ $w[1]=3$

i\j	0	1	2	3	4	5	6
0	0	0	0	0	0	0	0
1	0	0	0	6+0=6	6+0=6	6+0=6	6+0=6
2	0						
3	0						
4	0						

With `i=1`, the algorithm performs iteration `j` from 1 to `Wmax`:
- `j=1`: `w[1]>j`, `K[1,1]=0` (line #16)
- `j=2`: `w[1]>j`, `K[1,2]=0` (line #16)
- `j=3`: `w[1]=j`, `6+K[0,0]>K[0,3]`, `K[1,3]=6+0=6` (line #11)
- `j=4`: `w[1]<j`, `6+K[0,1]>K[0,4]`, `K[1,4]=6+0=6` (line #11)
- `j=5`: `w[1]<j`, `6+K[0,2]>K[0,5]`, `K[1,5]=6+0=6` (line #11)
- `j=6`: `w[1]<j`, `6+K[0,3]>K[0,6]`, `K[1,6]=6+0=6` (line #11)

Calculating row #2:

$i=2$ $\qquad$ $v[2]=5$ $\qquad$ $w[2]=2$

i\j	0	1	2	3	4	5	6
0	0	0	0	0	0	0	0
1	0	0	0	6	6	6	6
2	0	0	5+0=5	6	6	5+6=11	5+6=11
3	0						
4	0						

With `i=2`, the algorithm performs iteration `j` from 1 to `Wmax`:
- `j=1`: `w[2]>j`, `K[2,1]=0` (line #16)
- `j=2`: `w[2]=j`, `5+K[1,0]>K[1,2]`, `K[2,2]=5+0=5` (line #11)
- `j=3`: `w[2]<j`, `5+K[1,1]<K[1,3]`, `K[2,3]=6` (line #13)
- `j=4`: `w[2]<j`, `5+K[1,2]<K[1,4]`, `K[2,4]=6` (line #13)
- `j=5`: `w[2]<j`, `5+K[1,3]>K[1,5]`, `K[2,5]=5+6=11` (line #11)
- `j=6`: `w[2]<j`, `5+K[1,4]>K[1,6]`, `K[2,6]=5+6=11` (line #11)

Calculating row #3:

$$i=3 \qquad v[3]=9 \qquad w[3]=5$$

i\j	0	1	2	3	4	5	6
0	0	0	0	0	0	0	0
1	0	0	0	6	6	6	6
2	0	0	5	6	6	11	11
3	0	0	5	6	6	11	11
4	0						

With i=3, the algorithm performs iteration j from 1 to Wmax:
- j=1: w[3]>j, K[3,1]=0 (line #16)
- j=2: w[3]>j, K[3,2]=5 (line #16)
- j=3: w[3]>j, K[3,3]=6 (line #16)
- j=4: w[3]>j, K[3,4]=6 (line #16)
- j=5: w[3]=j, 9+K[2,0]<K[2,5], K[3,5]=11 (line #13)
- j=6: w[3]<j, 9+K[2,1]<K[2,6], K[3,6]=11 (line #13)

Calculating row #4:

$$i=4 \qquad v[4]=8 \qquad w[4]=4$$

i\j	0	1	2	3	4	5	6
0	0	0	0	0	0	0	0
1	0	0	0	6	6	6	6
2	0	0	5	6	6	11	11
3	0	0	5	6	6	11	11
4	0	0	5	6	8+0=8	11	8+5=13

With i=4, the algorithm performs iteration j from 1 to Wmax:
- j=1: w[4]>j, K[4,1]=0 (line #16)
- j=2: w[4]>j, K[4,2]=5 (line #16)
- j=3: w[4]>j, K[4,3]=6 (line #16)
- j=4: w[4]=j, 8+K[3,0]>K[3,4], K[2,5]=8+0=8 (line #11)
- j=5: w[4]<j, 8+K[3,1]<K[3,5], K[3,5]=11 (line #13)
- j=6: w[4]<j, 8+K[3,2]>K[3,6], K[2,5]=8+5=13 (line #11)

After array K is fully populated, the last value in the table (bottom right) is the maximum value of the items that can be carried in the knapsack. In this example, the knapsack with maximum weight 6 kgs can carry items with highest value of $13. Lines #20 to #26 from Algorithm 05-I reads array K to discover which items should be chosen to make that maximum value.

Selecting items for knapsack:

i\j	0	1	2	3	4	5	6
0	0	0	0	0	0	0	0
1	0	0	0	6	6	6	6
2	0	0	<u>5</u>	6	6	11	11
3	0	0	5	6	6	11	11
4	0	0	5	6	8	11	<u>13</u>

Starting from the value on bottom right:

- i=4. j=6. The value of K[4,6] is 13. Compare this value with the value from previous row (same column), K[4,6] (13) is greater than K[3,6] (11). Therefore, item #4 is selected for knapsack.
- The value of j is adjusted, j=j-w[i]=6-4=2.
- i=3. j=2. The value of K[3,2] is 5. Compare this value with the value from previous row (same column). K[3,2] (5) is not greater than K[2,2] (5). Therefore, item #3 is not selected for knapsack.
- i=2. j=2. The value of K[2,2] is 5. Compare this value with the value from previous row (same column). K[2,2] (5) is greater than K[1,2] (0). Therefore, item #2 is selected for knapsack.
- The value of j is adjusted, j=j-w[i]=2-2=0.
- i=1. j=0. The value of K[1,0] is 0. This meets the condition to stop the process in line #20.
- This algorithm finishes its calculation, choosing items #2 and #4 with total value of $13.

To understand more about solving 0/1 knapsack problem using dynamics programming, 3 completed examples are provided below.

Completed example A:

n = 7

Wmax = 10

(v1, v2, v3, v4, v5, v6, v7) = (37, 15, 22, 56, 29, 23, 14)

(w1, w2, w3, w4, w5, w6, w7) = (5, 2, 3, 6, 4, 3, 2)

i\j	0	1	2	3	4	5	6	7	8	9	10
0	0	0	0	0	0	0	0	0	0	0	0
1	0	0	0	0	0	37	37	37	37	37	37
2	0	0	15	15	15	37	37	52	52	52	52
3	0	0	15	22	22	37	37	52	59	59	74
4	0	0	15	22	22	37	**56**	56	71	78	78
5	0	0	15	22	29	37	56	56	71	78	**85**
6	0	0	15	23	29	38	56	56	71	79	85
7	0	0	15	23	29	38	56	56	71	79	85

Choosing items #4 and #5 produces maximum value of $85.

Completed example B:

n = 8

Wmax = 9

(v1, v2, v3, v4, v5, v6, v7, v8) = (63, 18, 41, 37, 55, 24, 32, 20)

(w1, w2, w3, w4, w5, w6, w7, w8) = (6, 2, 4, 3, 5, 2, 3, 2)

i\j	0	1	2	3	4	5	6	7	8	9
0	0	0	0	0	0	0	0	0	0	0
1	0	0	0	0	0	0	63	63	63	63
2	0	0	18	18	18	18	63	63	81	81
3	0	0	18	18	**41**	41	63	63	81	81
4	0	0	18	37	41	55	63	**78**	81	100
5	0	0	18	37	41	55	63	78	92	100
6	0	0	24	37	42	61	65	79	92	**102**
7	0	0	24	37	42	61	69	79	93	102
8	0	0	24	37	44	61	69	81	93	102

Choosing items #3, #4 and #6 produces maximum value of $102.

Completed example C:

$n = 8$

$\texttt{Wmax} = 9$

$(\texttt{v1, v2, v3, v4, v5, v6, v7, v8}) = (31, 60, 29, 18, 80, 17, 38, 26)$

$(\texttt{w1, w2, w3, w4, w5, w6, w7, w8}) = (5, 2, 3, 2, 6, 2, 4, 3)$

i\j	0	1	2	3	4	5	6	7	8	9
0	0	0	0	0	0	0	0	0	0	0
1	0	0	0	0	0	31	31	31	31	31
2	0	0	60	**60**	60	60	60	91	91	91
3	0	0	60	60	60	89	89	91	91	91
4	0	0	60	60	78	89	89	107	107	109
5	0	0	60	60	78	89	89	107	140	**140**
6	0	0	60	60	78	89	95	107	140	140
7	0	0	60	60	78	89	98	107	140	140
8	0	0	60	60	78	89	98	107	140	140

Choosing items #2 and #5 produces maximum value of $140.

Travelling Salesperson Problem

Given a list of locations and distances between each location, travelling salesperson problem (also known as travelling salesman problem or TSP) is trying to find the shortest possible path to visit each location exactly once and return to starting location. This problem was inspired by case study of a salesperson who tried to visit several locations to sell a product. It was mathematically formulated in 1930 and remains one of the most popular studies in optimisation.

TSP can be represented as graph or cost matrix. In graph model, each location is represented as a node. Cost to travel between two locations is represented using directed and weighted edge. It is possible for the cost from A to B to have different value from the cost from B to A. The direction of path matters in TSP, adding complexity to its calculation.

How is it possible for the cost from A to B is different from B to A?

In real life situations, it could be because going from A to B is an uphill walk while going from B to A is downhill. There could be other factors such as no-turn sign or other road situations which apply only for trip in particular direction. Note that edge weight is defined as cost instead of distance.

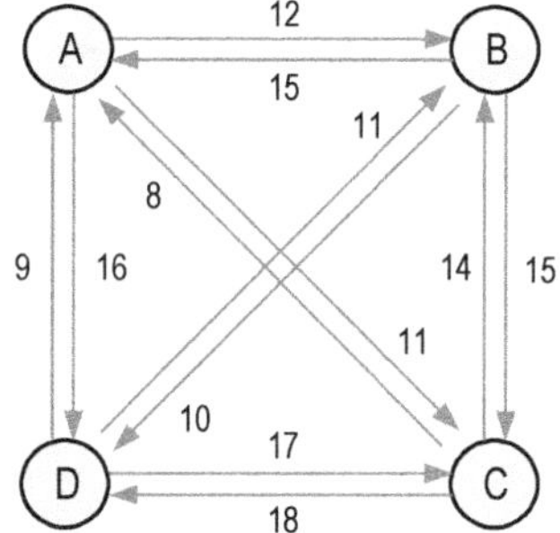

The above graph shows an example of travelling salesperson problem. A path always starts from node A, representing the current/home location of the salesperson.

The same graph can be represented using cost matrix:

$$\begin{bmatrix} \infty & 12 & 11 & 16 \\ 15 & \infty & 15 & 10 \\ 8 & 14 & \infty & 18 \\ 9 & 11 & 17 & \infty \end{bmatrix}$$

Main formula to solve TSP using dynamic programming:

```
p(i,L)=min[c(j,i)+p(j,L-{j})]
```

`p(i,L)` is the cost of path from start node to node `i` after visiting nodes in list `L`. `c(j,i)` is the cost from node `j` to node `i`. Note that `c(j,i)` is not the same as `c(i,j)` because *directed edges* between `i` and `j` have different costs. `L-{j}` is list `L` without node `j`.

The TSP solution for the above example is `p(A,{B,C,D})`. It can be read as the path cost from start node to node A after visiting B, C and D but not necessarily in that sequence (path with the lowest cost).

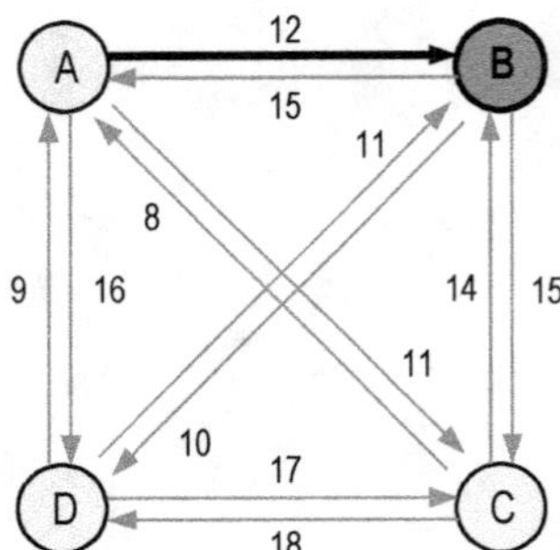

p(B,∅)=c(A,B)=12
This value represents total cost of the path from start node to node B.

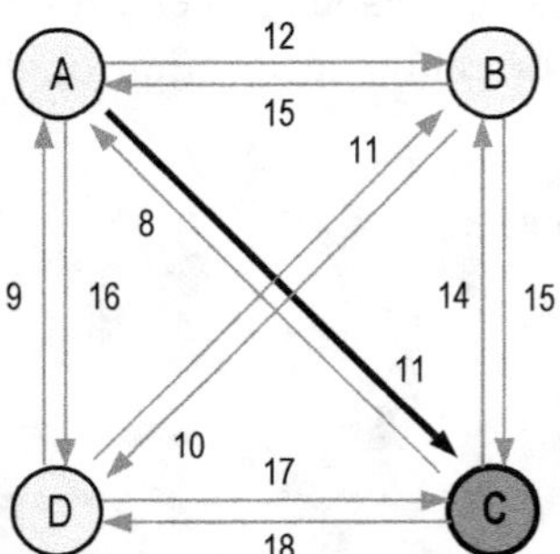

p(C,∅)=c(A,C)=11
This value represents total cost of the path from start node to node C.

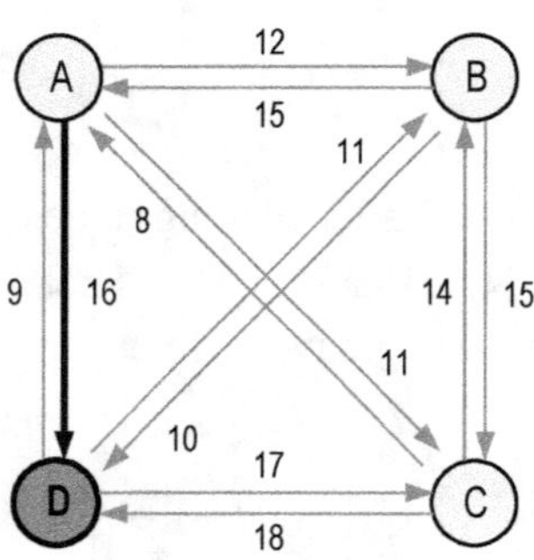

p(D,∅)=c(A,D)=16
This value represents total cost of the path from start node to node D.

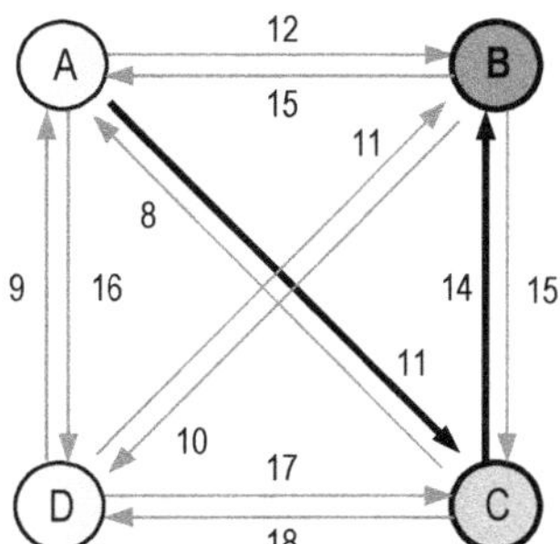

$p(B, \{C\}) = c(C,B) + p(C,\emptyset) = 25$

This value represents total cost of the path from start node to node B after visiting node C.

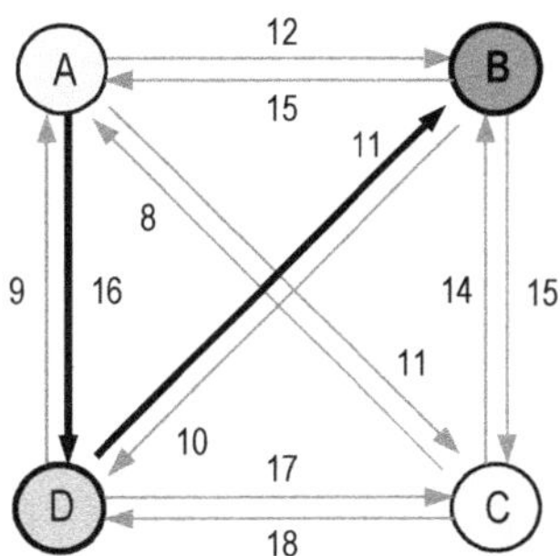

$p(B, \{D\}) = c(D,B) + p(D,\emptyset) = 27$

This value represents total cost of the path from start node to node B after visiting node D.

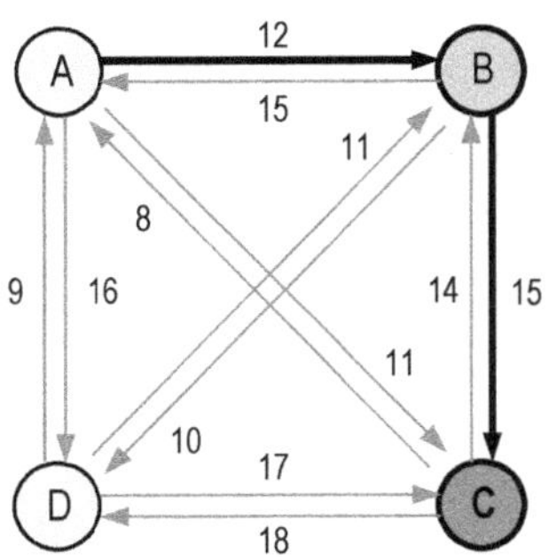

$p(C, \{B\}) = c(B,C) + p(B,\emptyset) = 29$

This value represents total cost of the path from start node to node C after visiting node B.

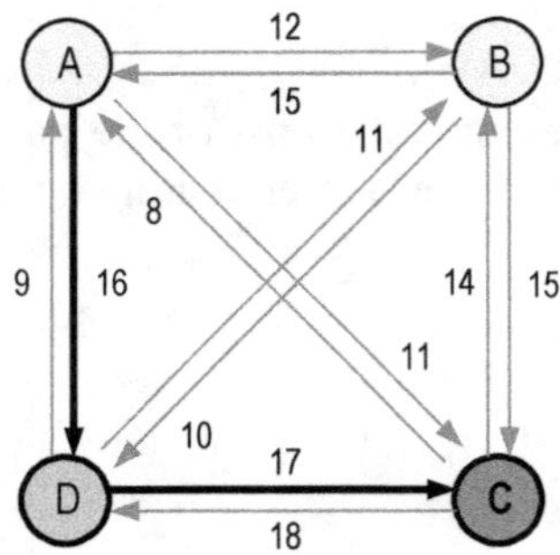

$p(C,\{D\})=c(D,C)+p(D,\emptyset)=33$
This value represents total cost of the path from start node to node C after visiting node D.

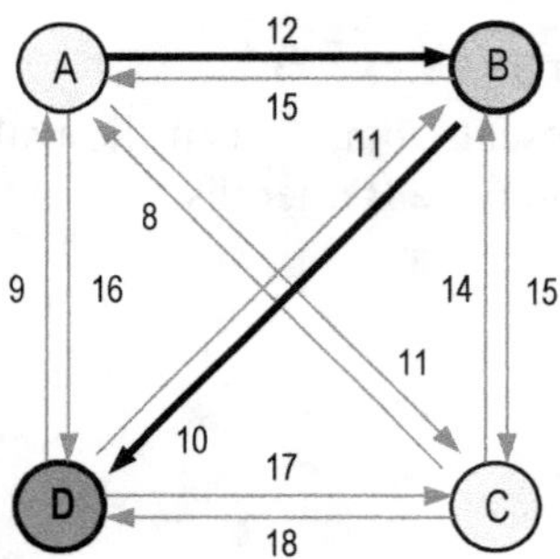

$p(D,\{B\})=c(B,D)+p(B,\emptyset)=22$
This value represents total cost of the path from start node to node D after visiting node B.

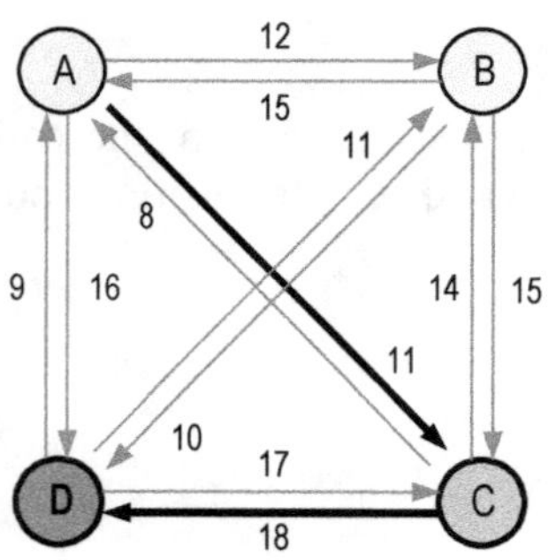

$p(D,\{C\})=c(C,D)+p(C,\emptyset)=29$
This value represents total cost of the path from start node to node D after visiting node C.

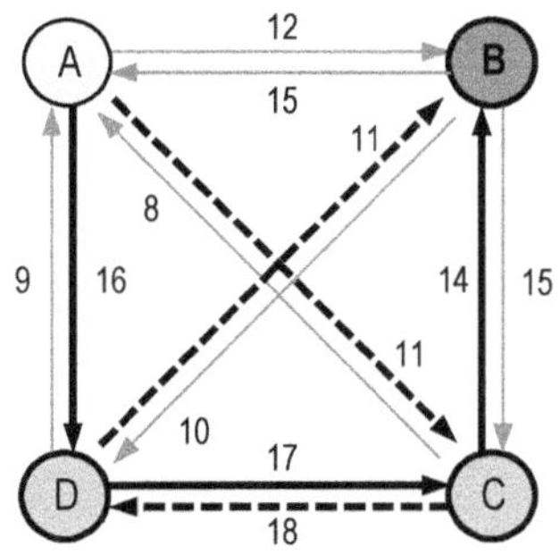

```
p(B,{C,D})=
min[c(C,B)+p(C,{D})|
     c(D,B)+p(D,{C})]=
min[14+33|11+29]=40
```

This value represents total cost of the path from start node to node B after visiting nodes C and D with the lowest cost.

`c(C,B)+p(C,{D})` → thicker lines.

`c(D,B)+p(D,{C})` → thicker medium-dotted lines.

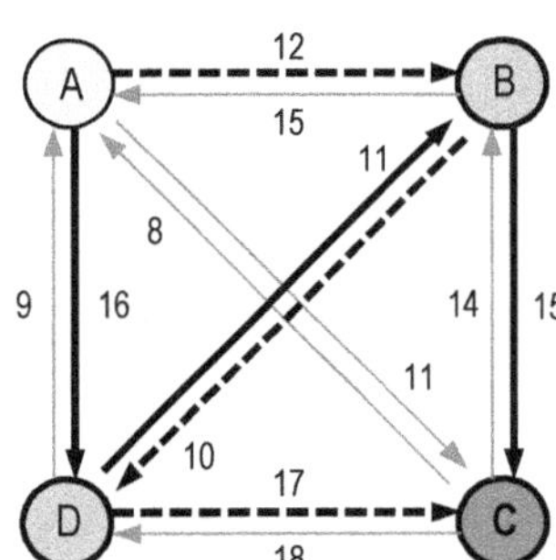

```
p(C,{B,D})=
min[c(B,C)+p(B,{D})|
     c(D,C)+p(D,{B})]=
min[15+27|17+22]=39
```

This value represents total cost of the path from start node to node C after visiting nodes B and D with the lowest cost.

`c(B,C)+p(B,{D})` → thicker lines.

`c(D,C)+p(D,{B})` → thicker medium-dotted lines.

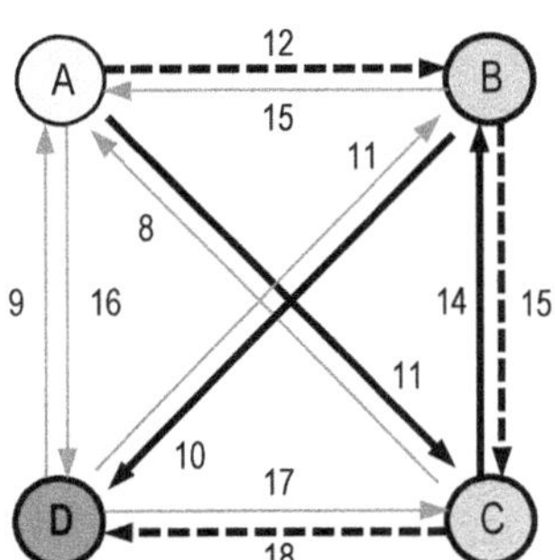

```
p(D,{B,C})=
min[c(B,D)+p(B,{C})|
     c(C,D)+p(C,{B})]=
min[10+25|18+27]=35
```

This value represents total cost of the path from start node to node D after visiting nodes B and C with the lowest cost.

`c(B,D)+p(B,{C})` → thicker lines.

`c(C,D)+p(C,{B})` → thicker medium-dotted lines.

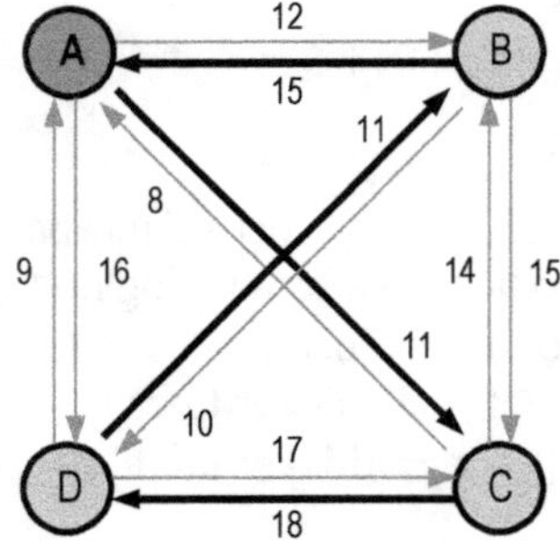 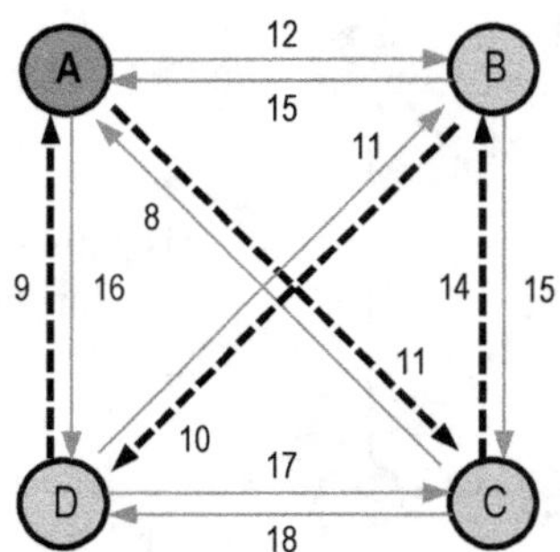

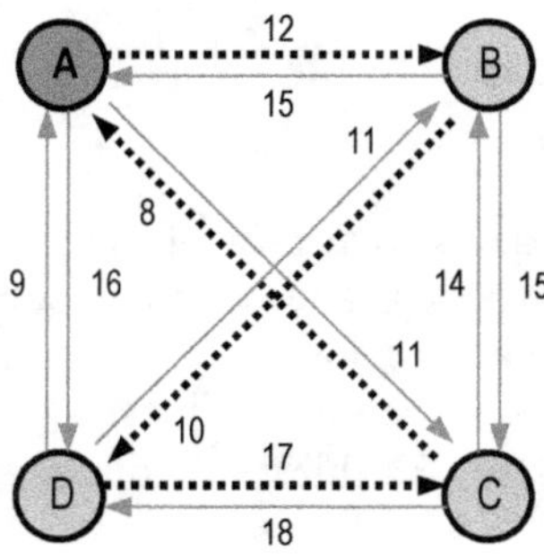

```
p(A,{B,C,D})=
min[c(B,A)+p(B,{C,D})|
     c(C,A)+p(C,{B,D})|
     c(D,A)+p(D,{B,C})]=
min[15+40|8+39|9+35]=44
```

This value represents total cost of the path from start node back to node A after visiting nodes B, C and D with the lowest cost.

`c(B,A)+p(B,{C,D})` → thicker lines.

`c(C,A)+p(C,{B,D})` → thicker medium-dotted lines.

`c(D,A)+p(D,{B,C})` → thicker short-dotted lines.

Lowest possible cost to travel from start node, visit all other nodes and return to node A is 44. The path can be analysed backward from previous calculations.

-
```
p(A,{B,C,D})= min[c(B,A)+p(B,{C,D})|
                  c(C,A)+p(C,{B,D})|
                  c(D,A)+p(D,{B,C})]
            = min[15+40|8+39|9+35]
            = 44
```

- The lowest cost comes from `c(D,A)+p(D,{B,C})`.
  D-A is part of the solution.

-
```
p(D,{B,C})= min[c(B,D)+p(B,{C})|
                c(C,D)+p(C,{B})]
          = min[10+25|18+27]
          = 35
```

- The lowest cost comes from `c(B,D)+p(B,{C})`.
  B-D-A is part of the solution.

- p(B,{C})=**c(C,B)+p(C,∅)=25**
- The lowest cost comes from c(C,B)+p(C,∅).
  C-B-D-A is part of the solution.
- p(C,∅)=**c(A,C)=11**
- The lowest cost comes from c(C,B)+p(C,∅).
  A-C-B-D-A is path with lowest possible cost.

To understand more about solving TSP using dynamic programming, a different example is presented below:

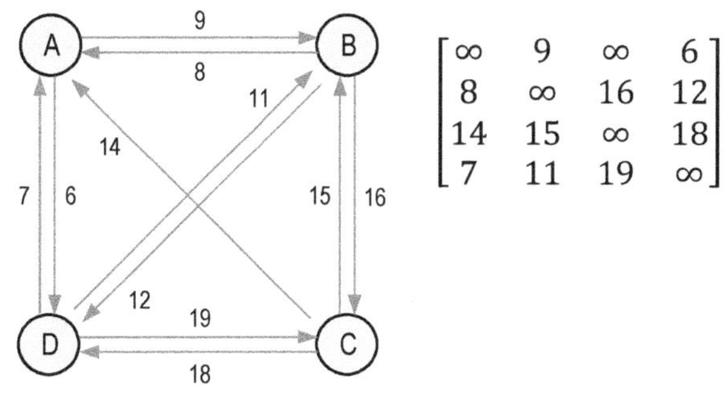


```
p(B,∅)=c(A,B)=9
p(D,∅)=c(A,D)=6
p(B,{D})=c(D,B)+p(D,∅)=17
p(C,{B})=c(B,C)+p(B,∅)=25
p(C,{D})=c(D,C)+p(D,∅)=25
p(D,{B})=c(B,D)+p(B,∅)=21
p(B,{C,D})= min[c(C,B)+p(C,{D})]
          = min[15+25] = 40
p(C,{B,D})= min[c(B,C)+p(B,{D})|c(D,C)+p(D,{B})]
          = min[16+17|19+21]  = 33
p(D,{B,C})= min[c(C,D)+p(C,{B})]
          = min[18+25]  = 43
p(A,{B,C,D})= min[c(B,A)+p(B,{C,D})|
                  c(C,A)+p(C,{B,D})|
                  c(D,A)+p(D,{B,C})]
            = min[8+40|14+33|7+43]
            = 47
```

TSP solution is A-D-B-C-A with total cost 47. Note that there is no edge from node A to node C. The cost from A to C is unlimited (cannot be travelled) instead of zero.

06. HUFFMAN CODING

How does data compression work? How can we save digital data using less storage without missing anything?

When a person types a sentence in a computer file, all letters from the characters will be saved as bits of 0 and 1 values. Capital letter A, for example, is character number #65 (also known as character encoding). It will be saved as 100 0001, which is the binary code for 65.

Who decides that letter A is has character number of 65? Why not 100, or even 250? Is it the same for every computer? Can someone build a computer which will save letter A as character #85?

Technically, any computer can have any translation between symbols and character encoding. However, if each computer uses different translation, then data from one computer will not be readable in others.

To enable communications between computers and other digital devices, some encoding standards were established. There are several popular encoding standards in the world, but for the purpose of keeping it simple, this chapter will only mention 3: ASCII, Latin-1 and UTF-8.

ASCII (American Standard Code for Information Interchange) is an encoding standard developed from telegraph code (from 1961 to 1967). This standard uses 7 bits binary to represent 95 printable characters and 33 command characters. Most newer encodings are based on ASCII with support for additional characters.

Latin-1 (also known as **ISO 8859-1**) is a newer encoding standard with 8 bits binary, capable to represent 256 different characters. The first half of Latin-1 is identical to ASCII standard, making it a superset of ASCII with some additions of alphabets from Western European languages.

UTF-8 (Unicode Transformation Format) is a modern character encoding capable of representing millions of characters and symbols from many languages. UTF-8 uses 1 to 4 bytes per character (1 byte = 8 bits). It is designed to be backward compatible with ASCII and Latin-1. **UTF-16** is a newer variant, it uses 2 bytes (16 bits) or 4 bytes (32 bits) for each character.

The below table shows binary encoding for printable characters in ASCII:

Binary	#	Char	Binary	#	Char	Binary	#	Char
0010 0000	32	sp	0100 0000	64	@	0110 0000	96	`
0010 0001	33	!	0100 0001	65	A	0110 0001	97	a
0010 0010	34	"	0100 0010	66	B	0110 0010	98	b
0010 0011	35	#	0100 0011	67	C	0110 0011	99	c
0010 0100	36	$	0100 0100	68	D	0110 0100	100	d
0010 0101	37	%	0100 0101	69	E	0110 0101	101	e
0010 0110	38	&	0100 0110	70	F	0110 0110	102	f
0010 0111	39	'	0100 0111	71	G	0110 0111	103	g
0010 1000	40	(	0100 1000	72	H	0110 1000	104	h
0010 1001	41	)	0100 1001	73	I	0110 1001	105	i
0010 1010	42	*	0100 1010	74	J	0110 1010	106	j
0010 1011	43	+	0100 1011	75	K	0110 1011	107	k
0010 1100	44	,	0100 1100	76	L	0110 1100	108	l
0010 1101	45	–	0100 1101	77	M	0110 1101	109	m
0010 1110	46	.	0100 1110	78	N	0110 1110	110	n
0010 1111	47	/	0100 1111	79	O	0110 1111	111	o
0011 0000	48	0	0101 0000	80	P	0111 0000	112	p
0011 0001	49	1	0101 0001	81	Q	0111 0001	113	q
0011 0010	50	2	0101 0010	82	R	0111 0010	114	r
0011 0011	51	3	0101 0011	83	S	0111 0011	115	s
0011 0100	52	4	0101 0100	84	T	0111 0100	116	t
0011 0101	53	5	0101 0101	85	U	0111 0101	117	u
0011 0110	54	6	0101 0110	86	V	0111 0110	118	v
0011 0111	55	7	0101 0111	87	W	0111 0111	119	w
0011 1000	56	8	0101 1000	88	X	0111 1000	120	x
0011 1001	57	9	0101 1001	89	Y	0111 1001	121	y
0011 1010	58	:	0101 1010	90	Z	0111 1010	122	z
0011 1011	59	;	0101 1011	91	[	0111 1011	123	{
0011 1100	60	<	0101 1100	92	\	0111 1100	124		
0011 1101	61	=	0101 1101	93	]	0111 1101	125	}
0011 1110	62	>	0101 1110	94	^	0111 1110	126	~
0011 1111	63	?	0101 1111	95	_			

Understanding Data Compression

Storing the word "Hello" in digital format (using ASCII/Latin-1) would require 40 bits of data:

```
0100 1000    0110 0101    0110 1100    0110 1100    0110 1111
    H            e            l            l            o
```

The very basic idea of digital data compression is to use temporary encoding to store data in a smaller number of bits.

Since the word "Hello" only uses 4 different characters, theoretically each character can be represented by 2 bits of data:

- H is assigned code 00.
- e is assigned code 01.
- l is assigned code 10.
- o is assigned code 11.

Then the word "Hello" can be stored in 10 bits instead of 40:

```
00    01    10    10    01
H     e     l     l     o
```

However, assigning arbitrary codes to store data will cause problems. When new data is added, the amount of bit encoding might not be sufficient to store them. For example, to store "Hello there", some new characters do not have assigned codes:

```
00    01    10    10    01    ??    ??    ??    01    ??    01
H     e     l     l     o           t     h     e     r     e
```

Note that empty space between words is also a character that needs to be stored. The letters t, h, r and space do not have assigned codes; hence they could not be stored.

Proper data compression techniques have consistent way to generate their bit encodings in such a way that new data can be added, and stored data can be successfully retrieved without any loss. The more possible characters to save, more combinations of bit encoding are required. More combinations will lead to longer bits encoding per character. Then how can data be stored in less bits without excluding some possible characters?

The key to digital data compression is to implement encoding with different length per character. Characters that likely will appear more frequent in a document gets shorter encoding so that total bits to store will be less than fixed-length encoding.

Huffman Algorithm

Huffman algorithm (also known as *Huffman code*) is one of the most popular techniques for data compression. This technique was invented by David A. Huffman in 1951 as an assignment for his PhD study in Massachusetts Institute of Technology (MIT). His professor in electrical engineering course (Robert M. Fano) offered students a choice of going through final exam or write term paper about efficient method of representing numbers, letters or other symbols using a binary code. Huffman wrote his term paper with a solution that is more optimal than what Fano was working on.

To produce his optimal binary code, Huffman uses binary tree (known as *Huffman tree*) to construct his encoding. This technique becomes the foundation of many other compression algorithms used in storing music (MP3), images (JPEG) and general compression (ZIP).

Steps to generate Huffman tree are categorised into preparation and execution.

Preparation:
- Make a list of all characters used in the message to store.
- Make sure to include space character and other symbols.
- Count the frequencies of how many times each character appears in the message.
- Sort the list of characters based on the frequencies (ascending order).

Execution:
- Create 2 tree nodes from the first 2 elements from the list and their frequencies.
- Connect those 2 new nodes with a new parent node.
- Remove the 2 elements from the list.
- Add the newly created parent node as new element in the list. The frequency of this new element is the sum of frequencies of its two child nodes.
- Repeat the execution steps until the list is empty.

Storing "**PROGRAMMING ALGORITHM BOOK**" message using ASCII/Latin-1 encoding with 1 byte per character would require $26 \times 8 = 208$ bits. Remember that space character also needs to be stored. The same message can be stored using less bits by generating Huffman tree to create new encoding with different length per character.

Applying preparation steps to the message would produce the below list:

P	N	L	T	H	B	K	A	I	sp	R	G	M	O
1	1	1	1	1	1	1	2	2	2	3	3	3	4

Steps of execution to build Huffman tree for the example message:

1. Create 2 tree nodes from elements P and N, each has frequency of 1. Connect the new nodes to a new parent node named *1 with frequency of 2 (1+1).

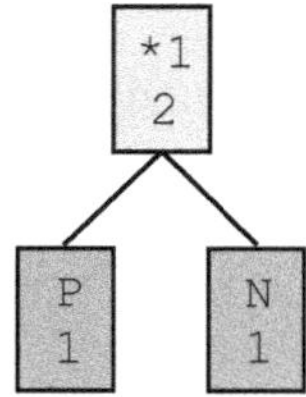

2. Remove elements P and N from list. Add the new node *1 into the list. Remember that the list needs to remain sorted by frequency in ascending order.

L	T	H	B	K	A	I	sp	*1	R	G	M	O
1	1	1	1	1	2	2	2	2	3	3	3	4

3. Create 2 tree nodes from elements L and T, each has frequency of 1. Connect the new nodes to a new parent node named *2 with frequency of 2 (1+1).

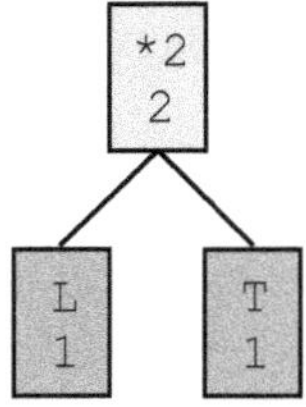

4. Remove elements L and T from list. Add the new node *2.

H	B	K	A	I	sp	*1	*2	R	G	M	O
1	1	1	2	2	2	2	2	3	3	3	4

5. Create 2 tree nodes from elements H and B, each has frequency of 1.
    Connect the new nodes to a new parent node named *3 with
    frequency of 2 (1+1).

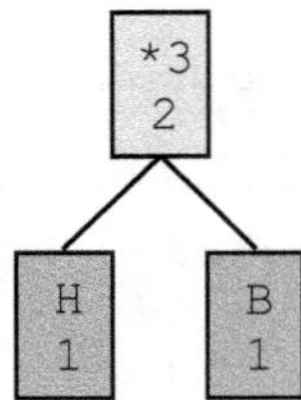

6. Remove elements H and B from list. Add the new node *3.

K	A	I	sp	*1	*2	*3	R	G	M	O
1	2	2	2	2	2	2	3	3	3	4

7. Create 2 tree nodes from elements K (frequency is 1) and A
    (frequency is 2). Connect the new nodes to a new parent node
    named *4 with frequency of 3 (1+2).

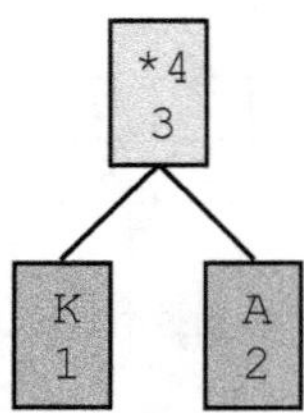

8. Remove elements K and A from list. Add the new node *4.

I	sp	*1	*2	*3	R	G	M	*4	O
2	2	2	2	2	3	3	3	3	4

9. Create 2 tree nodes from elements I and space, each has frequency
    of 2. Connect the new nodes to a new parent node named *5 with
    frequency of 4 (2+2).

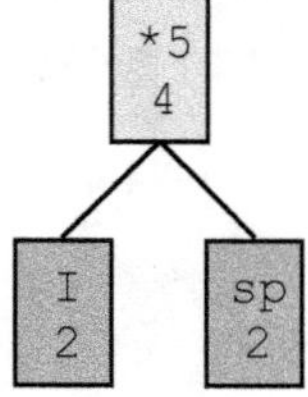

10. Remove elements I and space from list. Add the new node *5.

*1	*2	*3	R	G	M	*4	O	*5
2	2	2	3	3	3	3	4	4

11. Create 2 tree nodes from elements *1 and *2, each has frequency of 2. Connect the new nodes to a new parent node named *6 with frequency of 4 (2+2).

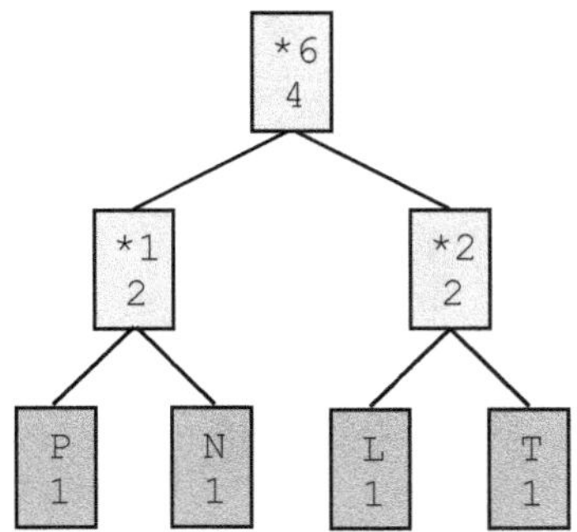

12. Remove elements *1 and *2 from list. Add the new node *6.

*3	R	G	M	*4	O	*5	*6
2	3	3	3	3	4	4	4

13. Create 2 tree nodes from elements *3 (frequency is 2) and R (frequency is 3). Connect the new nodes to a new parent node named *7 with frequency of 5 (2+3).

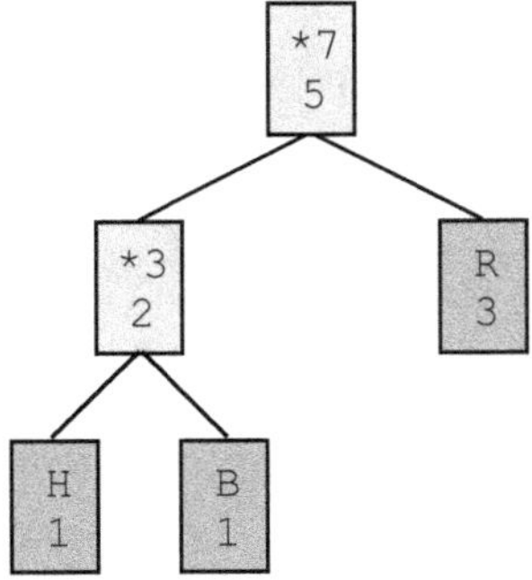

14. Remove elements ∗3 and R from list. Add the new node ∗7.

G	M	∗4	O	∗5	∗6	∗7
3	3	3	4	4	4	5

15. Create 2 tree nodes from elements G and M, each has frequency of 3. Connect the new nodes to a new parent node named ∗8 with frequency of 6 (3+3).

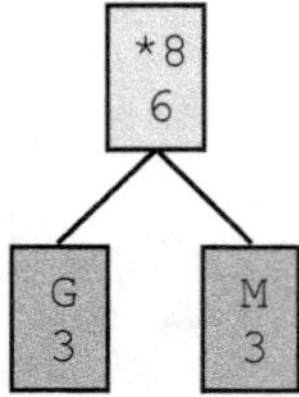

16. Remove elements G and M from list. Add the new node ∗8.

∗4	O	∗5	∗6	∗7	∗8
3	4	4	4	5	6

17. Create 2 tree nodes from elements ∗4 (frequency is 3) and O (frequency is 4). Connect the new nodes to a new parent node named ∗9 with frequency of 7 (3+4).

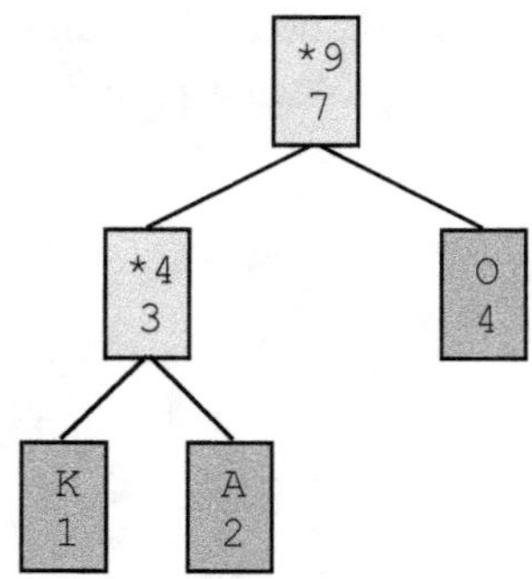

18. Remove elements ∗4 and O from list. Add the new node ∗9.

∗5	∗6	∗7	∗8	∗9
4	4	5	6	7

19. Create 2 tree nodes from elements *5 and *6, each has frequency of 4. Connect the new nodes to a new parent node named *10 with frequency of 8 (4+4).

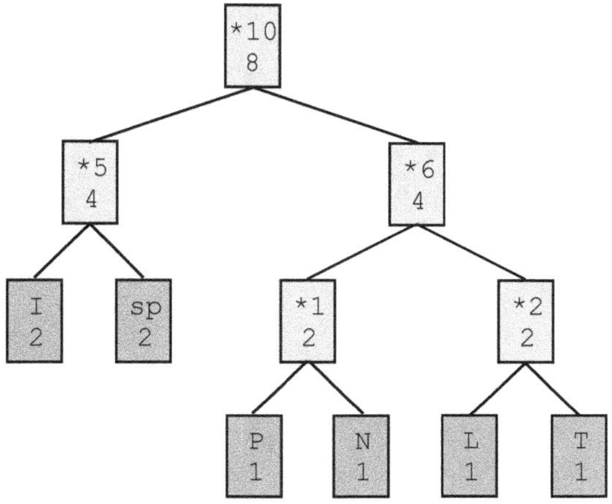

20. Remove elements *5 and *6 from list. Add the new node *10.

*7	*8	*9	*10
5	6	7	8

21. Create 2 tree nodes from elements *7 (frequency is 5) and *8 (frequency is 6). Connect the new nodes to a new parent node named *11 with frequency of 11 (5+6).

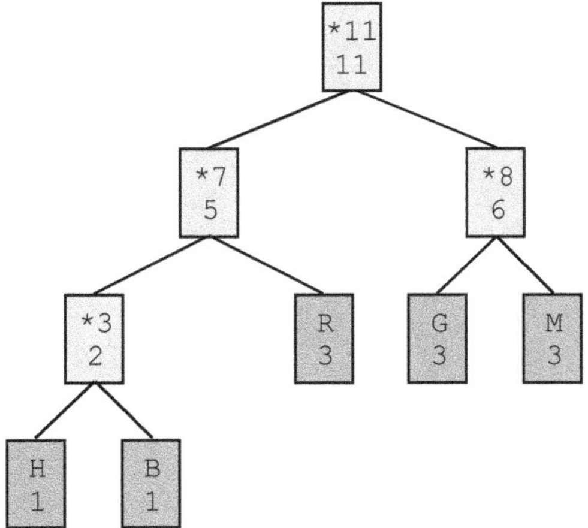

22. Remove elements *7 and *8 from list. Add the new node *11.

*9	*10	*11
7	8	11

23. Create 2 tree nodes from elements *9 (frequency is 7) and *10 (frequency is 8). Connect the new nodes to a new parent node named *12 with frequency of 15 (7+8).

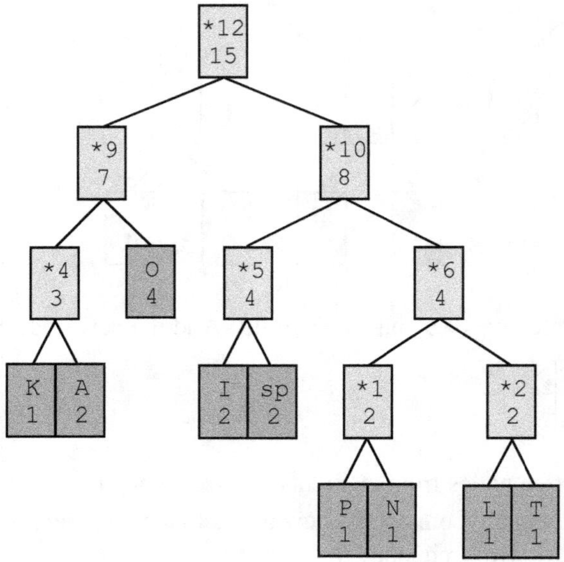

24. Remove elements *9 and *10 from list. Add the new node *12.

*11	*12
11	15

25. Create 2 tree nodes from elements `*11` (frequency is 11) and `*12` (frequency is 15). Connect the new nodes to a new parent node as root of the entire tree.

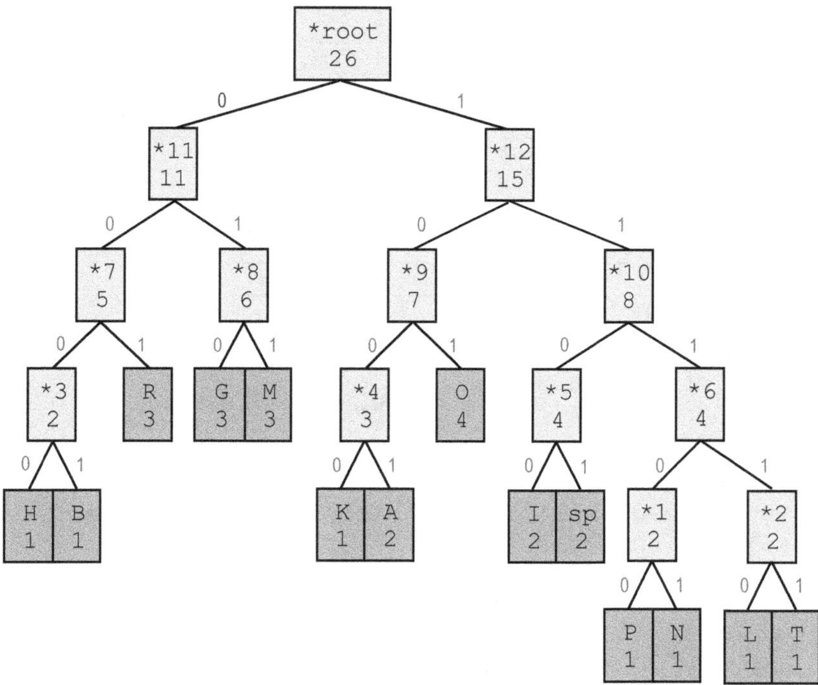

Completed Huffman tree is used to assign efficient codes to each character. The path from root to a character becomes its code. Every time a path goes from a node to its left child, add 0 to the code. If it goes to right child, add 1. Nodes closer to the root node will have shorter code. From the tree above, characters from "PROGRAMMING ALGORITHM BOOK" message will have codes between 3 to 5 bits.

Full list of binary codes for all characters from the message:

P	11100		A	1001
N	11101		I	1100
L	11110		sp	1101
T	11111		R	001
H	0000		G	010
B	0001		M	011
K	1000		O	101

Total bits required to store example message:

Character	Code	Length	Frequency	Bits required
P	11100	5	1	5
N	11101	5	1	5
L	11110	5	1	5
T	11111	5	1	5
H	0000	4	1	4
B	0001	4	1	4
K	1000	4	1	4
A	1001	4	2	8
I	1100	4	2	8
sp	1101	4	2	8
R	001	3	3	9
G	010	3	3	9
M	011	3	3	9
O	101	3	4	12
			Total	**95**

"PROGRAMMING ALGORITHM BOOK" message is stored as:
11100001101010001100101101111001110101011011001111100
10101001110011111000001111010001101011011000

Storing the message using codes from Huffman tree requires total of 95 bits. This is a 54% saving from 208 bits required to store the message using standard ASCII/Latin-1 with 1 byte per character.

Huffman algorithm will reach better efficiency when there are a few characters with significantly higher frequencies appearing in a set of data. Significantly higher frequencies will drive the calculation towards assigning shorter codes for those frequent characters. Shorter codes multiplied by high frequencies will allow better digital compression.

Decoding a stored message requires the Huffman tree from the compressing process. Each bit from stored message is treated as a movement from one parent node to a child node. 0 means move to the left and 1 means move to the right. Every time leaf node is reached (node with a character), that character is part of the original message. Reading process continues with the next bit, traversing the Huffman tree back from the root node.

07. SEARCH TREE

Some of the problems presented in previous chapters, such as shortest path, minimum spanning tree, and travelling salesperson problems, have shared characteristics that they are focusing on making several choices to end up with optimal solution. Choices are made in stages, one at a time. Each choice is impacted by previous stages and will impact next stages.

This model of making choices in multiple stages can be represented as a *search tree* (also known as *decision-making tree*). Each tree level is a stage, and each node is a possible choice. When all possible combinations of choices are mapped into a tree, the right solution is one of the nodes in the tree. Algorithms can be designed to search which node is the optimal solution.

N-Queen problem is a classic problem using the movement rule of a queen in chess game. A queen can move forward, backward, to the left, to the right and diagonal to any number of squares. Customised chessboard with n×n squares is used for this problem. The goal is to put n number of queens in such position that they would not threaten each other.

As an example, 4 queens can be placed in a 4×4 chessboard without threatening each other:

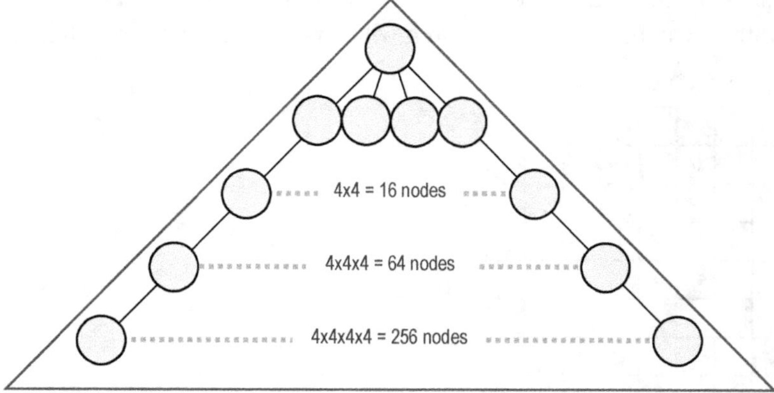

It is known that there can be only 1 queen in a row. Therefore, the problem of placing n queens in n×n chessboard is a problem with 4 decisions to make:

- Q1 should be placed in row #1, decision needs to be made about which column.
- Q2 should be placed in row #2, decision needs to be made about which column.
- Q3 should be placed in row #3, decision needs to be made about which column.
- Q4 should be placed in row #4, decision needs to be made about which column.

The 4 decisions can be mapped into search tree. After the root node, first level will have 4 nodes. Second level will have 4×4=16 nodes. Third level will have 4×4×4=64 nodes. Bottom level will have 4×4×4×4=256 nodes. Search tree will contain every possible solution. However, generating and finding valid solution in such large tree just for small chessboard is not most efficient way to solve the problem. When n is raised to 9000, for example, the size of search tree grows exponentially into 6,561,000,000,000,000 nodes in the fourth level.

There are techniques to explore search tree in such way to increase the possibility of finding the right solution as early as possible. Other techniques focus on quickly eliminating parts of search tree to significantly reduce the search area.

For the example of 4-queens, it is obvious that queens cannot be placed on the same column. Therefore, after the first decision with 4 choices (4 nodes), the second decision only has $4\times3=12$ valid possibilities. If first queen is placed on column #1, second queen can only be placed on columns #2, #3 and #4. Using the same logic, if the second queen is placed on column #2, there are only 2 possible options for the third choice: columns #3 or #4. After 3 decisions are made, there will be one column left for the fourth decision. Level 3 of search tree will have $4\times3\times2=24$ nodes. The last level will have $4\times3\times2\times1=24$ nodes. Note that queen's diagonal movements have not been considered.

N-Queen problem is chosen as example because of its simplicity. For many other problems, the process of reducing the size of search tree would require complex calculations. This chapter focuses on different techniques to find solution in search tree.

Tree Traversal

Any process of finding solution from a search tree starts with the ability to analyse nodes in a consistent pattern. *Tree traversal* is a systematic method to visit every node in a tree. It could be executed as a simple data reading technique, or some calculation/analysis could be performed during each visit.

Different methods of tree traversal:

- Pre-order Traversal
  This method visits parent node first, then goes to child nodes starting from left to right. Nodes will be visited until maximum depth before going back to parent node. This technique is also known as *Depth-First Search* (DFS). See illustration below.

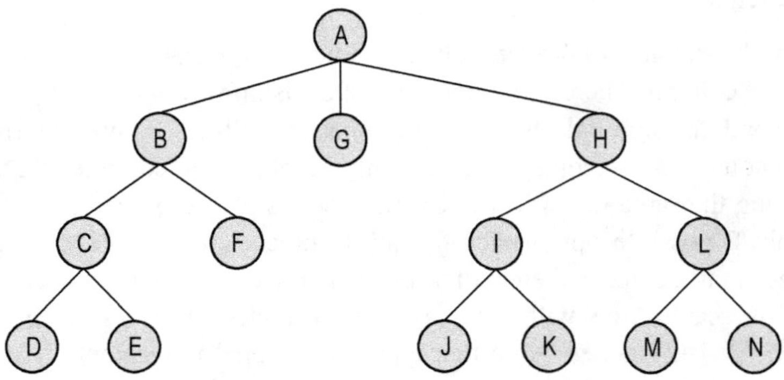

- Level-order Traversal
  This method visits parent node first, then goes to child nodes starting from left to right. Child nodes from the same level will be visited in consecutive order. This technique is also known as *Breadth-First Search* (BFS). See illustration below.

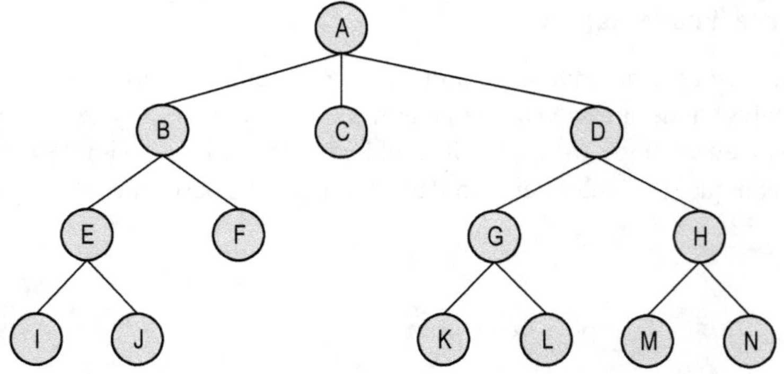

- In-order Traversal
  This method visits left child node first, then parent node, then right child node. In-order traversal only applies for binary tree because it assumes there is only 1 left child and 1 right child. See illustration below.

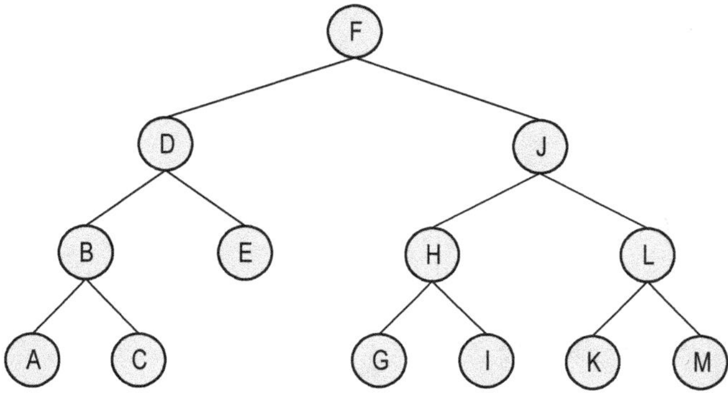

- Post-order Traversal
  This method visits all child nodes from left to right before visiting parent node. See illustration below.

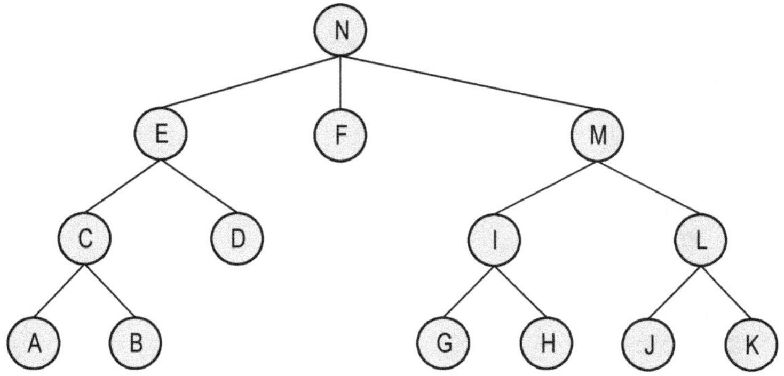

Depth-First Search with Stack

Depth-first search can be implemented in an algorithm using the help of *stack* data structure.

Steps of implementing depth-first search on tree using stack:
1. PUSH root node into the stack.
2. POP node X from stack.

3. If node X that is recently retrieved from the stack has child nodes, PUSH all child nodes of X to the stack.

4. Repeat from step #2 until all nodes are retrieved or until certain search criteria is met.

Example:

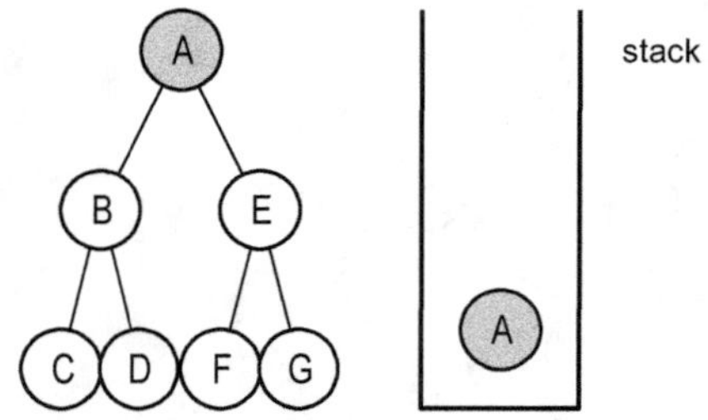

Step 1: PUSH node A to the stack.

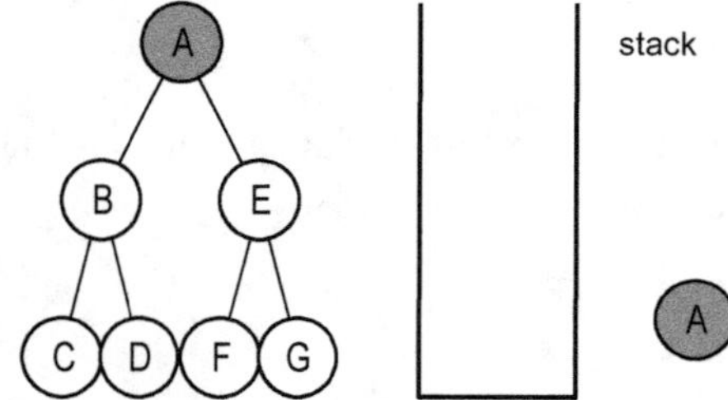

Step 2: POP node A from the stack.

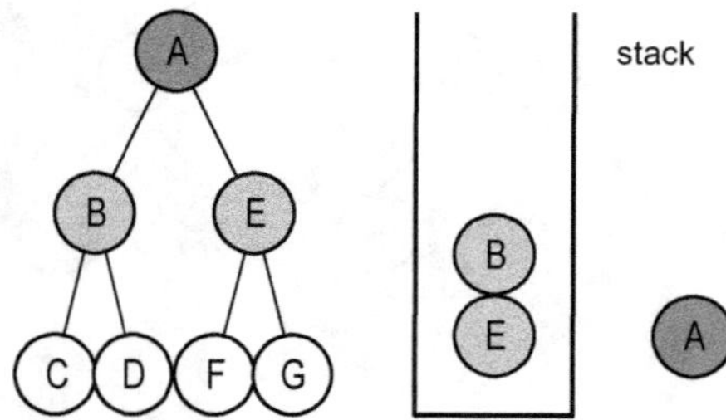

Step 3: PUSH nodes B and E (child nodes of node A) to the stack.

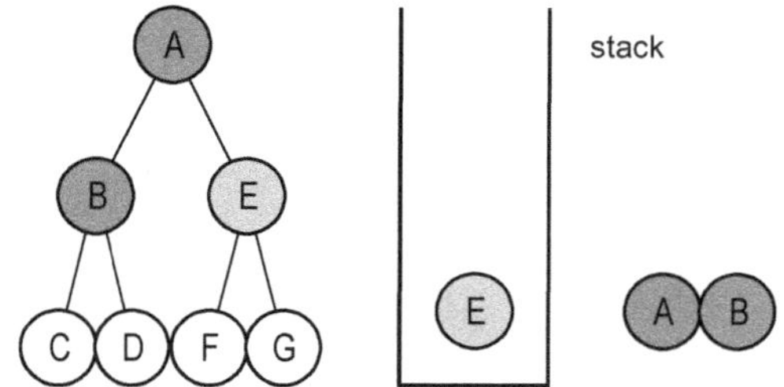

Step 4: POP node B from the stack.

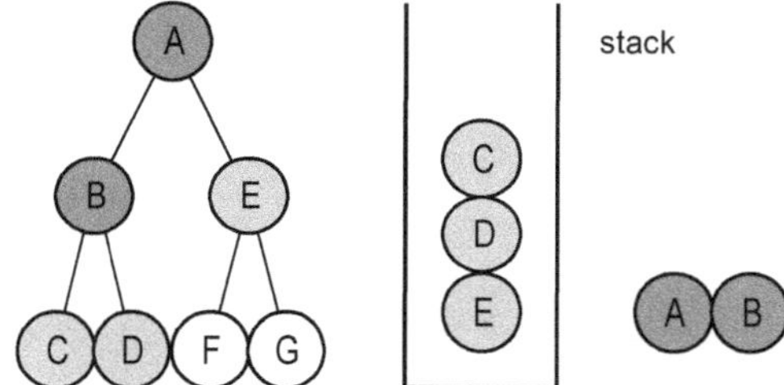

Step 5: PUSH nodes C and D (child nodes of node B) to the stack.

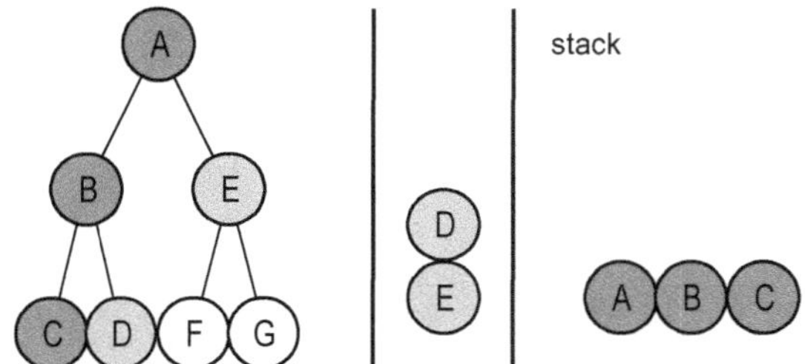

Step 6: POP node C from the stack.

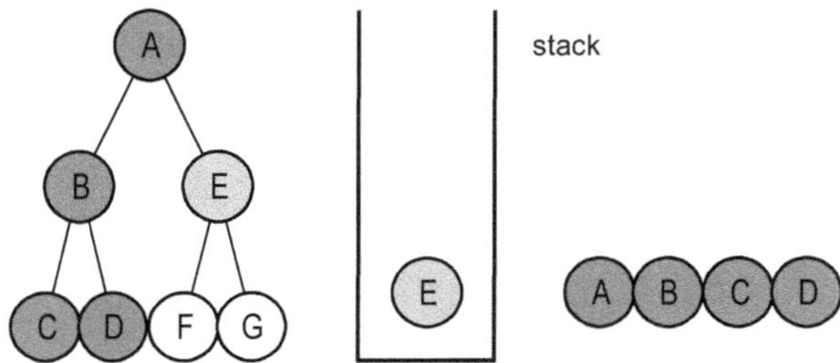

Step 7: Node C has no child node. POP node D from the stack.

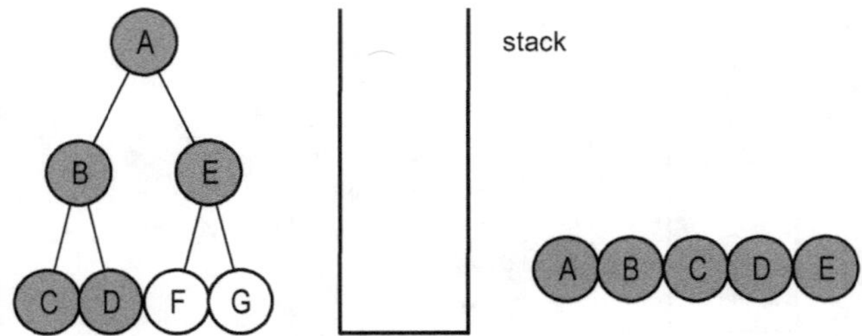

Step 8: Node D has no child node. POP node E from the stack.

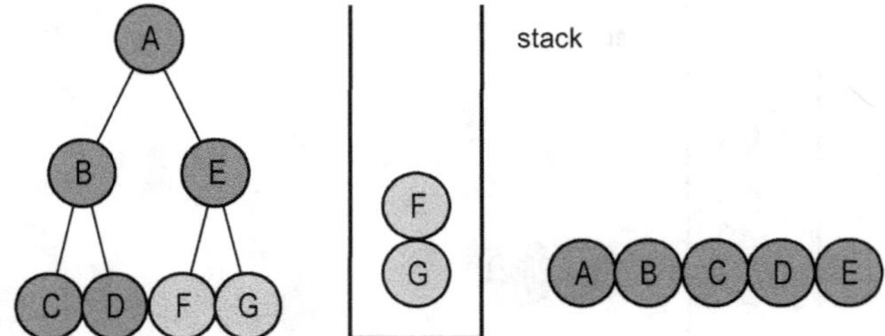

Step 9: PUSH nodes F and G (child nodes of node E) to the stack.

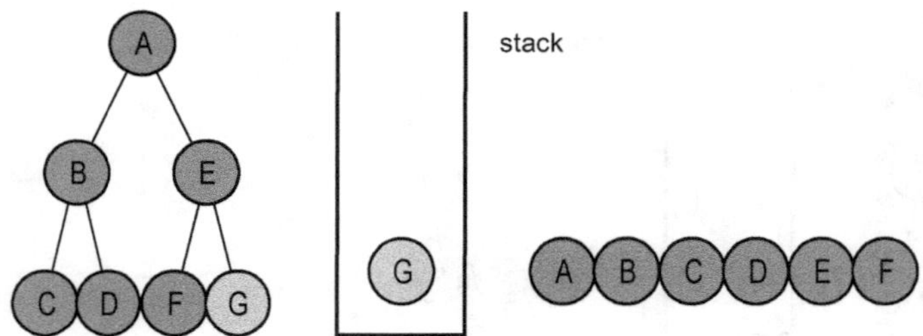

Step 10: POP node F from the stack.

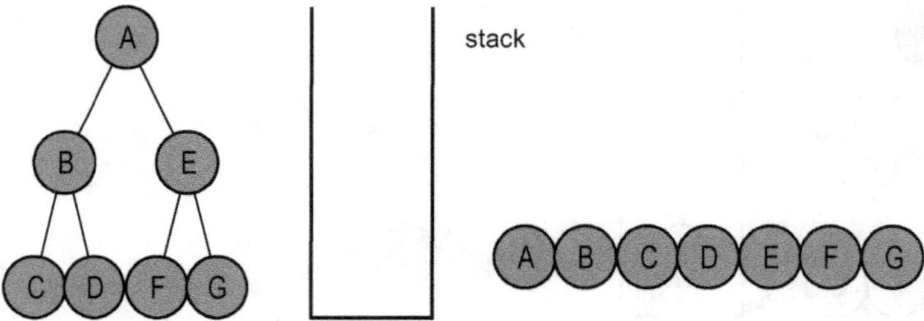

Step 11: Node F has no child node. POP node G from the stack. All tree nodes have been processed.

Breadth-First Search with Queue

Breadth-first search can be implemented in an algorithm using the help of *queue* data structure.

Steps of implementing breadth-first search on tree using queue:
1. PUSH root node into the queue.
2. POP node X from queue.
3. If node X that is recently retrieved from the queue has child nodes, PUSH all child nodes of X to the queue.
4. Repeat from step #2 until all nodes are retrieved or until certain search criteria is met.

Example:

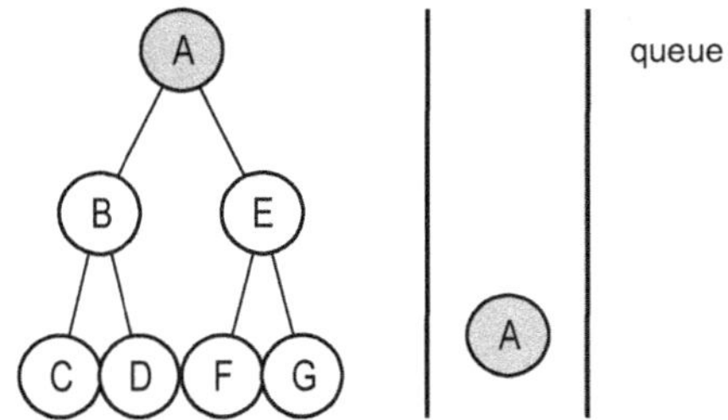

Step 1: PUSH node A to the queue.

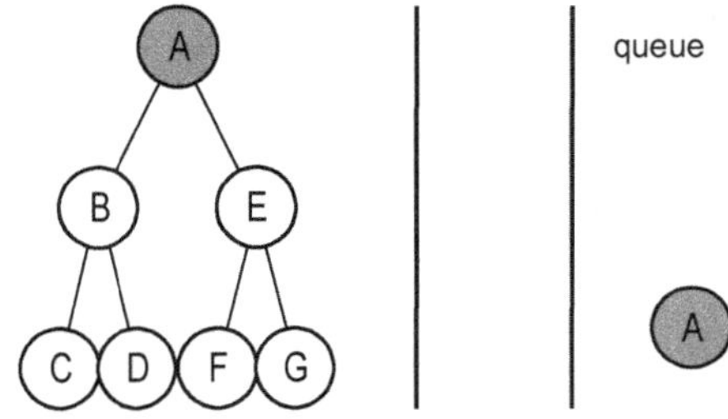

Step 2: POP node A from the queue.

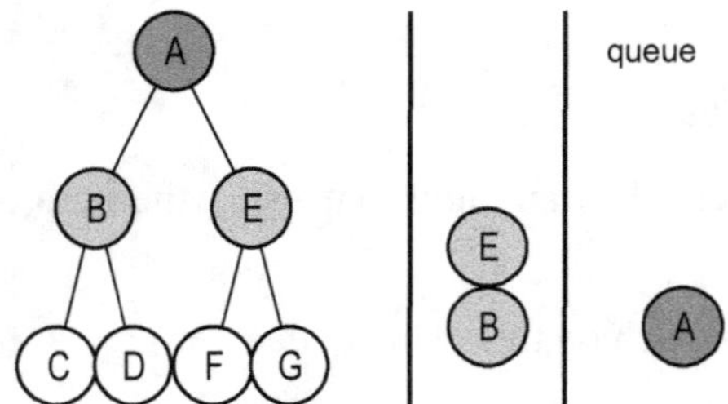

Step 3: PUSH nodes B and E (child nodes of node A) to the queue.

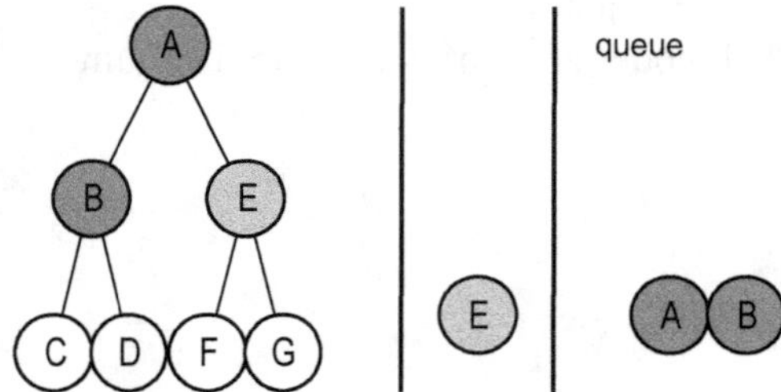

Step 4: POP node B from the queue.

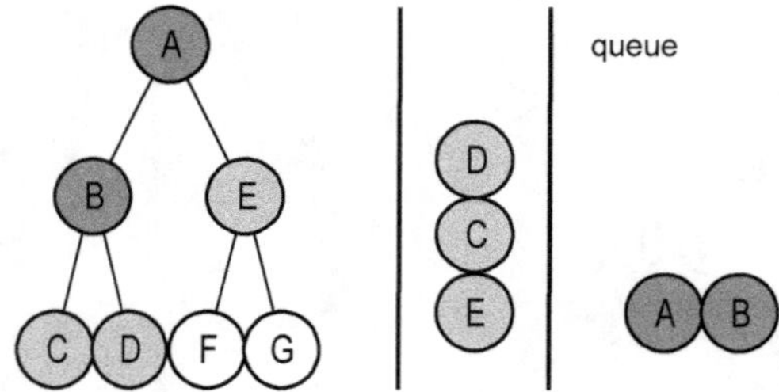

Step 5: PUSH nodes C and D (child nodes of node B) to the queue.

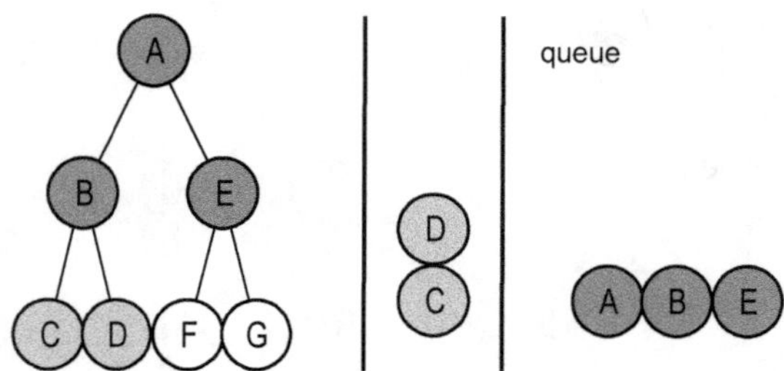

Step 6: POP node E from the queue.

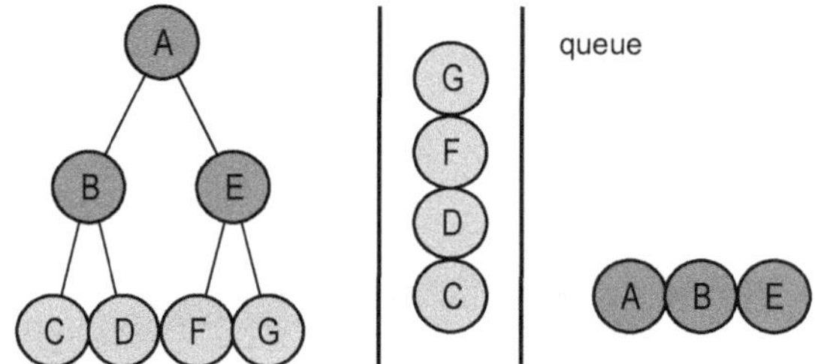

Step 7: PUSH nodes F and G (child nodes of node E) to the queue.

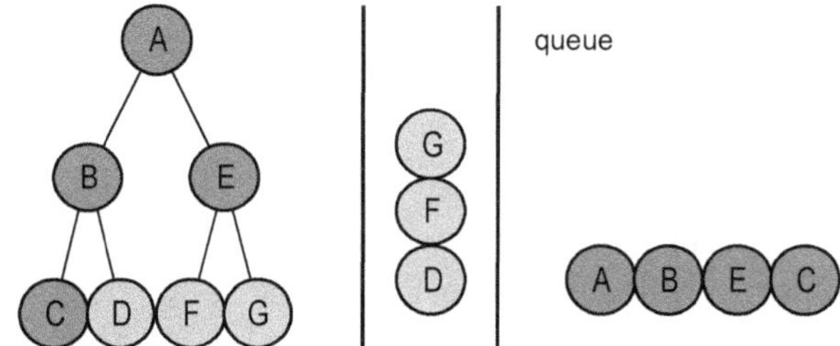

Step 8: POP node C from the queue.

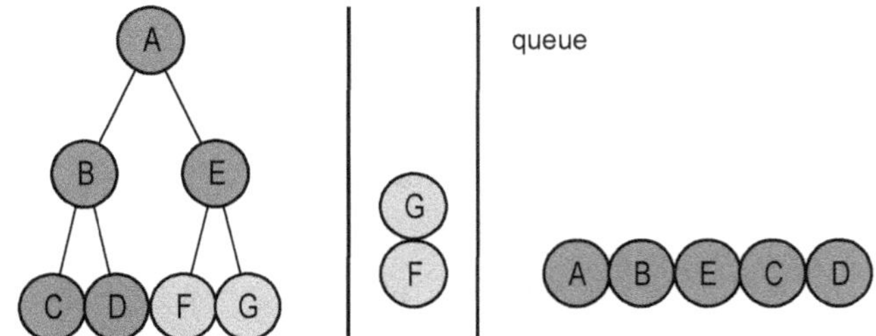

Step 9: Node C has no child node. POP node D from the queue.

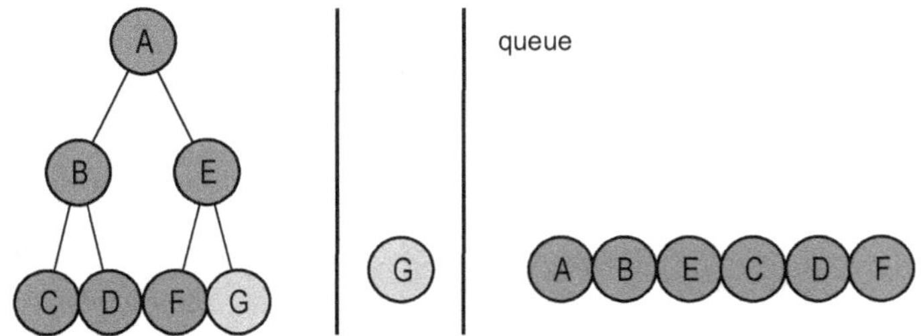

Step 10: Node D has no child node. POP node F from the queue.

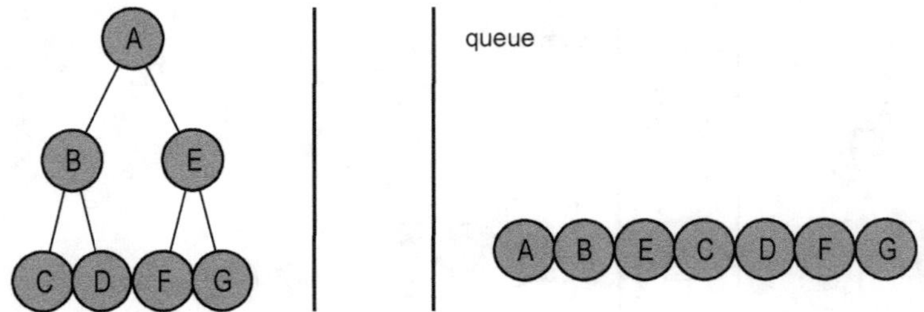

Step 11: Node F has no child node. POP node G from the queue. All tree nodes have been processed.

Depth-First Search in Graphs

Tree is technically an undirected graph in which any two nodes are connected by exactly one edge. Normal graphs that do not meet the specific criteria of a tree can also be traversed using similar technique. Depth-first search on graph can be implemented in an algorithm using the help of *stack* data structure.

Steps of implementing depth-first search on graph using stack:
1. PUSH root node into the queue. Mark the node as processed.
2. POP node X from stack.
3. If node X that is recently retrieved from the stack is directly connected to unprocessed nodes, PUSH all nodes directly connected to X to the stack. Mark these nodes as processed.
4. Repeat from step #2 until all nodes are retrieved or until certain search criteria is met.

Example:

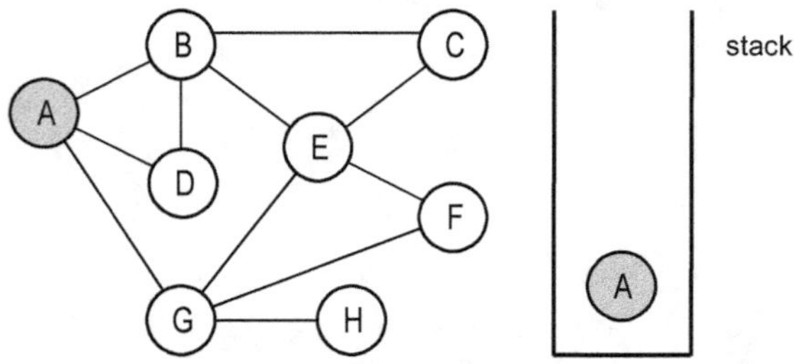

Step 1: PUSH node A to the stack.

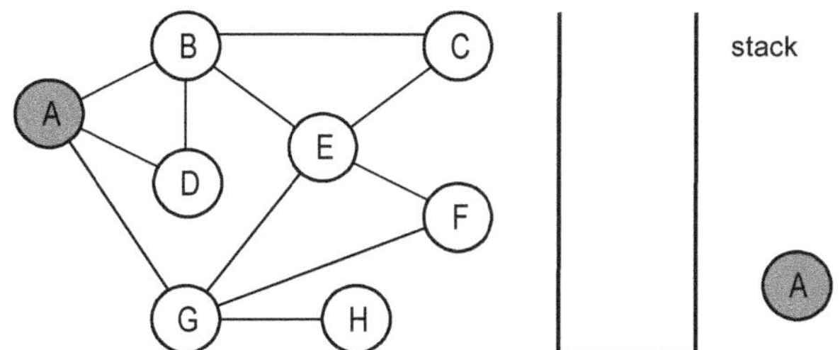

Step 2: POP node A from the stack.

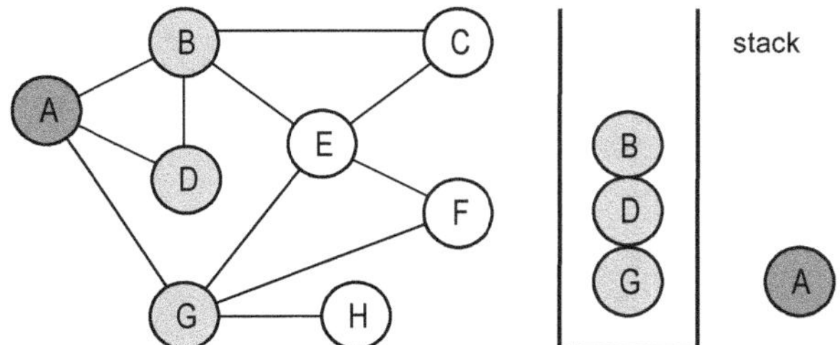

Step 3: PUSH nodes B, D and G (unprocessed nodes directly connected to node A) to the stack.

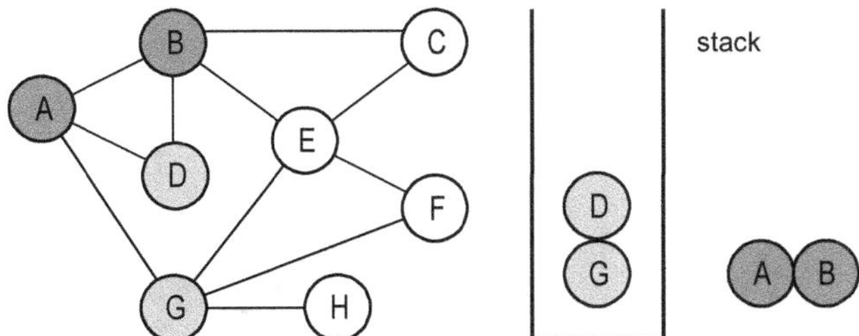

Step 4: POP node B from the stack.

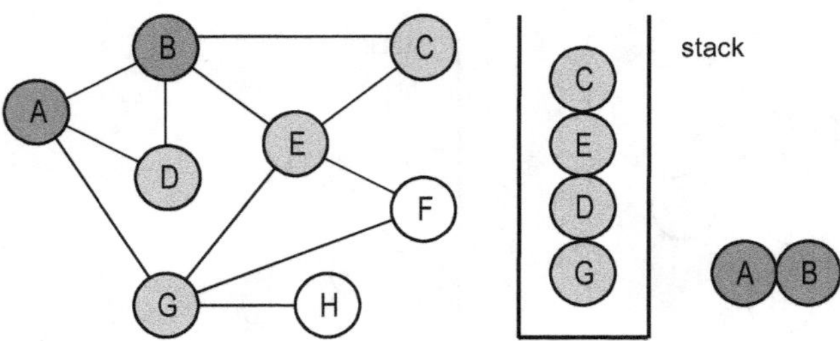

Step 5: PUSH nodes C and E (unprocessed nodes directly connected to node B) to the stack. Note that nodes A and D are already processed.

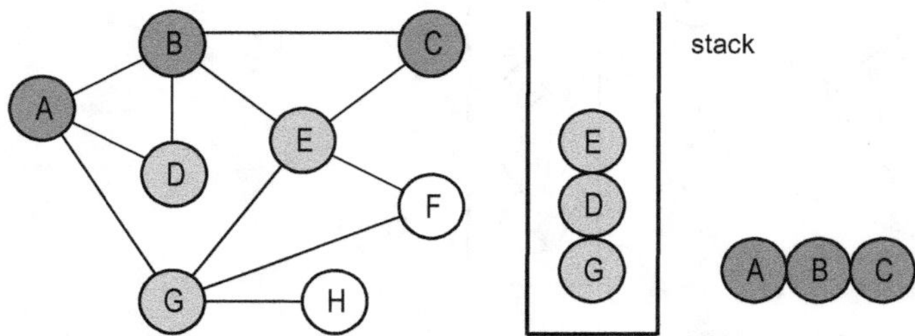

Step 6: POP node C from the stack.

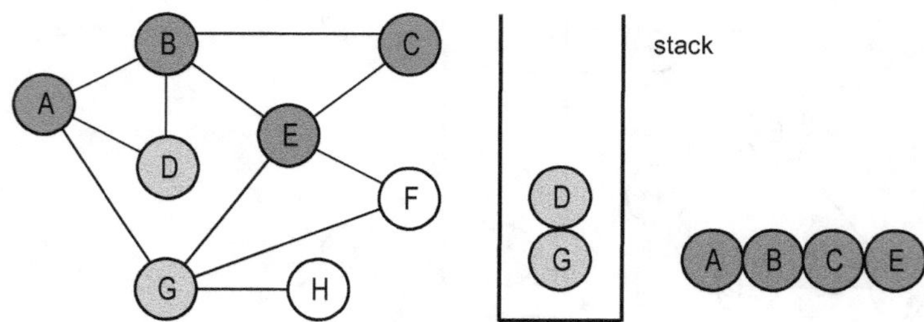

Step 7: Nodes directly connected to node C are already processed. POP node E from the stack.

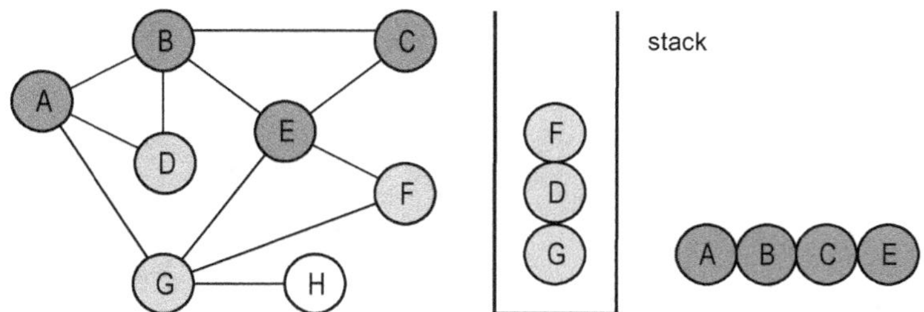

Step 8: PUSH node F (unprocessed node connected to E) to the stack.

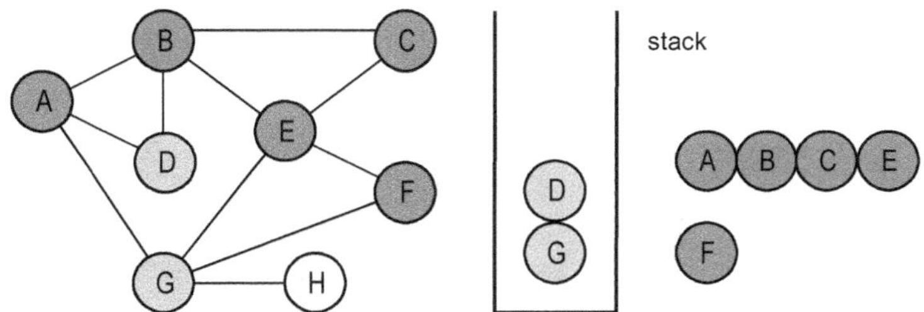

Step 9: POP node F from the stack.

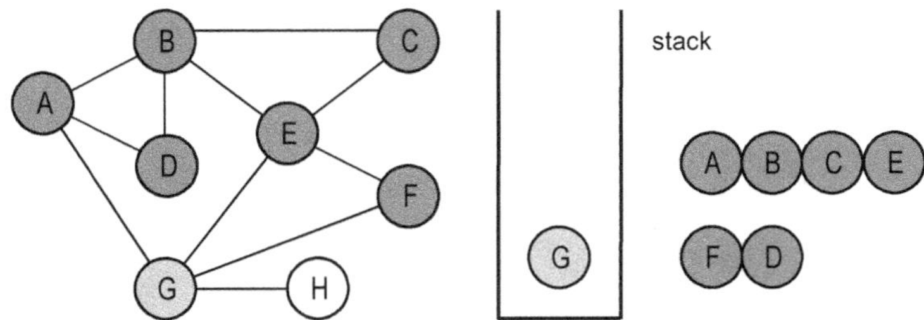

Step 10: Nodes directly connected to node F are already processed. POP node D from the stack.

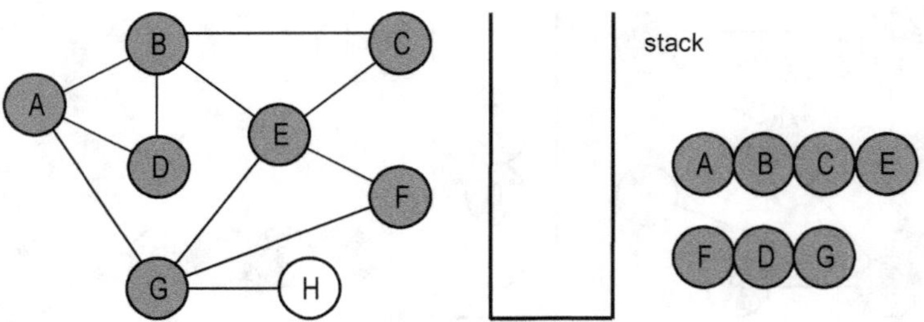

Step 11: Nodes directly connected to node D are already processed. POP node G from the stack.

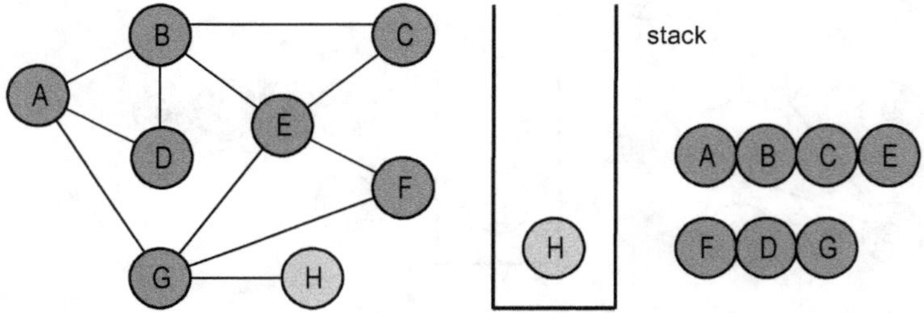

Step 12: PUSH node H (unprocessed node connected to G) to the stack.

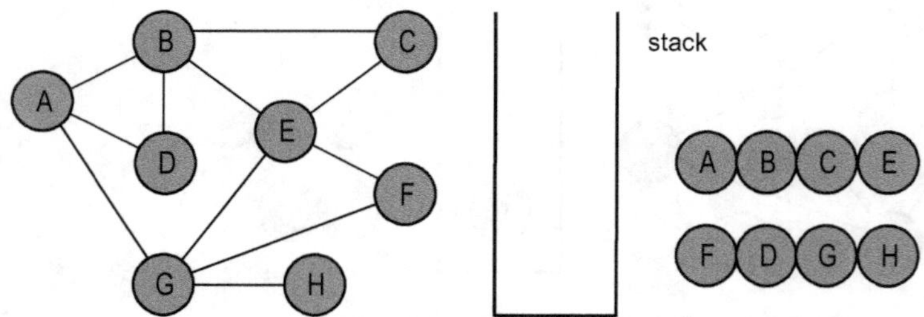

Step 13: POP node H from the stack. All graph nodes have been processed.

Breadth-First Search in Graphs

Breadth-first search on graph can be implemented in an algorithm using the help of *queue* data structure.

Steps of implementing breadth-first search on graph using queue:
1. PUSH root node into the queue. Mark the node as processed.
2. POP node X from queue.
3. If node X that is recently retrieved from the queue is directly connected to unprocessed nodes, PUSH all nodes directly connected to X to the queue. Mark these nodes as processed.
4. Repeat from step #2 until all nodes are retrieved or until certain search criteria is met.

Example:

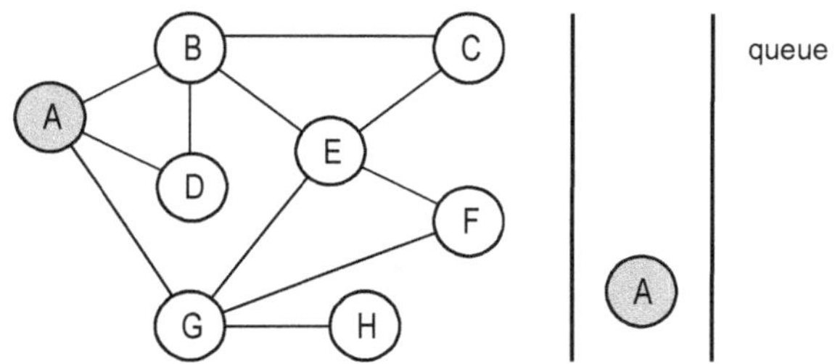

Step 1: PUSH node A to the queue.

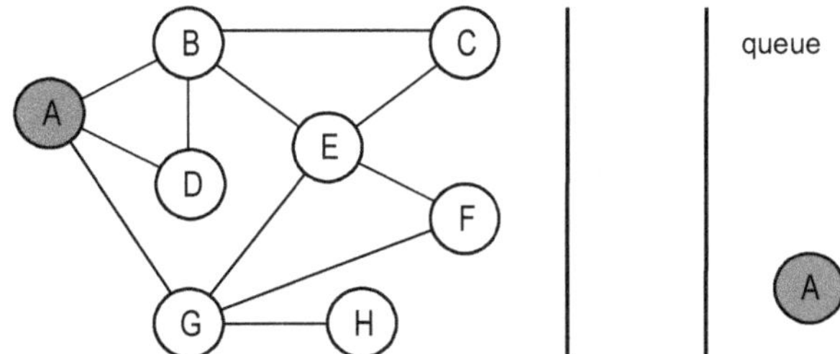

Step 2: POP node A from the queue.

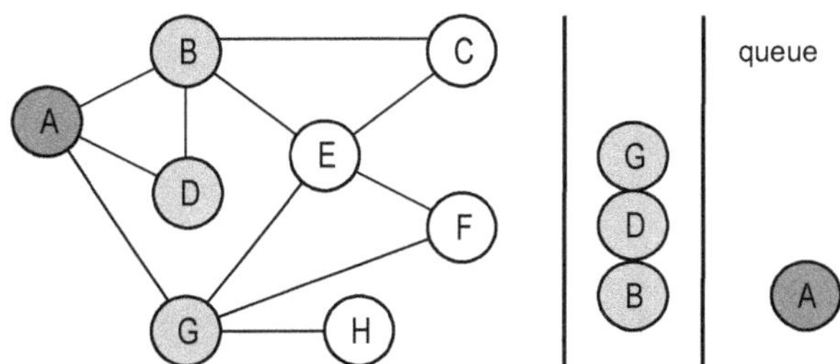

Step 3: PUSH nodes B, D and G (unprocessed nodes directly connected to node A) to the queue.

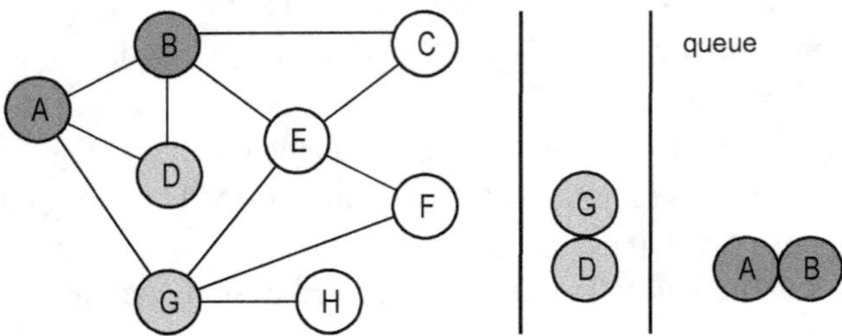

Step 4: POP node B from the queue.

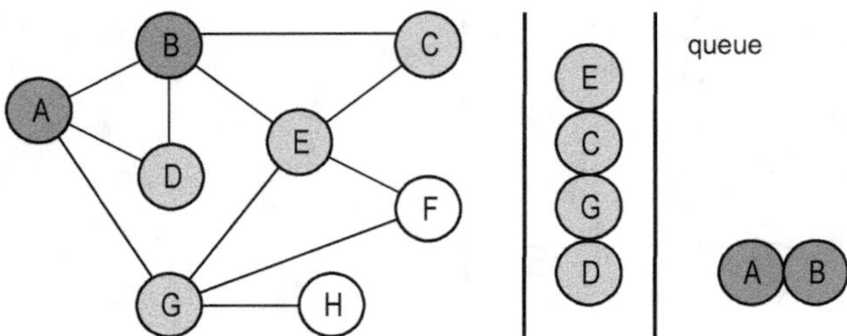

Step 5: PUSH nodes C and E (unprocessed nodes directly connected to node B) to the queue. Note that nodes A and D are already processed.

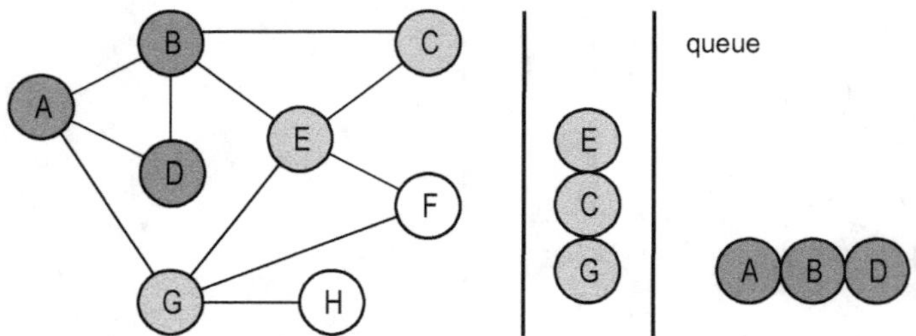

Step 6: POP node D from the queue.

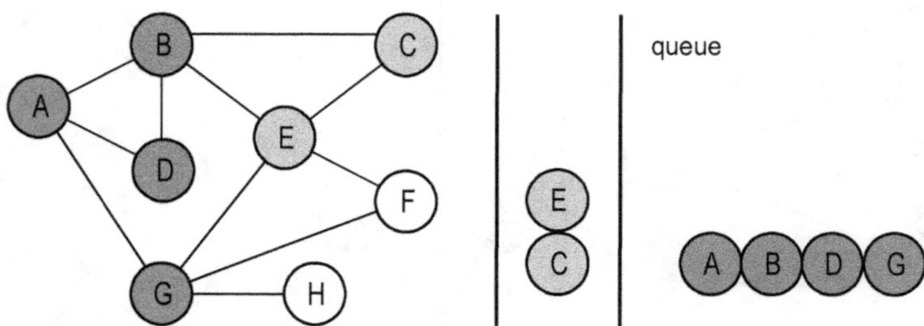

Step 7: Nodes directly connected to node D are already processed. POP node

G from the queue.

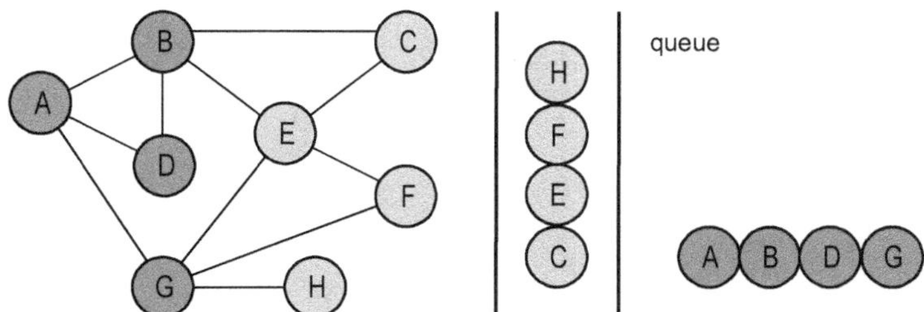

Step 8: PUSH nodes F and H (unprocessed nodes connected to G) to the queue.

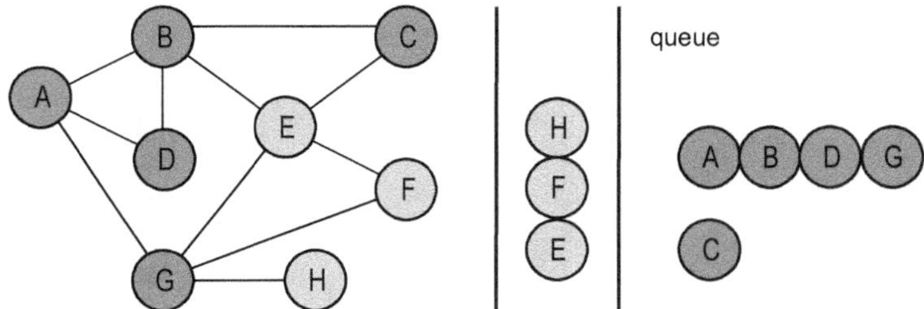

Step 9: POP node C from the queue.

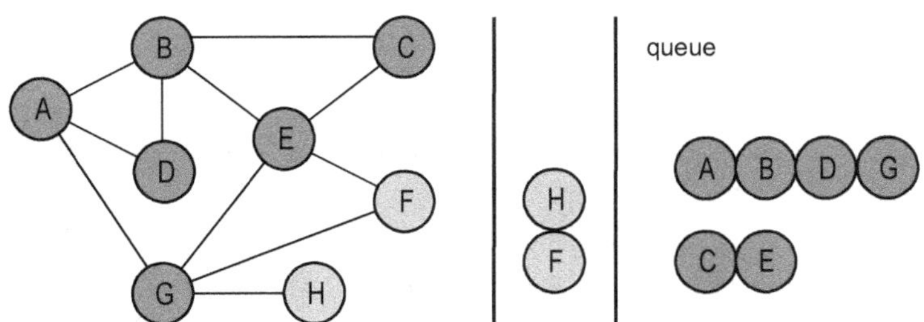

Step 10: Nodes directly connected to node C are already processed. POP node E from the queue.

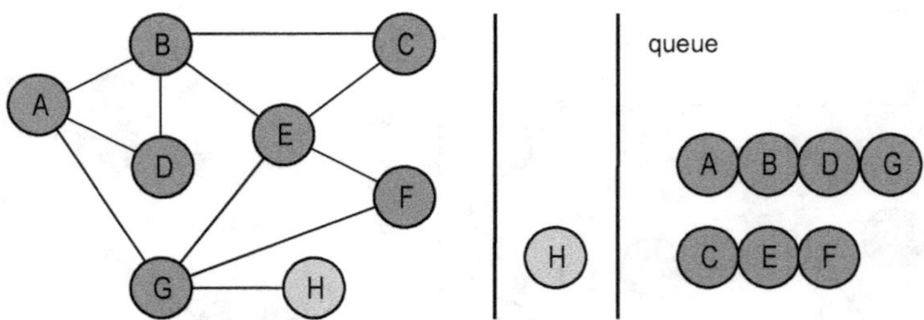

Step 11: Nodes directly connected to node E are already processed. POP node F from the queue.

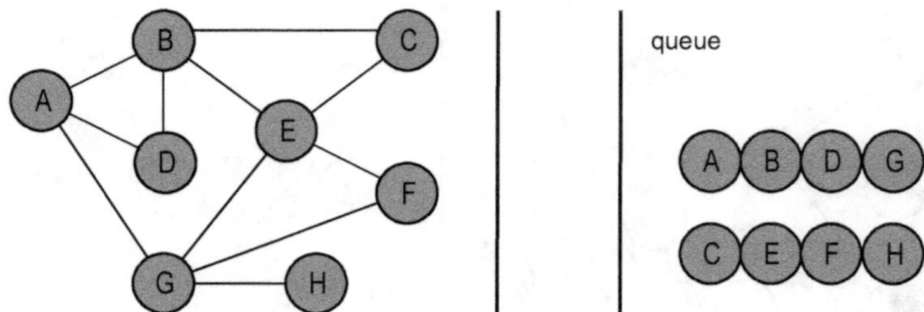

Step 12: Nodes directly connected to node F are already processed. POP node H from the queue. All graph nodes have been processed.

Backtracking

Finding an optimal solution by visiting every node in a search tree is clearly not the most efficient way. For complex problems, the number of nodes in the search tree will be too many for effective exploration, and the number will exponentially increase with more decision points to be made.

To increase speed and efficiency in solving a problem using search tree, algorithms can be developed to decrease the number of nodes that need to be visited. In *Partial Search Tree*, an algorithm will use the problem constraint to decide whether a node or a whole branch will not produce (or unlikely to lead to) optimal solution.

One of the popular implementations of partial search tree is *backtracking* technique. During each decision point, backtracking technique would calculate if a possible choice and its path downward is likely to lead to a solution or not. If a choice is unlikely to lead to a solution, algorithm will backtrack to the previous state and find other paths.

4-queens problem from the beginning of this chapter can be used to illustrate backtracking technique. If the first decision chooses to place Q1 in the location (1,1), then locations (2,1) and (2,2) are not valid for placing queen #2 because it will make two queens threatening each other, violating the constraint of n-queen problem.

If decision is made to place Q2 in location (2,3), then quick analysis will find out that there is no valid position for queen #3 in the third row. Therefore, algorithm will perform backtrack and undo the choice of placing Q2 in location (2,3).

Basic steps of backtracking technique:
- Start tree traversal using depth first search.
- On each visit to a node, check the constraint. If constraint is met, declare the node as active node.
- Otherwise, declare the node as dead node.
- If dead node is found, backtrack to the active node from previous level, explore the next branch.
- Repeat until a solution is found or all nodes in the tree have been visited.

Solving 4-queens problem using the steps above requires search tree with 4 levels because there are 4 decisions to make: the locations of 4 queens. From valid movements of a queen in chess, it can be concluded that each queen will have to be placed on different rows. Therefore, it can be modelled that each decision is to place one queen in a row.

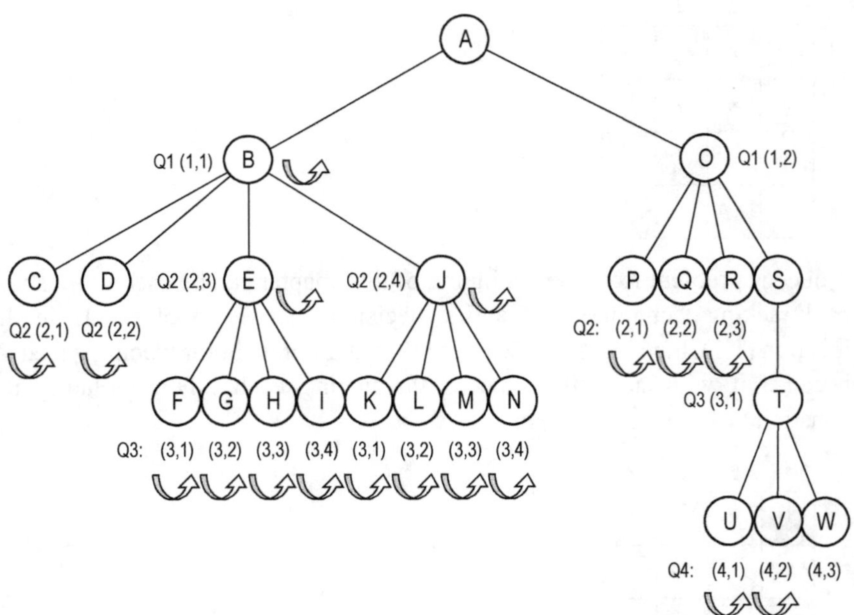

Starting from root node A, backtracking algorithm makes its first decision of placing the first queen (Q1). Instead of creating the whole search tree with every possibility, algorithm will start with the first possible option and expand on it. Child nodes are created as needed. When valid solution is no longer possible, the algorithm backtracks to previous level and explore another node.

Search tree traversal to solve 4-queens problem using backtracking:

- Algorithm starts from root node A.
- Node B: Q1 (1,1). This decision is valid because there is no other queen placed yet.
- Node C: Q1(1,1) and Q2 (2,1). This decision is not valid because it will make Q1 and Q2 threaten each other. There is no point of exploring any node below this because it cannot reach a valid solution anymore. Backtrack to node B.
- Node D: Q1(1,1) and Q2 (2,2). This decision is not valid because it will make Q1 and Q2 threaten each other. Backtrack to node B.
- Node E: Q1(1,1) and Q2 (2,3). This decision is valid. Q1 and Q2 do not threaten each other. Develop this branch further.
- Node F: Q1(1,1), Q2 (2,3) and Q3 (3,1). This decision is not valid because it will make Q1 and Q3 threaten each other. Backtrack to node E.

- Node G: Q1(1,1), Q2 (2,3) and Q3 (3,2). This decision is not valid because it will make Q2 and Q3 threaten each other. Backtrack to node E.
- Node H: Q1(1,1), Q2 (2,3) and Q3 (3,3). This decision is not valid because it will make Q1, Q2 and Q3 threaten each other. Backtrack to node E.
- Node I: Q1(1,1), Q2 (2,3) and Q3 (3,4). This decision is not valid because it will make Q2 and Q3 threaten each other. Backtrack to node E.
- All possible choices from node E had been explored. Backtrack to node B.
- Node J: Q1(1,1) and Q2 (2,4). This decision is valid. Q1 and Q2 do not threaten each other. Develop this branch further.
- Node K: Q1(1,1), Q2 (2,4) and Q3 (3,1). This decision is not valid because it will make Q1 and Q3 threaten each other. Backtrack to node J.
- Node G: Q1(1,1), Q2 (2,4) and Q3 (3,2). This decision is not valid because it will make Q1 and Q3 threaten each other. Backtrack to node J.
- Node H: Q1(1,1), Q2 (2,4) and Q3 (3,3). This decision is not valid because it will make Q1, Q2 and Q3 threaten each other. Backtrack to node J.
- Node I: Q1(1,1), Q2 (2,4) and Q3 (3,4). This decision is not valid because it will make Q2 and Q3 threaten each other. Backtrack to node J.
- All possible choices from node J had been explored. Backtrack to node B.
- All possible choices from node B had been explored. Backtrack to node A and explore the next possible choice for the first decision.
- Node O: Q1 (1,2). This decision is valid because there is no other queen placed yet.
- Node P: Q1(1,2) and Q2 (2,1). This decision is not valid because it will make Q1 and Q2 threaten each other. There is no point of exploring any node below this because it cannot reach a valid solution anymore. Backtrack to node O.
- Node Q: Q1(1,2) and Q2 (2,2). This decision is not valid because it will make Q1 and Q2 threaten each other. Backtrack to node O.
- Node R: Q1(1,2) and Q2 (2,3). This decision is not valid because it will make Q1 and Q2 threaten each other. Backtrack to node O.

- Node S: Q1(1,2) and Q2 (2,4). This decision is valid. Q1 and Q2 do not threaten each other. Develop this branch further.
- Node T: Q1(1,2), Q2 (2,4) and Q3 (3,1). This decision is valid. Q1, Q2 and Q3 do not threaten each other. Develop this branch further.
- Node U: Q1(1,2), Q2 (2,4), Q3 (3,1) and Q4 (4,1). This decision is not valid because it will make Q3 and Q4 threaten each other. Backtrack to node T.
- Node V: Q1(1,2), Q2 (2,4), Q3 (3,1) and Q4 (4,2). This decision is not valid because it will make Q1, Q2, Q3 and Q4 threaten each other. Backtrack to node T.
- Node W: Q1(1,2), Q2 (2,4), Q3 (3,1) and Q4 (4,3). This decision is valid. Q1, Q2, Q3 and Q4 do not threaten each other. Node W represents a valid solution.

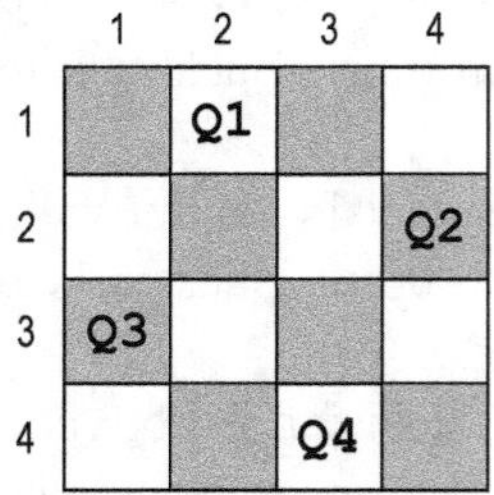

Finding a valid solution for 4-queens problem using backtracking technique visits 23 nodes. This is a significant improvement from the full search tree, which has 1 root node, 4 nodes in level 1, 16 nodes in level 2, 64 nodes in level 3 and 256 nodes in level 4 (total of 341 nodes).

Implementing smarter backtracking can improve efficiency even further. Suppose during each visit to a node, an algorithm will check whether that node have child node that may lead to a solution or not.

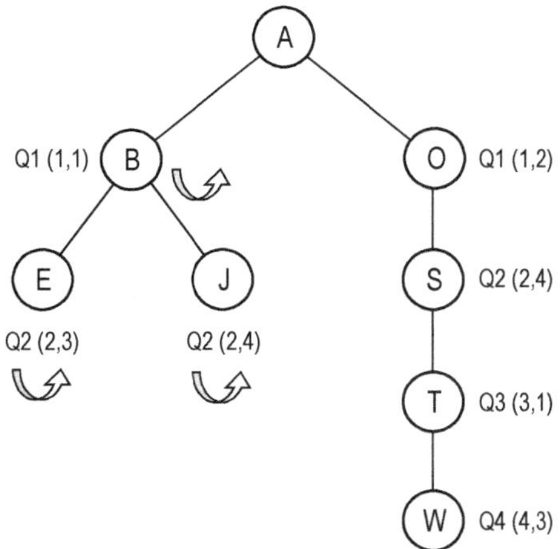

Using the same 4-queens problem, search tree traversal with smart backtracking will visit the following nodes:

- Algorithm starts from root node A. Node analysis calculates four child nodes could lead to solution: Q1 (1,1), Q1 (1,2), Q1 (1,3) and Q1 (1,4).
- Node B: Q1 (1,1). This decision is valid because there is no other queen placed yet. Node analysis calculates two child nodes could lead to solution: Q2 (2,3) and Q2 (2,4).
- Node E: Q1(1,1) and Q2 (2,3). This decision is valid. Q1 and Q2 do not threaten each other. Node analysis calculates that all child nodes of E will not lead to solution. Backtrack to node B.
- Next possible choice to make is Q2 (2,4).
- Node J: Q1(1,1) and Q2 (2,4). This decision is valid. Q1 and Q2 do not threaten each other. Node analysis calculates that all child nodes of E will not lead to solution. Backtrack to node B.
- All possible choices from node B had been explored. Backtrack to node A and explore the next possible choice for the first decision.
- Node O: Q1 (1,2). This decision is valid because there is no other queen placed yet. Node analysis calculates one child node could lead to solution: Q2 (2,4).
- Node S: Q1(1,2) and Q2 (2,4). This decision is valid. Q1 and Q2 do not threaten each other. Node analysis calculates one child node could lead to solution: Q3 (3,1).
- Node T: Q1(1,2), Q2 (2,4) and Q3 (3,1). This decision is valid. Q1, Q2 and Q3 do not threaten each other. Node analysis calculates one child node could lead to solution: Q4 (4,3).

- Node W: Q1(1,2), Q2 (2,4), Q3 (3,1) and Q4 (4,3). This decision is valid. Q1, Q2, Q3 and Q4 do not threaten each other. Node W represents a valid solution.

After adding node analysis calculation during each node visit, solution is reached after visiting only 8 nodes. Node analysis to find child nodes that could lead to solution is possible for n-queen problem, but it is not always possible for other problems. As general rule, smart analysis during each node visit is preferred for backtracking technique if the calculation does not require more computation than exploring the nodes itself.

Basic Principles of Branch and Bound

Branch-and-bound is one of the techniques available to find a valid solution from a search tree, usually for combinatorial optimisation problem. The *branch* part focuses on building heuristic calculation to quickly choose which tree branches have better chance of reaching a solution and explore them first. The *bound* part focuses on eliminating branches that will not lead to better solution compared to what has been found so far. This is particularly useful for problems to find maximum or minimum answer.

Travelling salesperson problem is one of the popular uses of branch-and-bound. To help with explaining the technique, the same example from chapter 05 is going to be used. Instead of working on the visual representation of the problem graph, branch-and-bound technique uses cost matrix to calculate possible solutions.

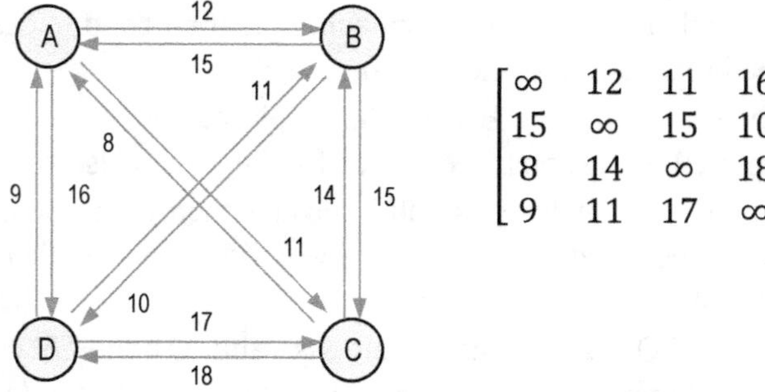

$$\begin{bmatrix} \infty & 12 & 11 & 16 \\ 15 & \infty & 15 & 10 \\ 8 & 14 & \infty & 18 \\ 9 & 11 & 17 & \infty \end{bmatrix}$$

The first step to solve travelling salesperson problem using branch-and-bound is calculating *reduced cost matrix* (RCM). RCM is calculated by subtracting the values of each row with the smallest value from the same row, then subtracting the values of each column with the smallest value from the same column. Total values reduced is summed as R.

∞	12	11	16
15	∞	15	10
8	14	∞	18
9	11	17	∞

→

∞	12	11	16
15	∞	15	10
8	14	∞	18
9	11	17	∞

R=11

→

∞	1	0	5
15	∞	15	10
8	14	∞	18
9	11	17	∞

R=11+10=21

→

∞	1	0	5
5	∞	5	0
8	14	∞	18
9	11	17	∞

R=21+8=29

∞	1	0	5
5	∞	5	0
0	6	∞	10
9	11	17	∞

R=29+9=38

→

∞	1	0	5
5	∞	5	0
0	6	∞	10
0	2	8	∞

R=38

→

∞	1	0	5
5	∞	5	0
0	6	∞	10
0	2	8	∞

R=38+0=38

→

∞	1	0	5
5	∞	5	0
0	6	∞	10
0	2	8	∞

R=38+1=39

∞	0	0	5
5	∞	5	0
0	5	∞	10
0	1	8	∞

R=39+0=39

→

∞	0	0	5
5	∞	5	0
0	5	∞	10
0	1	8	∞

R=39+0=39

→

∞	0	0	5
5	∞	5	0
0	5	∞	10
0	1	8	∞

R=39

Steps of RCM calculation:

- Row #1: the smallest value in the row is 11. Subtract 11 from all values from row #1. Total reduction R is 11.
- Row #2: the smallest value in the row is 10. Subtract 10 from all values from row #2. Total reduction R is 11+10=21.
- Row #3: the smallest value in the row is 8. Subtract 8 from all values from row #3. Total reduction R is 21+8=29.
- Row #4: the smallest value in the row is 9. Subtract 9 from all values from row #4. Total reduction R is 29+9=38.
- All rows have been reduced.
- Column #1: the smallest value in the column is already 0. Total reduction R remains 38.
- Column #2: the smallest value in the column is 1. Subtract 1 from all values from column #2. Total reduction R is 38+1=39.
- Column #3: the smallest value in the column is already 0. Total reduction R remains 39.
- Column #4: the smallest value in the column is already 0. Total reduction R remains 39.
- All columns have been reduced.

The first reduced cost matrix above becomes the root node (1) in the search tree to find solution for travelling salesperson problem using branch-and-bound technique. Starting from node A in the graph, there are 3 possible paths: AB, AC and AD. Each of these paths is represented with a child node under root node. These are labelled as nodes 2, 3 and 4. Note that search tree uses numbers instead of letters for its nodes to avoid confusion with the nodes from problem graph.

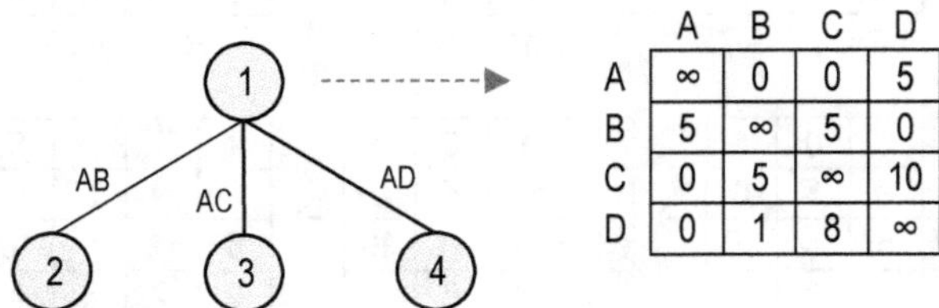

New (reduced) cost matrix of node X is calculated from the cost matrix of its parent node Y and the path it represents (an edge from node n1 to n2). For example, node 2 represents the choice of path AB from the problem graph.

Steps of calculating new (reduced) cost matrix:
- Start with the reduced cost matrix of parent node Y.
- Change all values in row n1 to ∞. This represents outgoing routes from node n1.
- Change all values in column n2 to ∞. This represents incoming routes to node n2.
- Change element (n2, n1) to ∞ (row n2, column n1). This represents change of focus from node n1 to node n2.
- Apply steps to calculate reduced cost matrix.

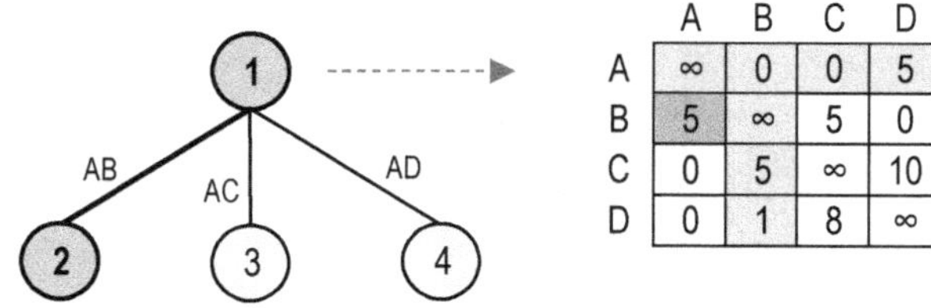

Calculating new cost matrix for node 2:
- Start with reduced cost matrix from parent node 1.
- Change all values in row A to ∞.
- Change all values in column B to ∞.
- Change element (B, A) to ∞.
- Apply steps to calculate reduced cost matrix (see below).

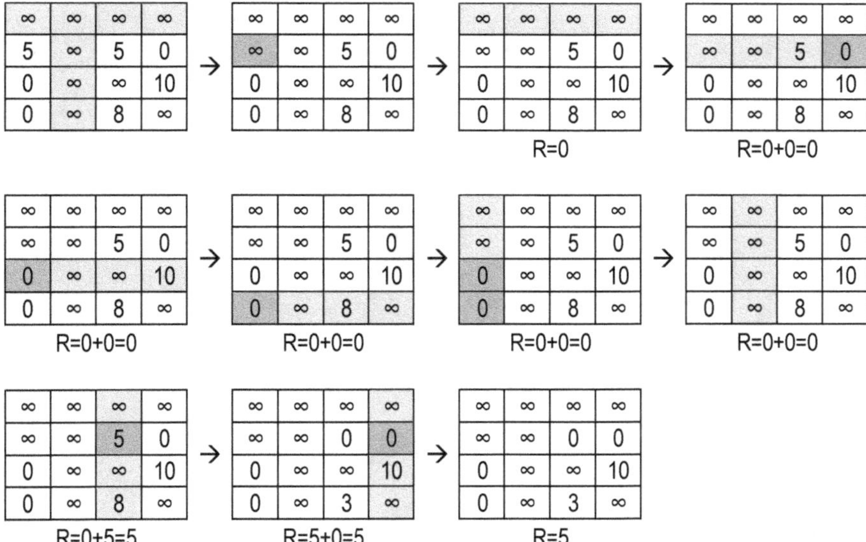

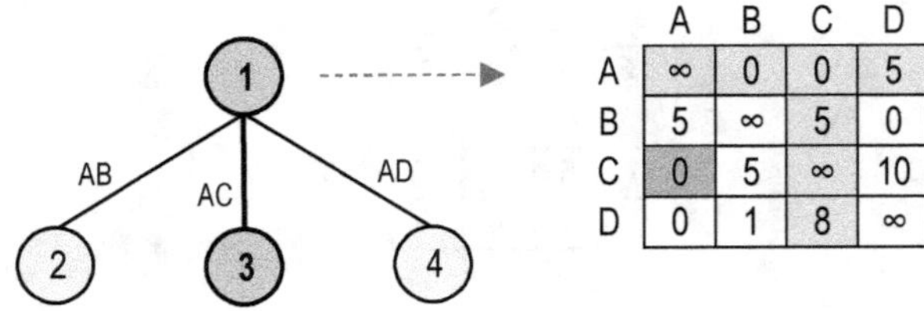

Calculating new cost matrix for node 3:

- Start with reduced cost matrix from parent node 1.
- Change all values in row A to ∞.
- Change all values in column C to ∞.
- Change element (C, A) to ∞.
- Apply steps to calculate reduced cost matrix (see below).

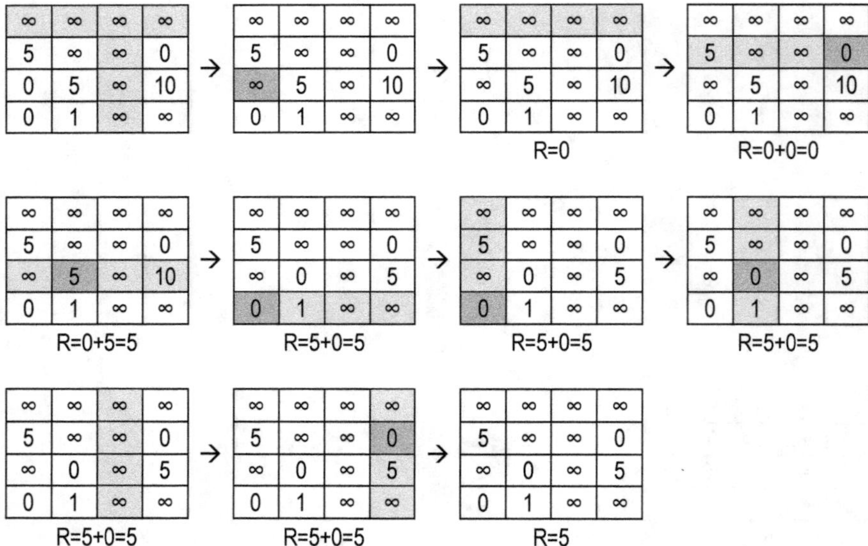

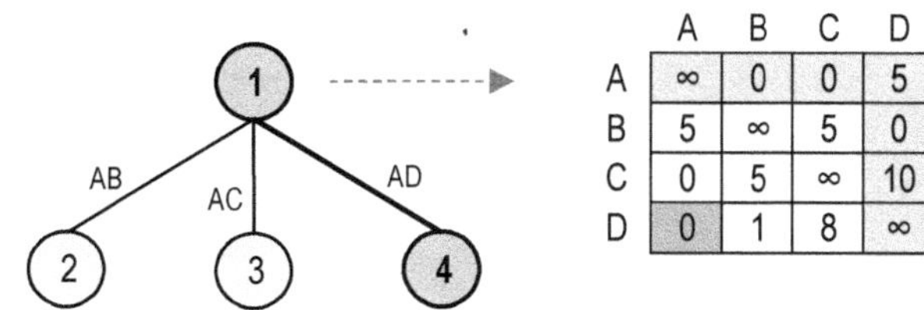

Calculating new cost matrix for node 4:

- Start with reduced cost matrix from parent node 1.
- Change all values in row A to ∞.
- Change all values in column D to ∞.
- Change element (D, A) to ∞.
- Apply steps to calculate reduced cost matrix (see below).

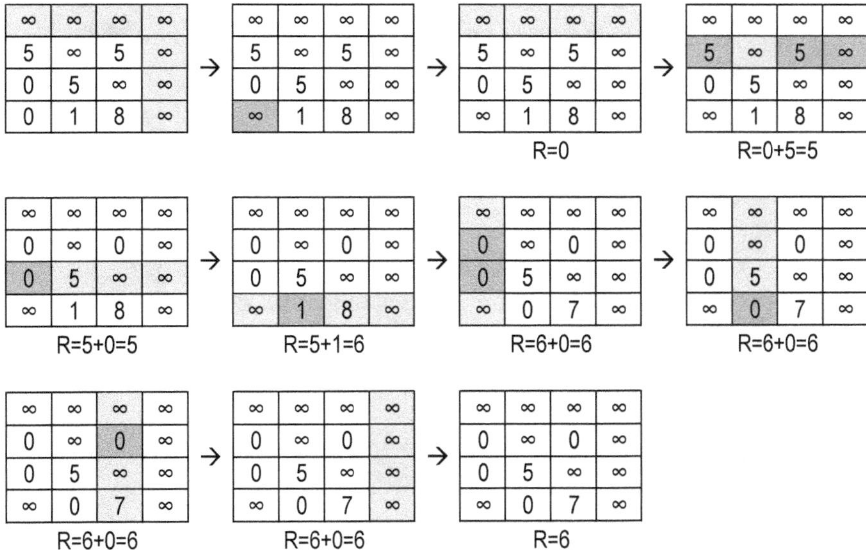

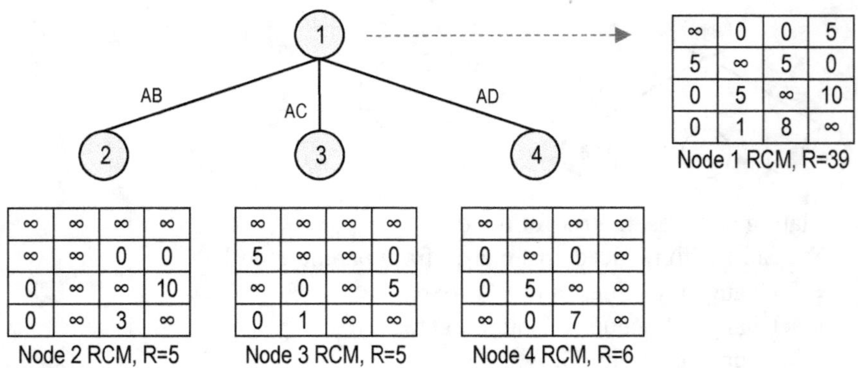

The next step in the branch process of the new nodes is calculating the path cost of each node. *Path cost* of a node is calculated from the R value of its parents plus reduced cost of the edge it represents plus the R value of the new node. For root node, path cost is equal to its R value.

```
PCost(X)=PCost(parent)+Element(parent,n1,n2)+R(X)
```

Calculating path cost for node 2:
- `PCost(node1)` is 39.
- Node 2 represents path AB. `Element(node1,A,B)` is the element from node 1's RCM at row A, column B. The value is 0.

	A	B	C	D
A	∞	0	0	5
B	5	∞	5	0
C	0	5	∞	10
D	0	1	8	∞

- `R(node2)` is 5.
- `PCost(node2)` is $39 + 0 + 5 = 44$.

Calculating path cost for node 3:
- `PCost(node1)` is 39.
- Node 3 represents path AC. `Element(node1,A,C)` is the element from node 1's RCM at row A, column C. The value is 0.

	A	B	C	D
A	∞	0	0	5
B	5	∞	5	0
C	0	5	∞	10
D	0	1	8	∞

- `R(node3)` is 5.
- `PCost(node3)` is $39 + 0 + 5 = 44$.

Calculating path cost for node 4:
- `PCost(node1)` is 39.
- Node 3 represents path AD. `Element(node1,A,D)` is the element from node 1's RCM at row A, column D. The value is 5.

	A	B	C	D
A	∞	0	0	5
B	5	∞	5	0
C	0	5	∞	10
D	0	1	8	∞

- `R(node4)` is 6.
- `PCost(node4)` is $39 + 5 + 6 = 50$.

Path costs are used to decide which nodes to explore next. In this case, nodes 2, 3 and 4 have path costs of 44, 44 and 50. This example aims to find path with lowest possible cost. Therefore, the algorithm choses nodes with smallest path cost. Nodes 2 and 3 have the same costs of 44. Since a tie is found, branch-and-bound algorithm can start with any of the two. Node 2 is chosen to be developed next.

Node 2 represents path AB. After taking this path, a salesperson can choose to go to nodes C or D from the problem graph. Therefore, node 2 has two child nodes. Node 5 represents path BC and node 6 represents path BD.

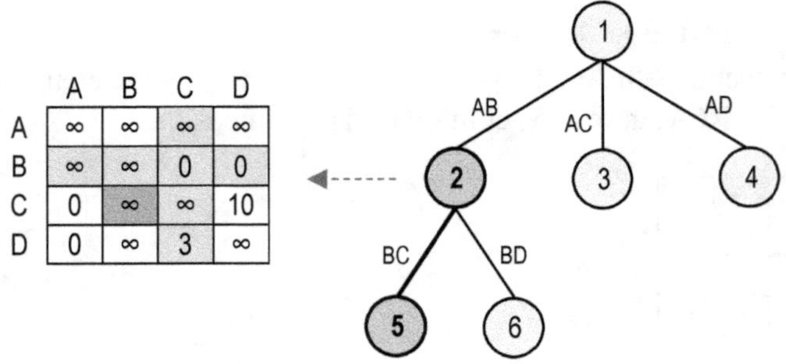

Calculating new cost matrix for node 5:
- Start with reduced cost matrix from parent node 2.
- Change all values in row B to ∞.
- Change all values in column C to ∞.
- Change element (C, B) to ∞.
- Apply steps to calculate reduced cost matrix (see below).

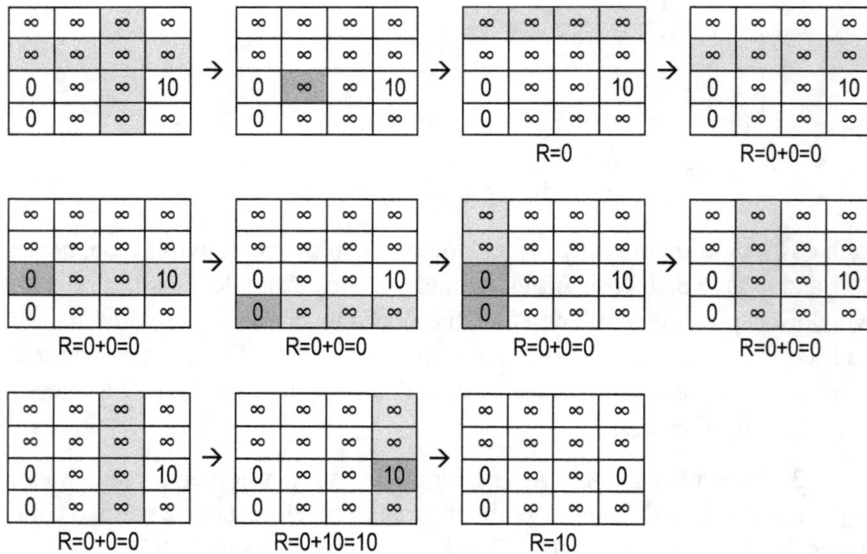

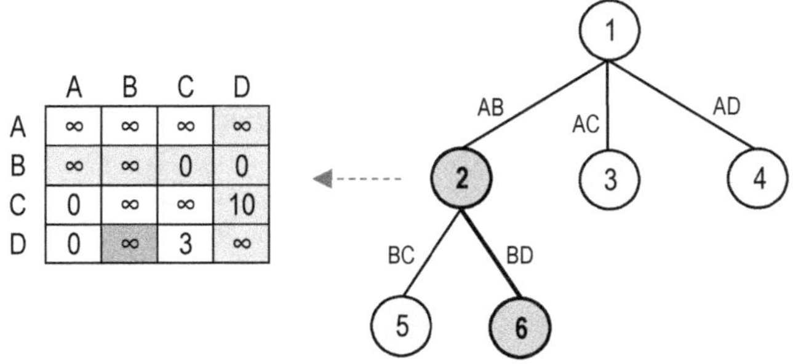

Calculating new cost matrix for node 6:

- Start with reduced cost matrix from parent node 2.
- Change all values in row B to ∞.
- Change all values in column D to ∞.
- Change element (D, B) to ∞.
- Apply steps to calculate reduced cost matrix (see below).

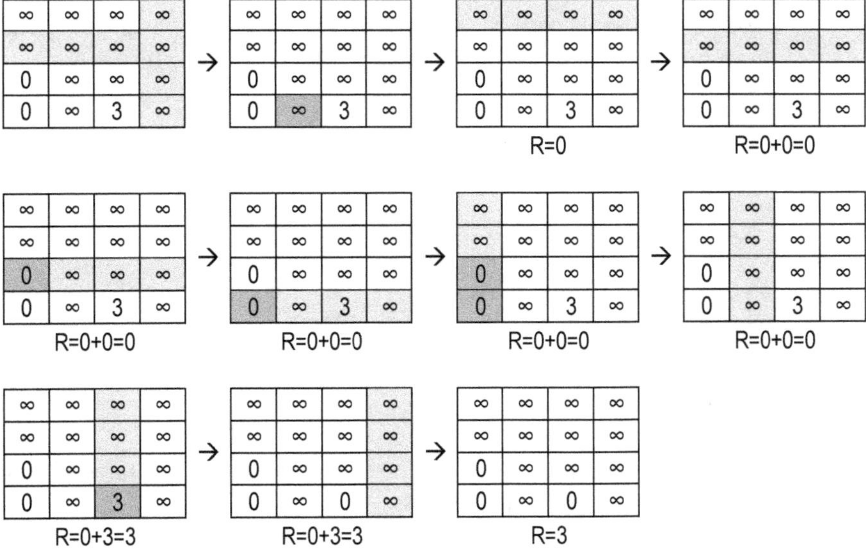

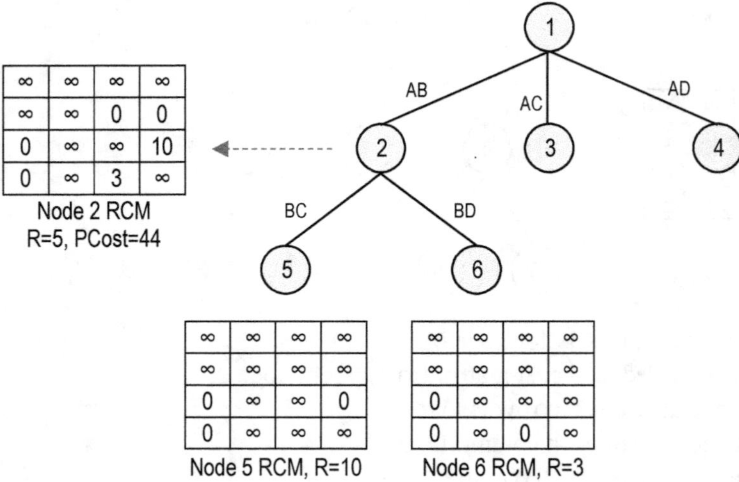

Node 2 RCM
R=5, PCost=44

Node 5 RCM, R=10   Node 6 RCM, R=3

Calculating path cost for node 5:

- `PCost(node2)` is 44.
- Node 5 represents path BC. `Element(node2,B,C)` is the element from node 2's RCM at row B, column C. The value is 0.

	A	B	C	D
A	∞	∞	∞	∞
B	∞	∞	0	0
C	0	∞	∞	10
D	0	∞	3	∞

- `R(node5)` is 10.
- `PCost(node2)` is $44 + 0 + 10 = 54$.

Calculating path cost for node 6:

- `PCost(node2)` is 44.
- Node 5 represents path BD. `Element(node2,B,D)` is the element from node 2's RCM at row B, column D. The value is 0.

	A	B	C	D
A	∞	∞	∞	∞
B	∞	∞	0	0
C	0	∞	∞	10
D	0	∞	3	∞

- `R(node5)` is 3.
- `PCost(node6)` is $44 + 0 + 3 = 47$.

Nodes 5 and 6 have path costs of 54 and 47. The algorithm choses nodes with smallest path cost. Nodes 6 is chosen to be developed next. This node represents path BD. After taking this path, a salesperson only has 1 node left to visit from the problem graph: node C. Therefore, node 6 has one child node (node 7) representing path DC.

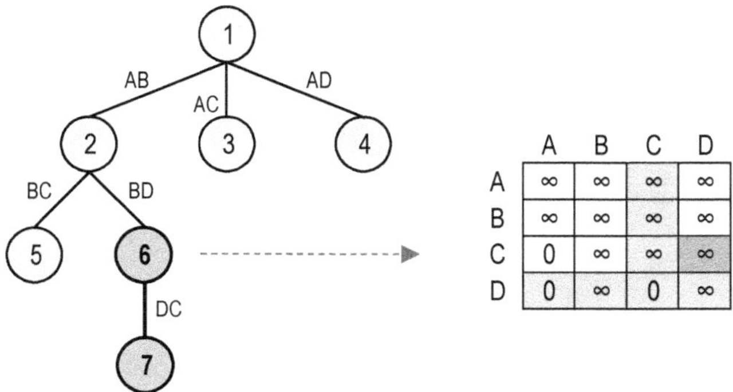

Calculating new cost matrix for node 7:
- Start with reduced cost matrix from parent node 6.
- Change all values in row D to ∞.
- Change all values in column C to ∞.
- Change element (C, D) to ∞.
- Apply steps to calculate reduced cost matrix (see below).

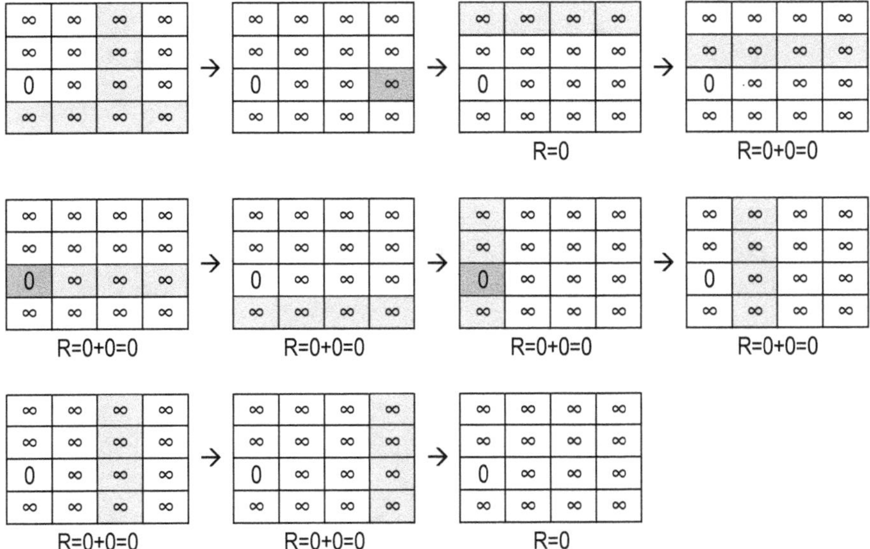

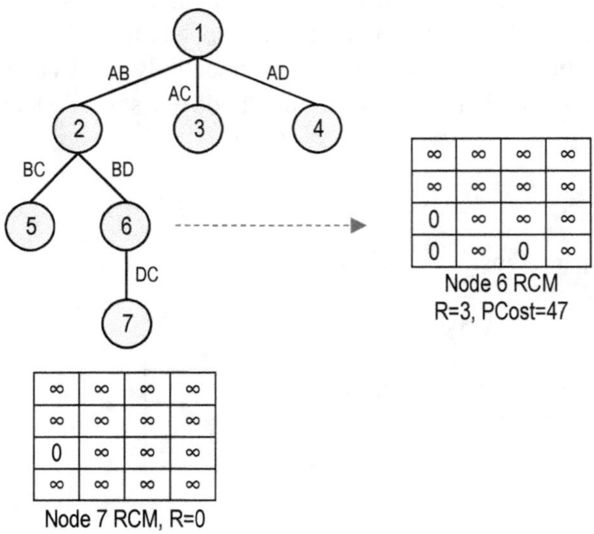

Calculating path cost for node 7:

- `PCost(node6)` is 47.
- Node 7 represents path DC. `Element(node6,D,C)` is the element from node 6's RCM at row D, column C. The value is 0.

	A	B	C	D
A	∞	∞	∞	∞
B	∞	∞	∞	∞
C	0	∞	∞	∞
D	0	∞	0	∞

- `R(node7)` is 0.
- `PCost(node7)` is $47 + 0 + 0 = 47$.

The path from node 1, node 2, node 6 and node 7 represents path A-B-D-C from the problem graph. The only step left (node 8) is to go back to node A because travelling salesman problem starts and ends at the same node.

Note that node 8 generation can be safely skipped in actual implementation of branch-and-bound algorithm because the reduced cost matrix of node 7 only contains infinity and zero values. Since there is nothing to reduce, the R value for the last edge is zero. This step is included in this book for explanation purpose.

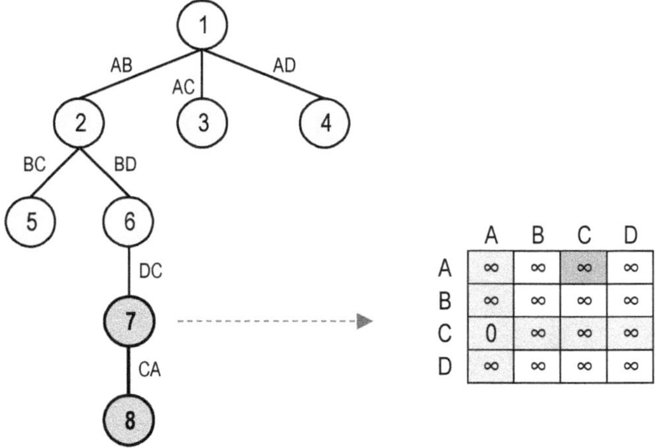

Calculating new cost matrix for node 8:

- Start with reduced cost matrix from parent node 7.
- Change all values in row C to ∞.
- Change all values in column A to ∞.
- Change element (A, C) to ∞.
- Apply steps to calculate reduced cost matrix (see below).

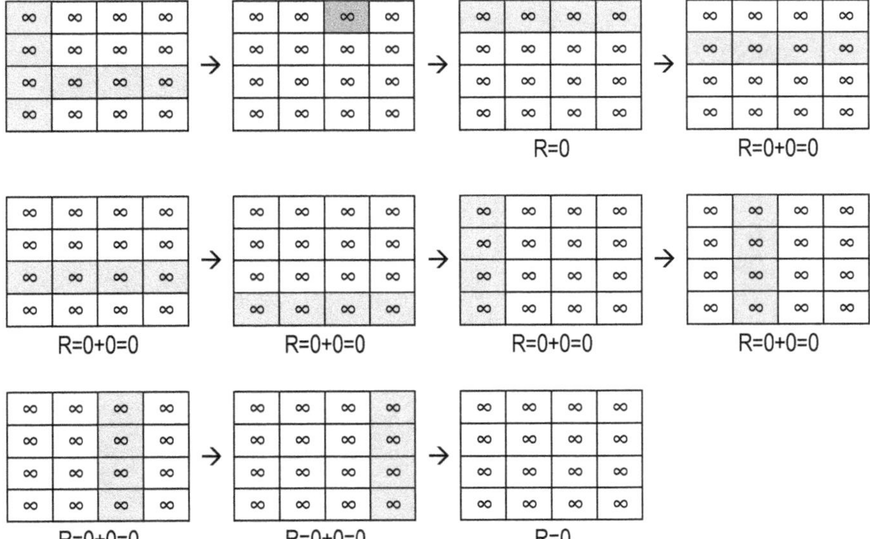

The final RCM of node 8 has infinity values in all elements:

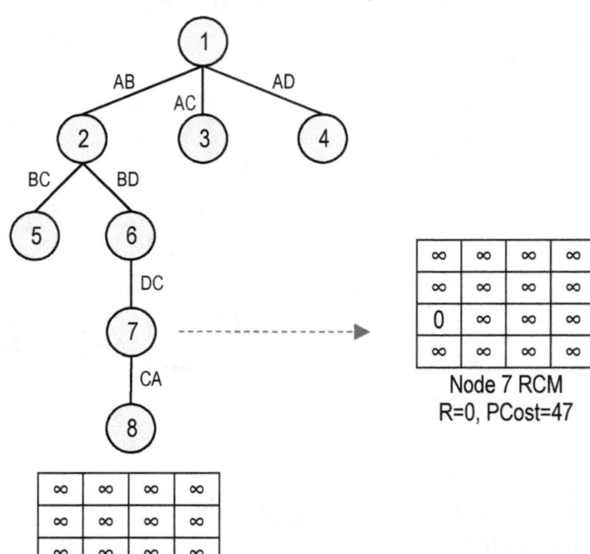

Calculating path cost for node 8:

- `PCost(node7)` is 47.
- Node 7 represents path CA. `Element(node7,C,A)` is the element from node 7's RCM at row C, column A. The value is 0.

- `R(node8)` is 0.
- `PCost(node8)` is $47 + 0 + 0 = 47$.

One possible solution is found: A-B-D-C-A with path cost 47. This means path A-B-D-C-A from the problem graph is a solution candidate with total cost of 47.

The steps discussed so far are the steps for *branch*. Since there is a solution candidate with path cost of 47. All unexplored nodes from the search tree with path cost greater than 47 can be ignored. There is no need to calculate the nodes below them because any path below would have greater or equal path cost. This is the *bound* step of branch-and-bound technique. Every time a new solution candidate is found, any unexplored branch worse than it are excluded from further calculation.

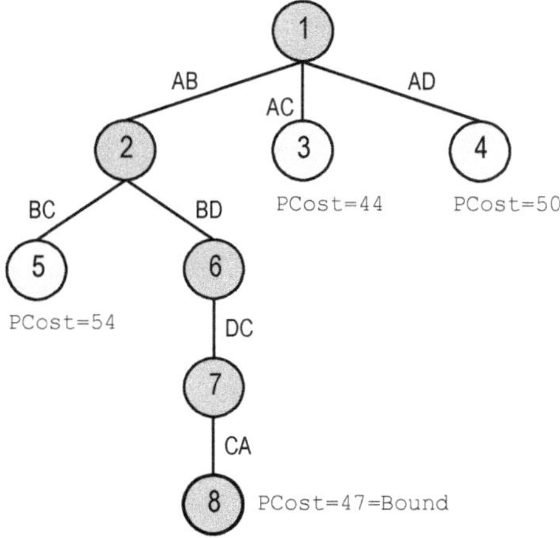

Nodes 3, 4 and 5 are unexplored. Based on *bound* limit (47), nodes 4 and 5 can be safely excluded.

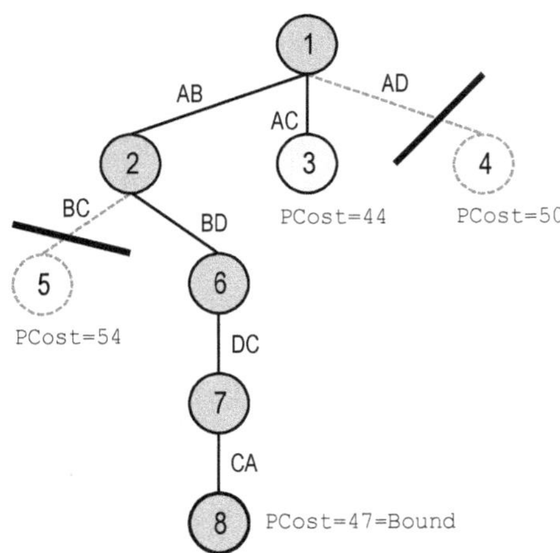

The next step of branch-and-bound technique is to explore node 3, which has the possibility to reach better solution because its path cost is lower than the *bound* limit (smallest path cost of solution candidates found so far).

Node 3 represents path AC. After taking this path, a salesperson can choose to go to nodes B or D from the problem graph. Therefore, node 3 has two child nodes. Node 9 represents path CB and node 10 represents path CD.

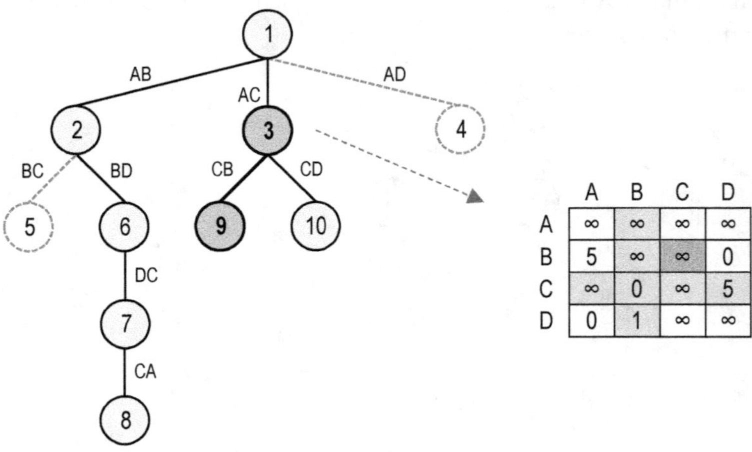

Calculating new cost matrix for node 9:

- Start with reduced cost matrix from parent node 3.
- Change all values in row C to ∞.
- Change all values in column B to ∞.
- Change element (B, C) to ∞.
- Apply steps to calculate reduced cost matrix (see below).

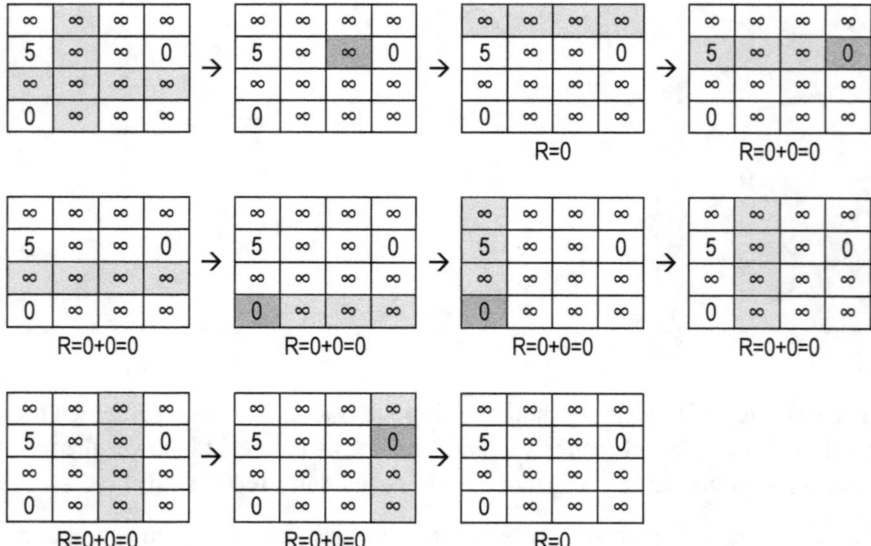

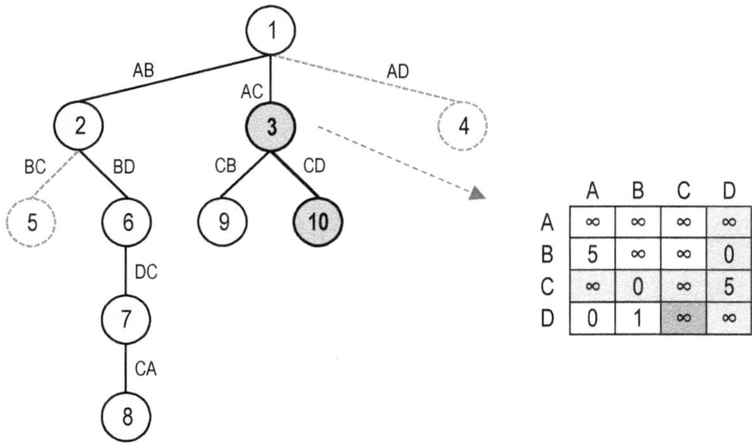

Calculating new cost matrix for node 10:

- Start with reduced cost matrix from parent node 3.
- Change all values in row C to ∞.
- Change all values in column D to ∞.
- Change element (D, C) to ∞.
- Apply steps to calculate reduced cost matrix (see below).

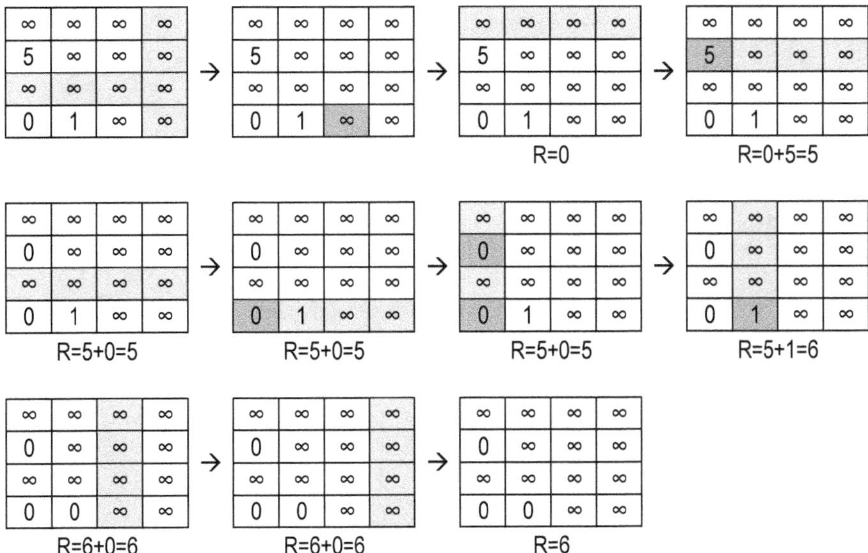

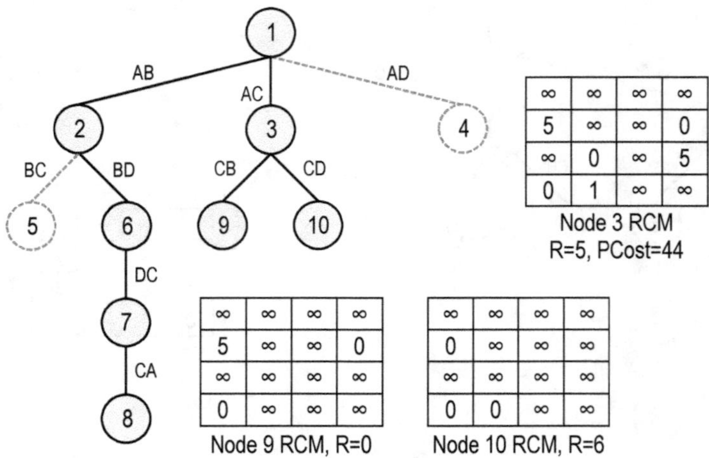

Calculating path cost for node 9:

- `PCost(node3)` is 44.
- Node 9 represents path CB. `Element(node3,C,B)` is the element from node 3's RCM at row C, column B. The value is 0.

	A	B	C	D
A	∞	∞	∞	∞
B	5	∞	∞	0
C	∞	0	∞	5
D	0	1	∞	∞

- `R(node9)` is 0.
- `PCost(node9)` is $44 + 0 + 0 = 44$.

Calculating path cost for node 10:

- `PCost(node3)` is 44.
- Node 10 represents path CD. `Element(node3,C,D)` is the element from node 3's RCM at row C, column D. The value is 5.

	A	B	C	D
A	∞	∞	∞	∞
B	5	∞	∞	0
C	∞	0	∞	5
D	0	1	∞	∞

- `R(node10)` is 6.
- `PCost(node10)` is $44 + 5 + 6 = 55$.

Node 9 is chosen to be developed next because it has smaller path cost.

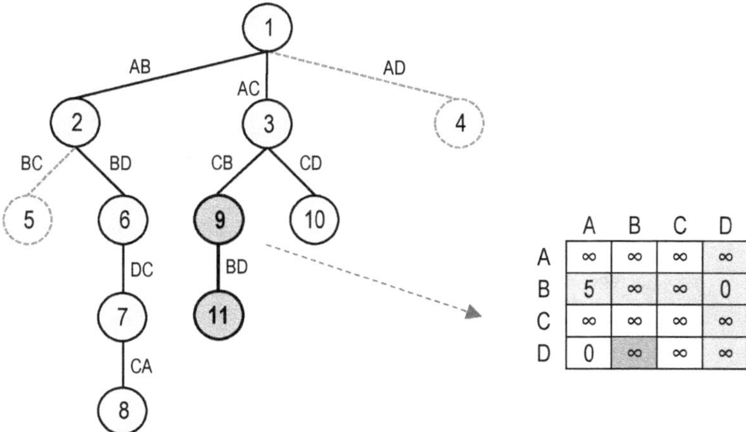

Calculating new cost matrix for node 11:
- Start with reduced cost matrix from parent node 9.
- Change all values in row B to ∞.
- Change all values in column D to ∞.
- Change element (D, B) to ∞.
- Apply steps to calculate reduced cost matrix (see below).

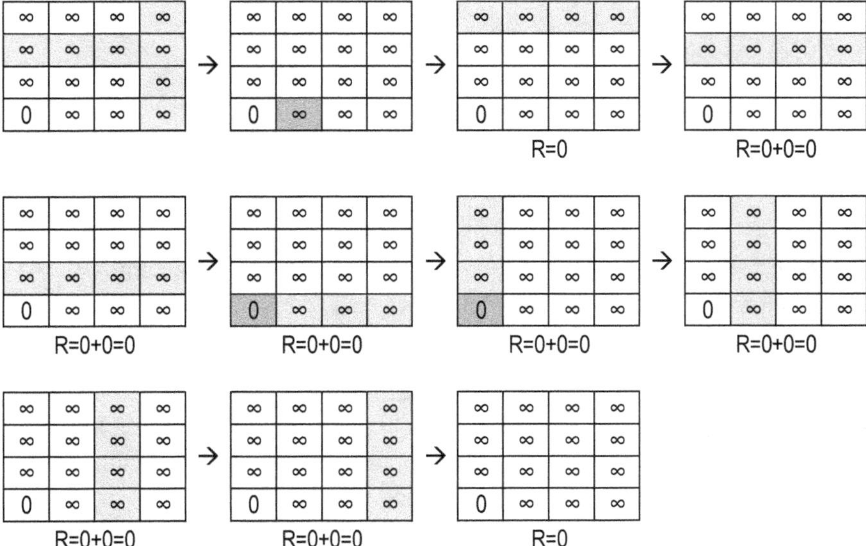

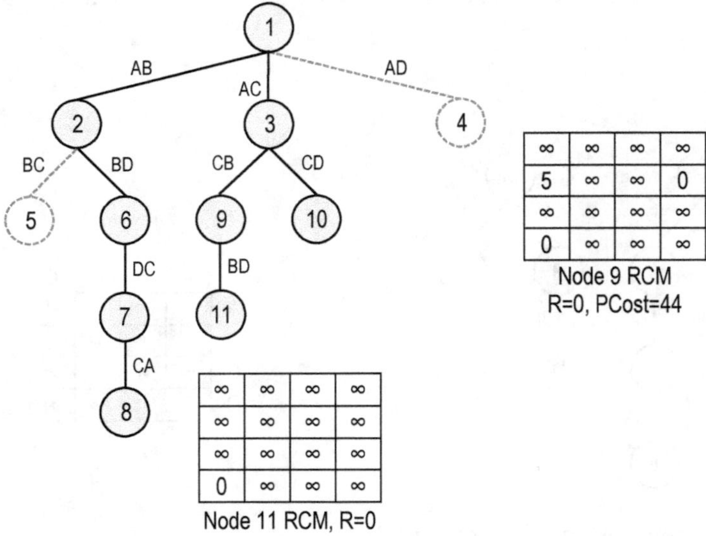

Calculating path cost for node 11:

- `PCost(node9)` is 44.
- Node 11 represents path BD. `Element(node3,B,D)` is the element from node 9's RCM at row B, column D. The value is 0.

	A	B	C	D
A	∞	∞	∞	∞
B	5	∞	∞	0
C	∞	∞	∞	∞
D	0	∞	∞	∞

- `R(node11)` is 0.
- `PCost(node11)` is $44 + 0 + 0 = 44$.

The path from node 1, node 3, node 9 and node 11 represents path A-C-B-D from the problem graph. The only step left (node 12) is to go back to node A because travelling salesman problem starts and ends at the same node.

Similar to the previous solution candidate, node 12 generation can be safely skipped in actual implementation of branch-and-bound algorithm because the reduced cost matrix of node 11 only contains infinity and zero values. This step is included in this book for explanation purpose.

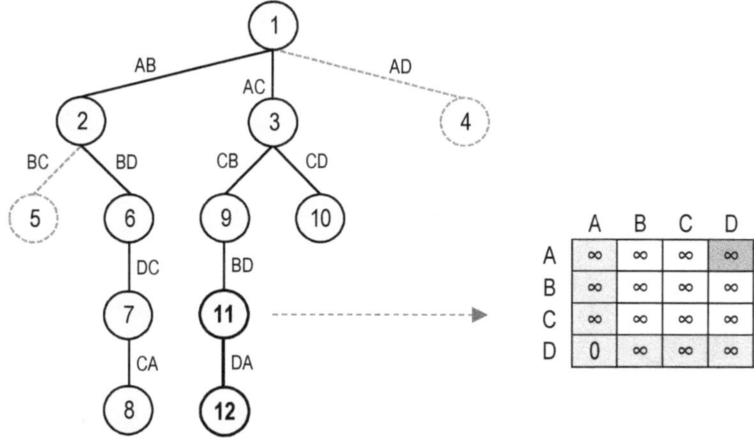

Calculating new cost matrix for node 12:

- Start with reduced cost matrix from parent node 11.
- Change all values in row D to ∞.
- Change all values in column A to ∞.
- Change element (A, D) to ∞.
- Apply steps to calculate reduced cost matrix (see below).

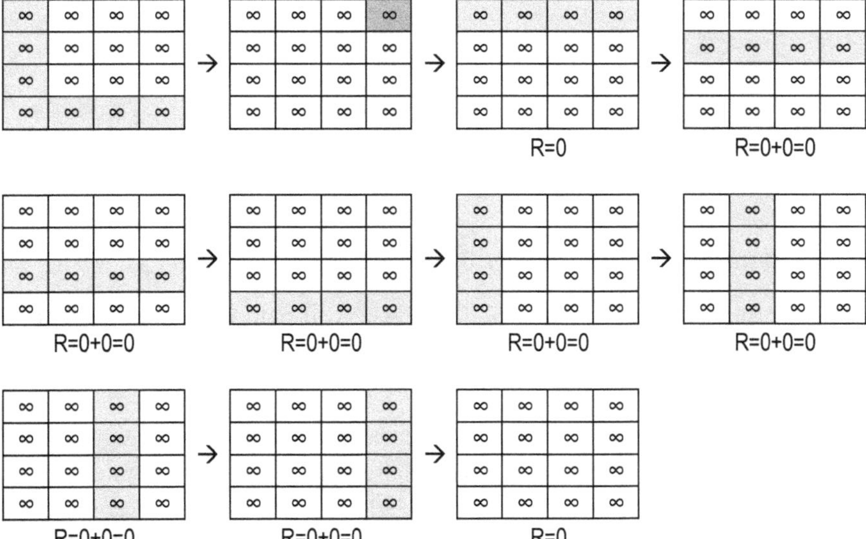

The final RCM of node 12 has infinity values in all elements:

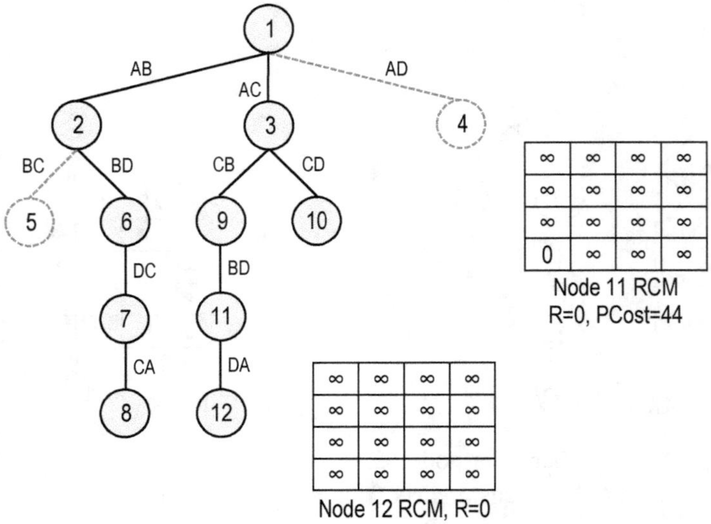

Node 11 RCM
R=0, PCost=44

Node 12 RCM, R=0

Calculating path cost for node 12:

- `PCost(node11)` is 44.
- Node 12 represents path DA. `Element(node11,D,A)` is the element from node 11's RCM at row D, column A. The value is 0.

- `R(node12)` is 0.
- `PCost(node12)` is $44 + 0 + 0 = 44$.

One possible solution is found: A-C-B-D-A with path cost 44. This means path A-C-B-D-A from the problem graph is a better solution candidate. The new *bound* limit is set to 44.

All unexplored nodes from the search tree with path cost greater than *bound* limit can be excluded from further calculation. There is no need to calculate the nodes below them because any path below would have greater or equal path cost.

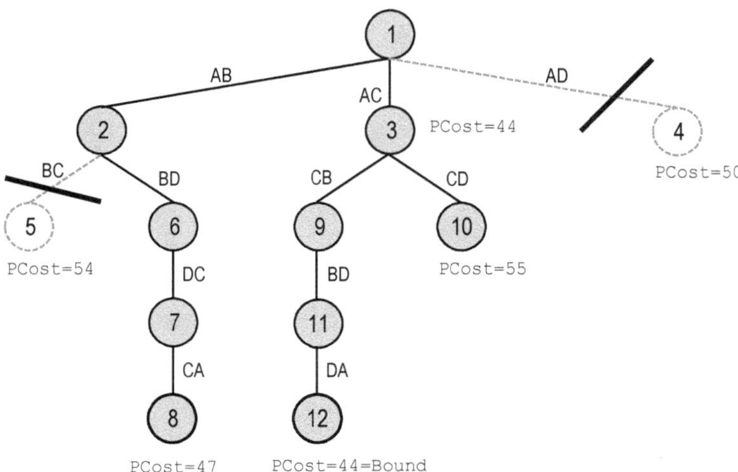

Node 10 is unexplored. Based on *bound* limit (44), it can be safely excluded.

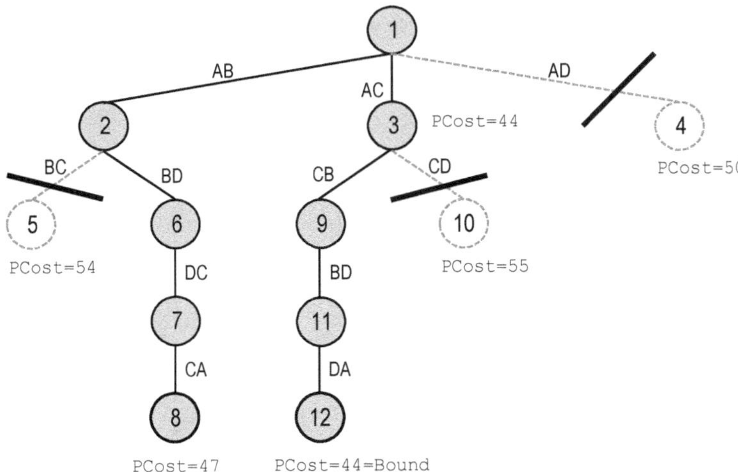

If search tree still has unexplored nodes, the process will continue to explore the next possible node with the smallest path cost. In this case, nodes 4, 5 and 10 are all already excluded because they have path cost greater than *bound* limit. Search tree exploration is completed with node 12 as final solution.

Branch-and-bound technique finds the optimal solution without having to explore the entire search tree. The *branch* steps calculate new RCM for each node and explore node with the smallest path cost. This will help the algorithm to find a feasible solution as early as possible to obtain the *bound* limit. Using the limit, *bound* steps aim to quickly exclude significant part of search tree because some branches will not lead to a better solution.

WRITING BETTER ALGORITHMS

08. ALGORITHM ANALYSIS

Before an algorithm is used in real world application, a software engineer needs to perform basic algorithm analysis to ensure 2 factors: correctness and quality. An algorithm is said to be *correct* if it generates correct outputs for ALL possible inputs, including error handling of all invalid inputs. Handling 99% possible inputs correctly, is considered as incorrect.

The process to check the correctness of an algorithm is referred to as *software testing* or quality assurance. There are different approaches and techniques to validate an algorithm while balancing the constraint of cost and time. This is a separate topic for the upcoming chapter 09.

An algorithm is said to have *good quality* if it consistently produces the correct outputs within the shortest possible time, using the minimum possible computing resources. Note that there are 2 main components of this definition (time and resources). The following discussion in this chapter starts from analysing execution speed and efficiency.

Computer needs time to process each line of instruction in the programming code. The number of processing time required to execute an algorithm is not equal to the number of lines in code because loops and branches will cause some lines to be executed multiple times or none at all.

The size of input is a key factor influencing how many instructions need to be executed by an algorithm to produce the output. An ideal algorithm would be able to finish its processes within reasonable time even when the input size is enormous. Unfortunately, this is often not achievable because larger size of inputs would require more iterations for the algorithm to process.

A certain algorithm needs 2 seconds to process n inputs. When given double the size of input data (2n), the algorithm requires 4 seconds to produce the results. Further increase of input data to 3n takes the algorithm 8 seconds to complete. The required time doubles with each additional n inputs. Why should this be a concern since the algorithm still only needs a few seconds to complete anyway?

It is not the actual time (in seconds, minutes or even hours) that should be a concern. The fact that an algorithm requires double execution time for each additional N input data shows that the algorithm's required effort to complete grows exponentially with the size of input. This can end up being astronomically large.

According to a legend, once upon a time a king was feeling bored, so he promised a big reward for anyone who can present a new game for him that he likes. Many citizens and nobles tried to invent games and presented them to please the king. None succeeded. A wise man brings a board with 8×8 squares and some pieces to be played on the board. The game is called chess.

The king is very impressed with this new game. He decides to offer a reward for the wise man. When given the opportunity to request a reward, the wise man asks for rice. He puts 1 single grain of rice on the first tile of his chess board. He then explains to the king that he would like to double the number of rice grain for each subsequent tile on the board and would like to receive the total rice from those 64 tiles.

Not realising the implication of this request, the king quickly agrees. How many grains of rice does the king owe the wise man? With simple math, we can calculate that the last tile on the board would have 2^{63} grains of rice. The total of rice of the requested reward is 1.8446744×10^{19} grains.

If one single grain of rice weighs 0.02 grams, the prize for the wise man weighs 368,934,881,474 tonnes. That is 368 billion tonnes of rice! For comparison, the world's annual rice production in 2022 was estimated around 515 million tonnes. The world needs more than 700 years to produce the required amount of rice.

The above story is a popular illustration to explain the possible impact of exponential growth. There are some variations of the story, such as the mention of wheat instead of rice, but the message remains the same.

Back to the discussion on execution time, the following algorithms will be used to compare 3 different scenarios:

- Algorithm 08-A takes an array of numeric values with N elements as input. The algorithm is designed to choose an element at random, and then display its text content to user.
- Algorithm 08-B takes an array of numeric values with N elements as input. This algorithm calculates each element multiplied by 2, and then display the results to user.
- Algorithm 08-C takes an array of numeric values with N elements as input. It performs bubble sort to rearrange the element values in ascending order before displaying the results to user.

```
1 read array A with n elements
2 RandomIndex=Random(n)
3 show A[RandomIndex]
```

Algorithm 08-A Choosing Random Elements

```
1 read array A with n elements
2 for i=1 to n-1 do
3    x=A[i]*2
4    show x
5 end for
```

Algorithm 08-B Calculate and Display Each Element

```
1 read array A with n elements
2 for i=2 to n-1 do
3    for j=n to i-1 do
4      if A[j-1]>A[j] then
5        swap(A[j-1],A[j])
6      end if
7    end for
8 end for
9 for i=1 to n do
10   show A[i]
11 end for
```

Algorithm 08-C Bubble Sort

Algorithm 08-A can take an array with 10 elements or an array with a million elements and the execution time remains the same. All it needs to do is choosing one random number from 1 to n, and then display the string value of the chosen element. It is said that this algorithm executes at *constant* time.

The running time of Algorithm 08-B is impacted by the size of input because the algorithm needs to iterate the instruction of multiplication and display to user n times. If a computer needs 1 nanosecond to execute an instruction, each iteration will require 3 nanoseconds: 1 for evaluating the `for` iteration with the counter variable, 1 for calculating the multiplication and storing the result in `x`, and 1 for displaying the result to user. An input array with 10 elements will take 3×10 nanoseconds to process. A larger input with a million elements needs $3 \times 1,000,000$ nanoseconds. More inputs require more processing time at the same proportion. It is said that this algorithm executes at *linear* time.

It is more difficult to analyse the execution time of Algorithm 08-C because it depends on both the size of the input array and the values within its elements. If the input array already has values sorted in ascending order, the swap instruction from line #5 would never execute (best case). An input array with values in descending order would trigger the swap instructions every time (worst case). Most input arrays with random values will require the swap instruction to be executed in some iterations, making the total time somewhere between the best and worst case.

Input size is still a key factor. The worst-case scenario for an array with 10 elements is likely better than the best-case execution time for a different input with 1 million elements.

Since most algorithms are designed to process wide range of inputs, it is important to understand how the algorithm will perform with different input sizes and characteristics of data within the set.

Big O Algorithmic Complexity

Execution time of an algorithm depends on the size of input and the data within the input set. The size of input determines the best-case and worst-case execution time of an algorithm based on its complexity (formed by the structure of branches and loops inside). The data within input set determines if one instance of execution would require execution time close to best-case or worse-case scenario.

Software engineering field uses 3 notations to describe algorithm's complexity:
- **Big O** notation is an indication of the upper bound of an algorithm's complexity (worst-case).
- **Omega (Ω)** notation is an indication of the lower bound of an algorithm's complexity (best-case).

- **Theta (Θ)** notation is an indication of the exact bound of an algorithm's complexity.

Best-case scenario tells us very little about the quality of an algorithm. If an algorithm performs extremely well because one specific set of input data happens to require very little computation, it can be said that the great performance comes from luck, not from efficient design.

The notation for the worst-case scenario is the most common notation to use. If an algorithm performs well enough for its worst-case situation, then most everyday use of that algorithm will show better performance. Big O notation basically states that larger input will grow execution time at most this much, but likely it could grow slower.

Time complexity of an algorithm is not the actual time to complete an algorithm. Different machine configurations and multitasking conditions make it virtually impossible to calculate exact time for an algorithm to complete its instructions. The focus of measuring Big O is to understand the relative change of execution time when the size of input data increases.

Basic Big O complexities from best to worst:
- Constant: `O(1)`
- Logarithmic: `O(log n)`
- Square root: `O($\sqrt{n}$)` or `O(sqrt(n))`
- Linear: `O(n)`
- Superlinear: `O(n log n)`
- Quadratic: `O(n`^{2}`)`
- Cubic: `O(n`^{3}`)`
- Polynomial: `O(n`^{c}`)` where c is a constant greater than 2
- Exponential: `O(c`^{n}`)` where c is a constant greater than 1
- Factorial: `O(n!)`

An algorithm is said to have *constant time* complexity if the input size of n has no impact to execution time. Algorithm 08-A is an example of constant time algorithm. As shown in Algorithm 08-B, an algorithm with *linear time* complexity requires execution time that increases linearly with the size of input.

Increasing input size by one element in this example will increase the execution time by 3 nanoseconds. It can be said that the required execution time is roughly equal to 3n. In obtaining Big O, we only care about the part with the <u>most impact</u> from a complexity formula. Therefore, we can safely ignore the coefficient of 3 and just use `O(n)` for the notation.

Is there a point in counting the exact number of instructions inside a loop? The structure of loops and branches matter more than the number of instructions inside them. If an algorithm's processing time can be represented by complexity formula of $4n^2 + 5n + 7$, we can safely ignore $5n + 7$ and the coefficient of 4 in front of n^2. This is because n^2 is the component with the biggest impact in the formula. It can be said that such algorithm has Big O notation of `O(n²)`, making it a quadratic time complexity.

Bubble sort in Algorithm 08-C has an iteration inside an iteration. The number of required iterations is impacted by n, the size of input data. The worst-case situation is to run n×n iterations and the `if-then` statement inside the nested loop evaluates as *true* every single time. Regardless of the number of instructions within each level of iteration, the biggest impact comes from the structure of 2 levels nested iteration. Bubble sort algorithm has Big O notation of `O(n²)`.

If adding more data into input size causes an algorithm execution time to grow at comparatively much slower pace, it is said that the algorithm has *logarithmic time* complexity. This Big O is considered as the golden standard to achieve when writing new algorithm.

Big O notations of `O(1)` (constant), `O(log n)` (logarithmic), `O(√n)` (square root), `O(n)` (linear) and `O(n log n)` (superlinear) are considered to be good quality, noting that `O(1)` is not really achievable for many real world situations. Algorithms with `O(n²)` (quadratic) are generally not desired, but sometimes cannot be avoided. Most experienced software engineers will try to avoid writing or using algorithms with `O(n³)` (cubic) or worse if better technique is technically feasible.

For reference: selection sort, insertion sort and bubble sort have Big O notation of `O(n²)`. Heap sort, merge sort and quick sort perform better at `O(n log n)`. Sequential search's time complexity is `O(n)` and binary search does better with `O(log n)`.

Resource Analysis

Algorithms require resources to complete its calculations. Many components in an algorithm require computing resource. This includes passing parameters and local variables during every instance of module calls. Some algorithm techniques save some calculations into memory to minimise the number of upcoming iterations. Fibonacci algorithm with memoisation from chapter 05 is a good example of using more resources to save time.

Big O notation for algorithm complexity is not limited for execution time. Another aspect to consider during algorithm design is how fast the *required resources* will increase with the size of input data.

Modern computing devices have more than sufficient resources for most use, excluding some heavy gaming or video rendering. Some low-end smartphones in today's market could have more memory than a desktop computer with decent specifications from 25 years ago. As a result, modern software developers would have less restrictions with resources compared to a few decades ago.

If an algorithm needs several two-dimensional arrays to process a one-dimensional input array with n elements, such algorithm is said to have quadratic resource complexity $O(n^2)$. Similar with time complexity, generally algorithms with $O(n^3)$ (cubic) or worse complexity should be avoided if better technique is technically achievable.

Algorithm	Big O (time)	Big O (resource)
Selection Sort	$O(n^2)$	$O(1)$
Insertion Sort	$O(n^2)$	$O(1)$
Bubble Sort	$O(n^2)$	$O(1)$
Heap Sort	$O(n\ log\ n)$	$O(1)$
Merge Sort	$O(n\ log\ n)$	$O(n)$
Quick Sort	$O(n\ log\ n)$	$O(log\ n)$
Sequential Search	$O(n)$	$O(1)$
Binary Search	$O(log\ n)$	$O(1)$

Sequential and binary search algorithms have resource complexity of $O(1)$. It means, the algorithm itself requires constant resources regardless of the size of input data. Note that the size of input data itself require some resources to store, but it is not considered as part of algorithm complexity.

Selection sort, insertion sort, bubble sort and even heap sort also have resource complexity of $O(1)$. These algorithms work directly on the input array and do not require additional storage that would increase with the size of input data.

Merge sort has resource complexity of $O(n)$ because its calculations take a lot of space. Executing merge sort using computers from 2 decades ago might cause slower operations for large input.

Quick sort also requires additional resource to calculate. A computing device would need to create stack data to store the local variables in its recursion technique. The Big O resource complexity is `O(log n)`.

There are times when a software engineer needs to make decisions between improving time complexity or resource complexity. If less-than-ideal Big O cannot be avoided, it is also an option to enforce maximum size of input, or minimum hardware requirements to run an algorithm.

Improvement Example: Prime Numbers Algorithm

The main purpose of doing algorithm analysis is to make improvements. Knowing how an algorithm will perform with large input data would help a software developer to optimise an algorithm to perform better.

An example of prime numbers algorithm is used in this chapter to illustrate possible steps and analysis in improving an algorithm. A *prime number* is a natural number greater than 1 that only have 2 factors. *Factor* of X is a positive number that can divide X with no remainder. It can also be identified as a number that can be multiplied by another whole number to make X. Using this definition, a prime number only has 1 and itself as factors.

Given a value of N from user input, an algorithm needs to display all prime numbers less than or equal to N.

```
 1 read N
 2 for x=1 to N do
 3    countFactor=0
 4    for i=1 to x do
 5      if (x mod i)=0 then
 6         countFactor=countFactor+1
 7      end if
 8    end for
 9    if countFactor=2 then
10       show x
11    end if
12 end for
```

Algorithm 08-D Prime Numbers from 1 to N (version 1)

The first attempt to write an algorithm to show all prime numbers from 1 to N works. The algorithm shows the prime numbers correctly. However, this algorithm is far from good quality because there are many unnecessary iterations that can be avoided.

A quick improvement can be made of the starting point of iteration on line #2. It is known that the smallest prime number is 2. There is no point of checking if 1 is a prime number.

Next, we know that every natural number can be divided by 1. We also do not need to check if a number can be divided by itself with no remainder because the answer is always yes. This algorithm can be improved by removing the first and last iteration of `i` from line #4 and adjusting the initial value of `countFactor` to 2, because the first 2 factors are always 1 and the number itself.

```
 1 read N
 2 for x=2 to N do
 3    countFactor=2
 4    for i=2 to x-1 do
 5      if (x mod i)=0 then
 6         countFactor=countFactor+1
 7      end if
 8    end for
 9    if countFactor=2 then
10       show x
11    end if
12 end for
```

Algorithm 08-E Prime Numbers from 1 to N (version 2)

No natural number can be divided without remainder by any whole number greater than half of it. This allows us to adjust line #4 further to exclude the second half of the iteration.

```
 1 read N
 2 for x=2 to N do
 3    countFactor=2
 4    for i=2 to (x div 2) do
 5      if (x mod i)=0 then
 6         countFactor=countFactor+1
 7      end if
 8    end for
 9    if countFactor=2 then
10       show x
11    end if
12 end for
```

Algorithm 08-F Prime Numbers from 1 to N (version 3)

Further improvement can be made by stopping the iteration if i after more than 2 factors are found. Prime number algorithm is only interested to find prime numbers after all. There is no point to continue further iterations when a number is already concluded as non-prime.

Using `for` statement in line #4 does not give the necessary flexibility to stop the iteration for non-prime numbers. To achieve this, `for` can be replaced with `while-do`.

```
 1 read N
 2 for x=2 to N do
 3    countFactor=2
 4    i=2
 5    while (countFactor=2) and (i<=(x div 2)) do
 6       if (x mod i)=0 then
 7          countFactor=countFactor+1
 8       end if
 9       i=i+1
10    end for
11    if countFactor=2 then
12       show x
13    end if
14 end for
```

Algorithm 08-G Prime Numbers from 1 to N (version 4)

By replacing `for-do` with `while-do`, the algorithm loses the convenience of having counter variable i that increases every cycle during iteration. Therefore, new line #4 is added to give initial value to i, and new line #9 is added to increase the counter for the next iteration.

The new inner loop uses `while-do`. It has two conditions with AND operator. The first operand checks if the `countFactor` is still 2, meaning no new factor has been found so far. The second operand limits the iteration to stop when i has reached x div 2, which is the biggest possible natural number that can be a factor of x.

If the iteration reaches x div 2 and `countFactor` remains 2, it means x is a prime number and needs to be displayed. If another factor was found before the iteration reaches x div 2, the `while` condition in line #5 evaluates as *false* and the loop will stop. This technique would save significant number of iterations especially when n is big.

Algorithm 08-G (version 4) is a common version algorithm to show prime numbers from 1 to n. This algorithm has time complexity of $O(n\sqrt{n})$, better than quadratic but worse than linear.

There is a completely different approach to solve the problem to display prime numbers between 1 and n. Instead of calculating each number (x) to find out whether x is a prime number or not, we can create an array of Boolean value with x elements and mark all multiplies of each prime number as *false*.

```
 1 read N
 2 A[1]=false
 3 for z=2 to N do
 4   A[z]=true
 5 end for
 6 for i=2 to (N div 2) do
 7   if A[i]=true then
 8     for j=2 to (N div i)do
 9       A[i*j]=false
10     end for
11   end if
12 end for
13 for k=2 to N do
14   if A[k]=true then
15     show A[k]
16   end if
17 end for
```

Algorithm 08-H Prime Numbers from 1 to N (version 5)

Array A is used to mark whether a natural number is a multiplication of other natural numbers except 1 and itself. Line #1 marks 1 as *false* because it is already known that 1 is not a prime number. Any number from 2 to n starts as *true* (lines #3 to #5) because they could be prime numbers until proven otherwise.

Line #6 starts a loop from 2 to n div 2 to mark all multiplications of prime numbers as false. The upper limit of n div 2 is because the largest natural number that can be a factor of n other than n itself is n div 2.

Inside the loop, if a number (i) is still marked as prime number ($A[i]$ is *true*), then mark all multiplications of i as *false* because i is found to be a factor of those numbers. The upper limit in line #8 uses N div i to ensure that the calculation of $i \times j$ will not exceed n.

Finally, lines #13 to #17 are going through every element of array A and display the number of the Boolean value stays *true* after the previous calculations are completed. This means, no other natural number was found to be a factor of that number.

1	2	3	4	5	6	7	8	9	10	11	12	13	14	15	16	17	18	19	20
F	T	T	T	T	T	T	T	T	T	T	T	T	T	T	T	T	T	T	T
21	22	23	24	25	26	27	28	29	30	31	32	33	34	35	36	37	38	39	40
T	T	T	T	T	T	T	T	T	T	T	T	T	T	T	T	T	T	T	T
41	42	43	44	45	46	47	48	49	50	51	52	53	54	55	56	57	58	59	60
T	T	T	T	T	T	T	T	T	T	T	T	T	T	T	T	T	T	T	T
61	62	63	64	65	66	67	68	69	70	71	72	73	74	75	76	77	78	79	80
F	T	T	T	T	T	T	T	T	T	T	T	T	T	T	T	T	T	T	T
81	82	83	84	85	86	87	88	89	90	91	92	93	94	95	96	97	98	99	100
F	T	T	T	T	T	T	T	T	T	T	T	T	T	T	T	T	T	T	T

To help with illustration, an array with 100 elements is displayed to show how the algorithm works with N=100. In the first step of the algorithm, all elements are marked as *true* except for the first element because 1 is not a prime number.

1	2	3	4	5	6	7	8	9	10	11	12	13	14	15	16	17	18	19	20
F	T	T	F	T	F	T	F	T	F	T	F	T	F	T	F	T	F	T	F
21	22	23	24	25	26	27	28	29	30	31	32	33	34	35	36	37	38	39	40
T	F	T	F	T	F	T	F	T	F	T	F	T	F	T	F	T	F	T	F
41	42	43	44	45	46	47	48	49	50	51	52	53	54	55	56	57	58	59	60
T	F	T	F	T	F	T	F	T	F	T	F	T	F	T	F	T	F	T	F
61	62	63	64	65	66	67	68	69	70	71	72	73	74	75	76	77	78	79	80
T	F	T	F	T	F	T	F	T	F	T	F	T	F	T	F	T	F	T	F
81	82	83	84	85	86	87	88	89	90	91	92	93	94	95	96	97	98	99	100
T	F	T	F	T	F	T	F	T	F	T	F	T	F	T	F	T	F	T	F

In the first iteration of i, the algorithm will mark all multiplications of 2 as *false*. This will essentially mark all even number as false except for 2 itself. Remember that 2 is the only even prime number.

1	2	3	4	5	6	7	8	9	10	11	12	13	14	15	16	17	18	19	20
F	T	T	F	T	F	T	F	F	F	T	F	T	F	F	F	T	F	T	F
21	22	23	24	25	26	27	28	29	30	31	32	33	34	35	36	37	38	39	40
F	F	T	F	T	F	F	F	T	F	T	F	F	F	T	F	T	F	F	F
41	42	43	44	45	46	47	48	49	50	51	52	53	54	55	56	57	58	59	60
T	F	T	F	F	F	T	F	T	F	F	F	T	F	T	F	F	F	T	F
61	62	63	64	65	66	67	68	69	70	71	72	73	74	75	76	77	78	79	80
T	F	F	F	T	F	T	F	F	F	T	F	T	F	F	F	T	F	T	F
81	82	83	84	85	86	87	88	89	90	91	92	93	94	95	96	97	98	99	100
F	F	T	F	T	F	F	F	T	F	T	F	F	F	T	F	T	F	F	F

During next iteration, the algorithm takes the number i=3 and will mark all multiplications of 3 as *false*. Note that there are several elements that is already marked as *false* from the previous iteration.

1	2	3	4	5	6	7	8	9	10	11	12	13	14	15	16	17	18	19	20
F	T	T	F	T	F	T	F	F	F	T	F	T	F	F	F	T	F	T	F
21	22	23	24	25	26	27	28	29	30	31	32	33	34	35	36	37	38	39	40
F	F	T	F	F	F	F	F	T	F	T	F	F	F	F	F	T	F	F	F
41	42	43	44	45	46	47	48	49	50	51	52	53	54	55	56	57	58	59	60
T	F	T	F	F	F	T	F	T	F	F	F	T	F	F	F	F	F	T	F
61	62	63	64	65	66	67	68	69	70	71	72	73	74	75	76	77	78	79	80
T	F	F	F	F	F	T	F	F	F	T	F	T	F	F	F	T	F	T	F
81	82	83	84	85	86	87	88	89	90	91	92	93	94	95	96	97	98	99	100
F	F	T	F	F	F	F	F	T	F	T	F	F	F	F	F	T	F	F	F

Iteration with i=4 does not do anything to the array because it does not satisfy the if condition from line #7. For i=5, the algorithm marks all multiplications of 5 as *false*.

1	2	3	4	5	6	7	8	9	10	11	12	13	14	15	16	17	18	19	20
F	T	T	F	T	F	T	F	F	F	T	F	T	F	F	F	T	F	T	F
21	22	23	24	25	26	27	28	29	30	31	32	33	34	35	36	37	38	39	40
F	F	T	F	F	F	F	F	T	F	T	F	F	F	F	F	T	F	F	F
41	42	43	44	45	46	47	48	49	50	51	52	53	54	55	56	57	58	59	60
T	F	T	F	F	F	T	F	F	F	F	F	T	F	F	F	F	F	T	F
61	62	63	64	65	66	67	68	69	70	71	72	73	74	75	76	77	78	79	80
T	F	F	F	F	F	T	F	F	F	T	F	T	F	F	F	F	F	T	F
81	82	83	84	85	86	87	88	89	90	91	92	93	94	95	96	97	98	99	100
F	F	T	F	F	F	F	F	T	F	F	F	F	F	F	F	T	F	F	F

Iteration with i=6 does not do anything to the array because it does not satisfy the if condition from line #7. For i=7, the algorithm marks all multiplications of 7 as *false*. Note that there are even more elements already marked as *false*.

1	2	3	4	5	6	7	8	9	10	11	12	13	14	15	16	17	18	19	20
F	T	T	F	T	F	T	F	F	F	T	F	T	F	F	F	T	F	T	F
21	22	23	24	25	26	27	28	29	30	31	32	33	34	35	36	37	38	39	40
F	F	T	F	F	F	F	F	T	F	T	F	F	F	F	F	T	F	F	F
41	42	43	44	45	46	47	48	49	50	51	52	53	54	55	56	57	58	59	60
T	F	T	F	F	F	T	F	F	F	F	F	T	F	F	F	F	F	T	F
61	62	63	64	65	66	67	68	69	70	71	72	73	74	75	76	77	78	79	80
T	F	F	F	F	F	T	F	F	F	T	F	T	F	F	F	F	F	T	F
81	82	83	84	85	86	87	88	89	90	91	92	93	94	95	96	97	98	99	100
F	F	T	F	F	F	F	F	T	F	F	F	F	F	F	F	T	F	F	F

The next few iterations find that numbers 8, 9 and 10 are not prime numbers. It continues with i=11 and try to mark all multiplications of 11 as *false*. However, there is no Boolean value to change because all multiplications of 11 up to 100 are already marked as *false*. Further calculations with numbers 13, 17, 19, 23, 29, 31, 47, 41, 43 and 47 observe similar pattern.

1	2	3	4	5	6	7	8	9	10	11	12	13	14	15	16	17	18	19	20
F	T	T	F	T	F	T	F	F	F	T	F	T	F	F	F	T	F	T	F
21	22	23	24	25	26	27	28	29	30	31	32	33	34	35	36	37	38	39	40
F	F	T	F	F	F	F	F	T	F	T	F	F	F	F	F	T	F	F	F
41	42	43	44	45	46	47	48	49	50	51	52	53	54	55	56	57	58	59	60
T	F	T	F	F	F	T	F	F	F	F	F	T	F	F	F	F	F	T	F
61	62	63	64	65	66	67	68	69	70	71	72	73	74	75	76	77	78	79	80
T	F	F	F	F	F	T	F	F	F	T	F	T	F	F	F	F	F	T	F
81	82	83	84	85	86	87	88	89	90	91	92	93	94	95	96	97	98	99	100
F	F	T	F	F	F	F	F	T	F	F	F	F	F	F	F	T	F	F	F

The iteration of lines #6 to #12 finishes with 25 numbers still marked as *true* in the array. The next part of this algorithm (lines #13 to #17) loops A one more time and display every number with *true* Boolean value.

Can this algorithm be optimised further? Yes. Prime numbers algorithm version 5 has several avoidable iterations. Remember that many times an array element is already marked as *false* and the algorithm proceeds with setting them *false* again. Technically, an `if-then` statement can be added to change the Boolean value only if needed.

```
 1 read N
 2 A[1]=false
 3 for z=2 to N do
 4    A[z]=true
 5 end for
 6 for i=2 to (N div 2) do
 7    if A[i]=true then
 8       for j=2 to (N div i)do
 9          if A[i*j]=true then
10             A[i*j]=false
11          end if
12       end for
13    end if
14 end for
15 for k=2 to N do
16    if A[k]=true then
17       show A[k]
18    end if
19 end for
```

Algorithm 08-I Prime Numbers from 1 to N (version 6)

Algorithm 08-I (version 6) adds a little check (line #9) to see if an element is already marked as *false* and skip the process to set it to *false* again. This improvement does change its Big O time complexity and offers no significant change to the actual run time because checking the condition whether A[i*j] is *true* also requires computation time.

A better improvement is to prevent useless iterations from happening in the first place. Some mathematical analysis is proven to be useful to improve this calculation.

Suppose $x \times y = N = \sqrt{N} \times \sqrt{N}$.

If $x \geq \sqrt{N}$ then $y = \frac{xy}{x} \leq \frac{N}{\sqrt{N}}$. Therefore $y \leq \sqrt{N}$.

In simple term, for x×y to be equal to N, one of x or y must be smaller than √N. When an algorithm already processed all the numbers less than or equal to √N, all numbers greater than √N that needs to be set to *false* are already marked before. With this additional knowledge, the upper limit of for iteration (line #6) can be adjusted to sqrt(N).

```
 1 read N
 2 A[1]=false
 3 for z=2 to N do
 4   A[z]=true
 5 end for
 6 for i=2 to sqrt(N) do
 7   if A[i]=true then
 8     for j=2 to (N div i)do
 9       if A[i*j]=true then
10         A[i*j]=false
11       end if
12     end for
13   end if
14 end for
15 for k=2 to N do
16   if A[k]=true then
17     show A[k]
18   end if
19 end for
```

Algorithm 08-J Prime Numbers from 1 to N (version 7)

Algorithm 08-J is a significant improvement because it removes many redundant iterations. With N=100, version 6 would process 50 iterations while version 7 can stop after 10.

When observing i=3, the algorithm does not actually need to check if A[6] is already *false* because 6 is already marked by the previous process. Similarly, when doing the marking process for i=5, the algorithm can safely skip 10, 15 and 20 (multiplication numbers less than 25). This improvement uses similar theory to create version 7, any non-prime numbers less than i^2 should already been found because for any pair of $x \times y = i^2$ (other than 1 and i^2 itself), one of x or y must be smaller than i. Instead of starting j from 2 (line #8), it can start from i to commence the marking process from i^2.

```
 1 read N
 2 A[1]=false
 3 for z=2 to N do
 4   A[z]=true
 5 end for
 6 for i=2 to sqrt(N) do
 7   if A[i]=true then
 8     for j=i to (N div i)do
 9       if A[i*j]=true then
10         A[i*j]=false
11       end if
12     end for
13   end if
14 end for
15 for k=2 to N do
16   if A[k]=true then
17     show A[k]
18   end if
19 end for
```

Algorithm 08-K Prime Numbers from 1 to N (version 8)

In Algorithm 08-K, line #8 starts the j loop from the value of i to save several loops inside the big iteration of i. It is fascinating that changing one single character in an algorithm would bring such significant impact. That is the power of a correct algorithm with good quality. Sometimes, the thinking and planning steps during the creation (and improvement) of algorithm takes more time and effort than writing the code itself.

At this point, the `if-then` statement to check whether an element is already marked as *false* (lines #9 and #11) is either useless or doing more harm than good. The nested loops of i and j are already optimised in such a way that many redundant iterations would not happen in the first place. This `if-then` branch will not prevent many redundant executions and will only increase total computation because it doubles the effort to mark an element from *true* to *false*, having to check its value first.

```
 1 read N
 2 A[1]=false
 3 for z=2 to N do
 4    A[z]=true
 5 end for
 6 for i=2 to sqrt(N) do
 7    if A[i]=true then
 8       for j=i to (N div i)do
 9          A[i*j]=false
10       end for
11    end if
12 end for
13 for k=2 to N do
14    if A[k]=true then
15       show A[k]
16    end if
17 end for
```

Algorithm 08-L Prime Numbers from 1 to N (version 9)

Version 9 removes the `if-then` branch which checks whether the Boolean value of an element before setting it to *false*. An improvement does not always involve adding more checks or changing conditions. Removing unnecessary checks can sometimes make an algorithm perform better.

This technique of prime number algorithm is known as *Sieve of Eratosthenes* with time complexity of `O(n log (log n))`. It works significantly better than the last version without Boolean mapping (version 4).

09. ALGORITHM TESTING

No matter how fast an algorithm can perform, it does not bring much value if users cannot trust it to deliver correct results consistently. Testing an algorithm helps to verify its correctness and discover defects and logic faults in it.

An algorithm is normally implemented into code using chosen programming language. Such code can be part of a module or object, and then integrated into a larger solution following some architectural design.

Testing is a discipline in software engineering with some universities dedicating research centres and major fields for students. This chapter serves only as introduction to a few topics limited to algorithm-level testing. Other areas such as code implementation (unit testing), module testing, integration testing, system testing, acceptance testing, and test automation are not covered in this discussion.

Broadly speaking, activities of testing are categorised into verification and validation. There are a few different interpretations of these terms. This book defines algorithm *verification* as the effort to evaluate an algorithm to ensure that it meets specified requirements. This activity is taken during the process of development.

Algorithm *validation* checks if an algorithm meets the true needs and expectations of the intended user. This activity happens after the completion of an algorithm or a module. Note that even an algorithm is correct, validation can still conclude that it fails the test because it does not satisfy user's need and the requirements need to be adjusted.

The main intent of testing activities is to find issues in an algorithm. These issues are called *bugs* when an algorithm is still in development, and called defects when a solution is already completed. A static bug or defect in an algorithm is referred to as a *fault*. When a fault causes an incorrect behaviour observable by user or tester, it is called a *failure*. A failure that happens when a solution is in production (used with real data in real operations) is called an *incident*.

A fault can remain undetected in an algorithm if testing process fails to observe it. Therefore, testing activities actually try to observe failures in order to find faults.

There are at least three conditions to observe a failure:
- *Reachability*. This condition states that testing activity must be able to reach the location of a fault.
- *Infection*. Testing activity must reach the location of the fault with incorrect state of the algorithm. This is normally achieved by controlling the inputs.
- *Propagation*. For a fault to be observed as a failure, the incorrect state must cause some incorrect outputs.

The above principles are commonly known as the *RIP model*. A tester would use and implement these principles to design test cases that meets certain coverage criteria.

White-box testing assumes that testers have sufficient knowledge and access to algorithm details and its code implementations. *Black-box testing* goes on different direction. This testing approach uses the specification documents, list of requirements and high-level design to come up with test cases.

Top-down testing activity starts from the main algorithm, then continue with each module calls. On the other hand, *bottom-up testing* starts by evaluating each module that does not call any other module, then progress with the callers up to the main algorithm (root).

Control Flow Coverage

The previous chapters in this book have explained about branches, loops and other strategies to build an algorithm. When an algorithm executes an `if-then` statement, the flow of algorithm depends on how the conditions evaluate. Different inputs will cause different lines of the algorithm to be executed.

Consider representing lines in a pseudocode as nodes in a graph. Add edges connecting those nodes for every possible flow that an algorithm execution can take. Traversing the tree can show paths that might happen during algorithm execution. One of the early steps in testing activity is to define those paths and choose some of them to be tested.

Should tester just test all paths instead of choosing some? Complex algorithms would translate into complex graphs with massive number of possible paths. Doing a complete testing is ideal, but often not feasible because it will make testing process requiring significantly more time and effort than the development of the algorithm itself.

```
 1 read X, Y
 2 if X>5 then
 3    call moduleStrawberry
 4 else
 5    call moduleBanana
 6 end if
 7 if Y<8 then
 8    call moduleApple
 9 else if Y<12 then
10    call moduleKiwi
11 else
12    call moduleOrange
13 end if
14 call moduleMango
```

Algorithm 09-A Translating Algorithm into Directed Graph for Testing

The above algorithm uses the value of X and Y to decide which module to call. Executing the algorithm with different input values of X and Y would result in different flow. This can be represented using a *control flow* graph below.

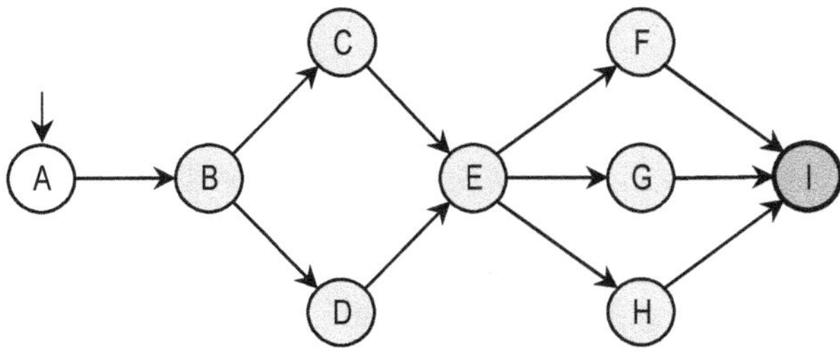

The graph is called a control flow graph because it maps how the algorithm control its flow during execution depending on branch criteria. Each node represents a state in an algorithm, that is a line in pseudocode (or a block of lines that do not have branches, loops or module calls). Each edge represents transition between states.

In this example, the directed graph above maps to lines from Algorithm 09-A:
- Line #1 is represented by node A.
- Line #2 is represented by node B.
- Line #3 is represented by node C.
- Line #5 is represented by node D.
- Line #7 is represented by node E.
- Line #8 is represented by node F.
- Line #10 is represented by node G.
- Line #12 is represented by node H.
- Line #14 is represented by node I.

List of valid paths:
- [A, B, C, E, F, I]
- [A, B, C, E, G, I]
- [A, B, C, E, H, I]
- [A, B, D, E, F, I]
- [A, B, D, E, G, I]
- [A, B, D, E, H, I]

By creating test cases to ensure that the above paths are traversed, a tester is said to meet the **complete path coverage** of the control flow graph representing the tested algorithm. The number of all valid paths of a complex algorithm can get quite large.

If testing all valid paths is not feasible, a tester can choose one of the other coverage criteria of a control flow:
- *Node Coverage*: test set must contain paths with all reachable nodes in control flow graph.
- *Edge Coverage*: test set must contain paths with all reachable edges in control flow graph.
- *Edge-Pair Coverage*: test set must contain paths with all reachable sub-paths with length 0, 1 and 2 in control flow graph. A sub-path with length 0 is essentially a node; sub-path with length 1 is an edge. Therefore, this coverage covers (sometimes also called subsumes) both node coverage and edge coverage criteria.
- *Prime Path Coverage*: test set must contain all prime paths in control flow graph. A prime path is a simple path (does not include a loop as a sub-path) with maximum length (not a sub-path of another simple path).

- *Complete Path Coverage*: test set must contain all valid paths in control flow graph. This is the most complete testing coverage.

Calculating Prime Path Coverage

A tester creates a control flow graph as part of testing activity. It starts from node A and ends at node H. The test plan is to identify all prime paths from this graph to define a set of test paths.

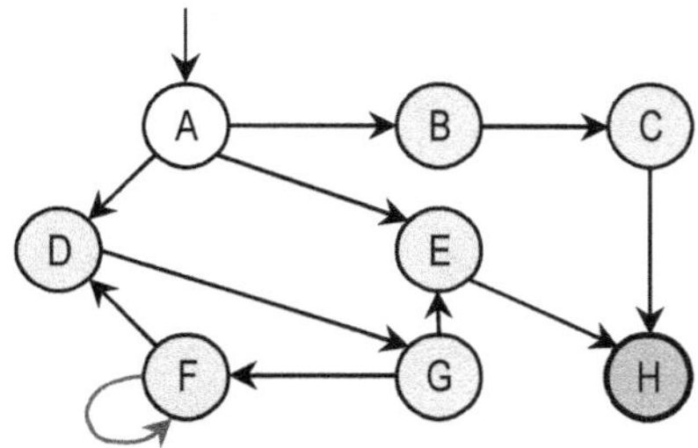

The process of finding all prime paths starts from listing simple paths with the shortest length. It continues with the longer paths until longest possible paths are listed.

Simple paths with length = 0:
1. [A]
2. [B]
3. [C]
4. [D]
5. [E]
6. [F]
7. [G]
8. [H] !

Paths that end with the final node (H) is marked with exclamation point (!) symbol. These paths cannot be extended further.

Simple paths with length = 1:
9. [A, B]
10. [A, D]
11. [A, E]
12. [B, C]
13. [C, H] !
14. [D, G]
15. [E, H] !

16. [F, D]
17. [F, F] *
18. [G, E]
19. [G, F]

A simple path cannot contain a loop as sub-path, but a whole path itself forming a loop counts as a simple path. Loop paths are indicated with asterisk (*) symbol.

Paths of length 2 are obtained by extending each path of length 1 without symbol. In this example, [A, B] is extended to [A, B, C]; [A, D] is extended to [A, D, G] and so on.

Simple paths with length = 2:
20. [A, B, C]
21. [A, D, G]
22. [A, E, H] !
23. [B, C, H] !
24. [D, G, E]
25. [D, G, F]
26. [F, D, G]
27. [G, E, H] !
28. [G, F, D]

In a similar way, paths of length 3 are obtained by extending each path of length 2 without symbol. [D, G, F] can be extended to [D, G, F, D], but not [D, G, F, F] because it would have [F, F] loop as a sub-path.

Simple paths with length = 3:
29. [A, B, C, H] !
30. [A, D, G, E]
31. [A, D, G, F]
32. [D, G, E, H] !
33. [D, G, F, D] *
34. [F, D, G, E]
35. [F, D, G, F] *
36. [G, F, D, G] *

There are 3 paths of length 3 to be extended. [A, D, G, F] cannot be extended to [A, D, G, F, D] because sub-path [D, G, F, D] is a loop. Similarly, [A, D, G, F, F] is also not a valid simple path because of sub-path [F, F].

Simple paths with length = 4:
37. [A, D, G, E, H] !
38. [F, D, G, E, H] !

All paths with symbols (* or !) are prime paths. In this example, we can list the following prime paths:

- Path #8 [H]
- Path #13 [C, H]
- Path #15 [E, H]
- Path #17 [F, F]
- Path #22 [A, E, H]
- Path #23 [B, C, H]
- Path #27 [G, E, H]
- Path #29 [A, B, C, H]
- Path #32 [D, G, E, H]
- Path #33 [D, G, F, D]
- Path #35 [F, D, G, F]
- Path #36 [G, F, D, G]
- Path #37 [A, D, G, E, H]
- Path #38 [F, D, G, E, H]

From its definition, prime path can start and end with any node from a control flow graph. A test path is different from prime path because it needs to start from first node (A) and ends with last node (H). To perform testing that meets prime paths coverage, a tester needs to create a test set, which is a set of test paths (from A to H) that travels through all prime paths.

The next step to find test paths is eliminating all prime paths that are sub-path of another prime path:

- ~~Path #8 [H]~~ can be removed because it is a sub-path of #13.
- ~~Path #13 [C, H]~~ can be removed because it is a sub-path of #23.
- ~~Path #15 [E, H]~~ can be removed because it is a sub-path of #22.
- Path #17 [F, F]
- Path #22 [A, E, H] is a valid test path (from A to H).
- ~~Path #23 [B, C, H]~~ can be removed because it is a sub-path of #28.
- ~~Path #27 [G, E, H]~~ can be removed because it is a sub-path of #32.
- Path #29 [A, B, C, H] is a valid test path (from A to H).
- ~~Path #32 [D, G, E, H]~~ can be removed because it is a sub-path of #37.
- Path #33 [D, G, F, D]
- Path #35 [F, D, G, F]
- Path #36 [G, F, D, G]
- Path #37 [A, D, G, E, H] is a valid test path (from A to H).
- Path #38 [F, D, G, E, H]

Paths #22, #29 and #37 can be added into the test set. Tester still needs more testing path to traverse paths #17, #33, #35, #36 and #38. The easiest way to achieve this is by extending the longest remaining prime path to the start and end node. The longest remaining prime path from the example is [F, D, G, E, H]. This can be extended to [A, D, G, F, D, G, E, H], forming path #39:

- Path #17 [F, F]
- ~~Path #33 [D, G, F, D]~~ can be removed because it is a sub-path of #39.
- Path #35 [F, D, G, F]
- ~~Path #36 [G, F, D, G]~~ can be removed because it is a sub-path of #39.
- ~~Path #38 [F, D, G, E, H]~~ can be removed because it is a sub-path of #39.
- Path #39 [A, D, G, F, D, G, E, H] this is a test path from extending longest remaining prime path.

Paths #33, #36 and #39 are removed from list. Path #39 is added into test set as one of the test paths. Now there are only 3 prime paths remaining: #17 and #35. Path #35 is the longest remaining prime path and can be extended to [A, D, G, F, D, G, F, D, G, E, H].

The updated list will look as follow:

- Path #17 [F, F]
- ~~Path #35 [F, D, G, F]~~ can be removed because it is a sub-path of #40.
- Path #40 [A, D, G, F, D, G, F, D, G, E, H] this is a test path from extending longest remaining prime path.

Unfortunately, the new path #40 still does not cover path #17. Therefore, this process needs to be repeated one more time. The longest remaining prime path [F, F] can be extended to [A, D, G, F, F, D, G, E, H].

Final list:

- ~~Path #17 [F, F]~~ can be removed because it is a sub-path of #41.
- Path #41 [A, D, G, F, F, D, G, E, H] this is a test path from extending longest remaining prime path.

Test set to satisfy the **prime path coverage**:

- Test path #22 [A, E, H]
- Test path #29 [A, B, C, H]
- Test path #37 [A, D, G, E, H]
- Test path #39 [A, D, G, F, D, G, E, H]
- Test path #40 [A, D, G, F, D, G, F, D, G, E, H]
- Test path #41 [A, D, G, F, F, D, G, E, H]

Data Flow Coverage

Data flow coverage focuses on variables and their values. Data flow graph maps the location where variables are defined or assigned values within an algorithm and where those values are used. This is different from control flow graph that focuses on the flow of execution.

In pseudocode, variable definition happens when:
- A variable appears on the left side of an assignment instruction.
- A variable is used as a parameter in a module definition. It sets the values to be used locally within module execution.
- A variable's value is changed after a module call completes.

Variable use happens when:
- A variable appears on the right side of an assignment instruction.
- A variable appears in a condition to be evaluated.
- A variable is used as a parameter in a module call.
- A variable is an output of an algorithm or module.

Data flow testing relies on the fact that values are carried from definition points to whether they are used. In other words: from *defs* to *uses*. A path in data flow coverage from where a particular value is assigned to a variable to a node where that value is used is called a *du-pair*.

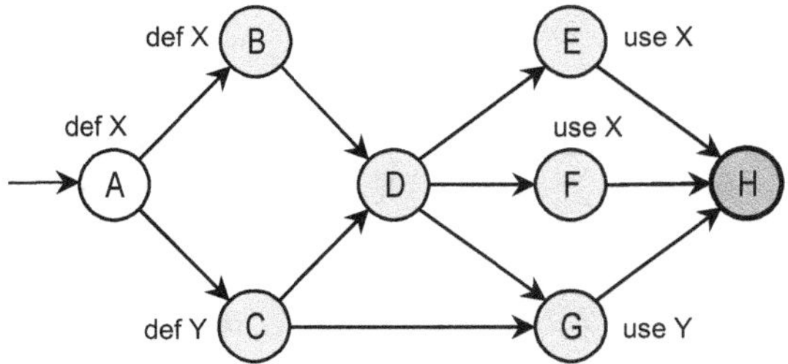

There are 2 variables in the above data flow graph: X and Y. X is defined in nodes B and C and used in nodes E and F. Y is defined in C and used in G.

To test using data flow coverage criteria, a tester can define a test set with test paths that meets one of these coverage criteria:
- *All-Defs Coverage*: test set must contain paths that cover at least one du-path from each node with definition.
- *All-Uses Coverage*: test set must contain paths that cover at least one du-path to each node with variable use.

- *All-du-Paths Coverage*: test set must contain paths that cover all possible du-pairs.

Each test path needs to travel the graph from start node to finish node. Since there are only two nodes with *def* in this example, all-defs coverage can be satisfied by a test set that contains test paths that travel through those.

List of all du-pairs:
1. [B, D, E]
2. [B, D, F]
3. [C, D, G]
4. [C, G]

The definition of X in node A never has any use because the value is changed immediately after. Du-pair tracks particular value of a variable until the next time the value changes. Since the value from node A is not used, there is no du-pair involving node A.

There are 2 du-pairs coming from def node B. For all-defs coverage, tester can choose one of them and extend it to become a test path. [B, D, E] is extended to [A, B, D, E, H]. The other def node is C. Tester can choose between du-pairs #3 or #4. Du-pair #3 is extended to [A, C, D, G, H].

This test set with 2 test paths meets the **all-defs coverage** criteria:
- [A, B, D, E, H]
- [A, C, D, G, H]

For all-uses coverage, at least 1 du-pair from each use node must be used. There are 3 nodes with use in the example graph: E, F, and G. Therefore, tester needs to use at least 1 du-pair for each of those nodes and extend the path to the start and end node.

This test set with 3 test paths meets the **all-uses coverage** criteria:
- [A, B, D, E, H]
- [A, B, D, F, H]
- [A, C, D, G, H]

All-du-paths coverage is simpler. Testers need to use all du-pairs and extend them to become a test path. The below test set satisfies the **all-du-paths coverage** criteria:
- [A, B, D, E, H]
- [A, B, D, F, H]
- [A, C, D, G, H]
- [A, C, G, H]

This example makes data flow coverage appears simpler than control flow coverage. In real world testing, data flow graph will look far more complex than this example because even some simple algorithms would use more variables and update them often.

Logic Coverage

Logic coverage focuses on testing the conditions in branches and loops. As explained in the first chapter, an algorithm uses selections and iterations with conditions to control its flow. These conditions use variables from user inputs or from prior calculations, which means that one possible testing methods is to verify whether the logic in a condition is implemented correctly.

A logic *predicate* is an expression that contains variables and values and evaluates as Boolean value *true* or *false*. This is essentially the whole condition itself in a branch or loop statements. A *clause* is a component of predicate that does not contain any logical operator (NOT, AND, OR, XOR, NAND, NOR and XNOR). If a condition does not have any logical operator, then the condition is a predicate and a clause.

```
(X≤9)    AND    ( (Y>3)    OR    (Z≥15) )
clause A              clause B         clause C
```

The above example shows a predicate with 3 clauses. The possible evaluation of the predicate is listed in the below truth table:

#	A	B	C	A and (B or C)
1	T	T	T	T
2	T	T	F	T
3	T	F	T	T
4	T	F	F	F
5	F	T	T	F
6	F	T	F	F
7	F	F	T	F
8	F	F	F	F

To test using logic coverage criteria, a tester needs to prepare test set with a collection of test data to meet one of these coverage criteria:

- *Predicate Coverage*: test set must contain test data to make the predicate evaluates as *true* and *false*.
- *Clause Coverage*: test set must contain test data to make each clause evaluates as *true* and *false*.

- *Combinational Coverage*: test set must contain test data to make all possible combination of truth values for each clause in a predicate.

To test the above predicate with test set that meets the **predicate coverage** criteria, tester only needs to pick 2 sets of values. One set to make the whole predicate evaluates to *true*, and another to make it *false*:

- X=8, Y=5, Z=20. These test data will make the predicate evaluates as *true*.
- X=10, Y=2, Z=7. These test data will make the predicate evaluates as *false*.

The below test set meets **clause coverage** criteria:

- X=8, Y=2, Z=7.
  - These test data will make clause A evaluates as *true*.
  - These test data will make clause B evaluates as *false*.
  - These test data will make clause C evaluates as *false*.
  - The predicate evaluates as *false*.
- X=10, Y=5, Z=20.
  - These test data will make clause A evaluates as *false*.
  - These test data will make clause B evaluates as *true*.
  - These test data will make clause C evaluates as *true*.
  - The predicate evaluates as *false*.

Note that these test set has the same number of test data as the set to satisfy predicate coverage. However, the values are different. Clauses A, B and C evaluates as *true* and *false* using the test data. The fact that the predicate evaluates as *false* to both does not violate clause coverage criteria.

Best method for logic coverage testing is combinatorial coverage. This means tester must define test data to cover every combination listed in the truth table.

The below test set meets **combinatorial coverage** criteria:

- X=8, Y=4, Z=18.
  - These test data will make clause A evaluates as *true*.
  - These test data will make clause B evaluates as *true*.
  - These test data will make clause C evaluates as *true*.
  - The predicate evaluates as *true*.
- X=5, Y=7, Z=6.
  - These test data will make clause A evaluates as *true*.
  - These test data will make clause B evaluates as *true*.
  - These test data will make clause C evaluates as *false*.
  - The predicate evaluates as *true*.

- X=1, Y=2, Z=15.
    - o   These test data will make clause A evaluates as *true*.
    - o   These test data will make clause B evaluates as *false*.
    - o   These test data will make clause C evaluates as *true*.
    - o   The predicate evaluates as *true*.
- X=2, Y=1, Z=9.
    - o   These test data will make clause A evaluates as *true*.
    - o   These test data will make clause B evaluates as *false*.
    - o   These test data will make clause C evaluates as *false*.
    - o   The predicate evaluates as *false*.
- X=10, Y=20, Z=17.
    - o   These test data will make clause A evaluates as *false*.
    - o   These test data will make clause B evaluates as *true*.
    - o   These test data will make clause C evaluates as *true*.
    - o   The predicate evaluates as *false*.
- X=15, Y=12, Z=7.
    - o   These test data will make clause A evaluates as *false*.
    - o   These test data will make clause B evaluates as *true*.
    - o   These test data will make clause C evaluates as *false*.
    - o   The predicate evaluates as *false*.
- X=11, Y=0, Z=19.
    - o   These test data will make clause A evaluates as *false*.
    - o   These test data will make clause B evaluates as *false*.
    - o   These test data will make clause C evaluates as *true*.
    - o   The predicate evaluates as *false*.
- X=12, Y=2, Z=10.
    - o   These test data will make clause A evaluates as *false*.
    - o   These test data will make clause B evaluates as *false*.
    - o   These test data will make clause C evaluates as *false*.
    - o   The predicate evaluates as *false*.

Using combinatorial coverage is not always feasible due to the fact that predicate with n clauses would have 2^n combinations of truth values. Some techniques such as *active clause coverage* and *inactive clause coverage* are developed to mitigate this challenge.

In a complex predicate with many clauses, some clauses have greater impact to influence the value of the whole predicate than others. If we change test data in such a way to change the Boolean value of a clause and the whole predicate changes value, then the clause is said to be a *major clause* which *determines* the predicate.

It is important to that the value of a major clause and its predicate does not have to be equal. This definition only requires that changing the value of a major clause also changes the value of its predicate.

To define test set to satisfy active clause coverage, tester analyses the example predicate and finds the required test data for each clause when treated as major clause.

First, to treat clause A as major clause, tester would need to find the values of clauses B and C which will make clause A to determine the value of predicate:

- If B is *true* and C is *true*, changing the value of A will change the value of the predicate.
    - If these values of B and C are chosen, then [A is *true*, B is *true*, C is *true*] and [A is *false*, B is *true*, C is *true*] can be added into the test set (pair #1).
- If B is *true* and C is *false*, changing the value of A will change the value of the predicate.
    - If these values of B and C are chosen, then [A is *true*, B is *true*, C is *false*] and [A is *false*, B is *true*, C is *false*] can be added into the test set (pair #2).
- If B is *false* and C is *true*, changing the value of A will change the value of the predicate.
    - If these values of B and C are chosen, then [A is *true*, B is *false*, C is *true*] and [A is *false*, B is *false*, C is *true*] can be added into the test set (pair #3).

Up to this point, tester has 3 pairs of candidates to be added to test set. Before making decision, it is best to continue with other clauses to allow minimum number of test data to satisfy active clause coverage.

To treat B as major clause, A must be *true*, and C must be *false*. There is no other value combinations of A and C that makes changing the value of B changes the value of the whole predicate. Therefore, [A is *true*, B is *true*, C is *false*] and [A is *true*, B is *false*, C is *false*] are added into test set. Decision can be made immediately because there are no other options to meet active clause coverage criteria.

Similarly, to treat C as major clause, A must be *true*, and B must be *false*. [A is *true*, B is *false*, C is *true*] and [A is *true*, B is *false*, C is *false*] are added into test set. Note that [A is *true*, B is *false*, C is *false*] is already in the test set.

#	A	B	C	A and (B or C)	Test Set	Candidate	Major Clause
1	T	T	T	T		Pair #1	A
2	T	T	F	T	Added	Pair #2	A and B
3	T	F	T	T	Added	Pair #3	A and C
4	T	F	F	F	Added		B and C
5	F	T	T	F		Pair #1	A
6	F	T	F	F		Pair #2	A
7	F	F	T	F		Pair #3	A
8	F	F	F	F			

Remember that test data candidates from clause A come in pairs. As shown in the truth table, choosing pair #2 or #3 is more beneficial because it overlaps with test data already in the test set. This example continues with choosing pair #2.

List of test data that satisfies active clause coverage:
- [A is *true*, B is *true*, C is *false*]
  This is implemented as X=6, Y=5, Z=8.
- [A is *true*, B is *false*, C is *true*]
  This is implemented as X=3, Y=1, Z=16.
- [A is *true*, B is *false*, C is *false*]
  This is implemented as X=9, Y=2, Z=5.
- [A is *false*, B is *true*, C is *false*]
  This is implemented as X=17, Y=8, Z=7.

There are many variations on the implementation of active clause coverage. The technique demonstrated in this chapter is intended as early introduction. Interested readers can find out more about correlated active clause coverage, restricted active clause coverage and inactive clause coverage.

Input Space Partitioning

At the fundamental level, an algorithm receives inputs, performs some processes or calculations, and then produces outputs. All possible inputs for an algorithm are referred to as *input domain*. In most cases, there are infinite number of possible inputs so that testing all possible combinations is not considered feasible.

Input space partitioning focuses on partitioning the input domain so that it can be separated into multiple partitions and blocks. These blocks must cover the entire domain and they should not overlap. The goal of this exercise is to choose a subset of input from the domain in such that the execution of an algorithm using selected inputs will reveal as many faults as possible.

Partitioning can be achieved using some known characteristics of the algorithm being tested. Some common questions during this process:
- Is input X a positive number, zero or negative number?
- Is input Y null?
- Is input Z is within the maximum limit requested by an algorithm or exceeding?
- Does the input array A contain elements already sorted in ascending order, or descending order, or random, or all elements have the same value?

Input domain modelling starts from identifying all testable modules in an algorithm and all the parameters. Model can be created by considering each parameter as separate entities (interface-based) or by identifying the characteristics of the intended functionality of a module or an algorithm (functionality-based).

Some real-world examples on domain partitioning:
- Calculator app
  - Partition 1: basic arithmetic operations.
  - Blocks in partition 1: addition, subtraction, multiplication, division).
  - Partition 2: division by zero
  - Blocks in partition 2: zero value for division, non-zero value for division.
  - Partition 3: large number calculation
  - Blocks in partition 3: numbers requiring up to 16-bit memory (-32,768 to 32,767), numbers requiring more than 16-bit and up to 32-bit memory, numbers requiring more than 32-bit memory and up to 64-bit memory, numbers requiring more than 64-bit memory.
- Calendar app
  - Partition 1: adding new events.
  - Blocks in partition 1: all-day event, specific hours event, multi-day event, recurring event.
  - Partition 2: setting reminders.
  - Blocks in partition 2: time-based reminder in the past, time-based reminder at present or in the future, location-based reminder at home location, location-based reminder at locations other than home.

- o Partition 3: editing events.
- o Blocks in partition 3: editing date, editing time, editing title, editing location, editing recurrence.
- o Partition 4: deleting events.
- o Blocks in partition 4: deleting single event, deleting recurring event.

After domain model is defined and partition blocks are identified, test input values can be identified by:

- Include at least one set of valid values. Consider if valid values can be partitioned further into smaller blocks.
- Identify values that has potential to create problems (edge cases).
- Ensure that values frequently used during normal use is tested.
- Add wrong values to test an algorithm's ability to validate inputs.

As an example, input space partitioning has identified 3 partitions with blocks {A1, A2, A3}, {B1, B2} and {C1, C2, C3}.

A tester can create a test set with input values that cover one value from each block for each partition to meet **each choice coverage** criteria. This coverage is very relaxed and there are many ways to satisfy this coverage. The below test set is one of the possibilities:

- [A1, B1, C1]
- [A2, B1, C2]
- [A3, B2, C3]

Going to the other extreme, **all combinations coverage** requires a test set to have all possible combinations of blocks from all partitions. Test case to meet this coverage is listed below:

- [A1, B1, C1]
- [A1, B1, C2]
- [A1, B1, C3]
- [A1, B2, C1]
- [A1, B2, C2]
- [A1, B2, C3]
- [A2, B1, C1]
- [A2, B1, C2]
- [A2, B1, C3]
- [A2, B2, C1]
- [A2, B2, C2]
- [A2, B2, C3]
- [A3, B1, C1]
- [A3, B1, C2]
- [A3, B1, C3]
- [A3, B2, C1]
- [A3, B2, C2]
- [A3, B2, C3]

Models with more partitions and more blocks will require significantly higher number of test cases to meet all combinations coverage. If the total is still testable, it is recommended to use this coverage. Otherwise, there are several different coverage criteria trying to minimise the number of tests while still aiming to reveal as many issues as possible.

Pair-wise coverage makes pairs of blocks between 2 partitions, then chooses the minimum number of test data that contains all those pairs. For this example, the pairs are:

- #1 (A1, B1)
- #2 (A1, B2)
- #3 (A1, C1)
- #4 (A1, C2)
- #5 (A1, C3)
- #6 (A2, B1)
- #7 (A2, B2)
- #8 (A2, C1)
- #9 (A2, C2)
- #10 (A2, C3)
- #11 (A3, B1)
- #12 (A3, B2)
- #13 (A3, C1)
- #14 (A3, C2)
- #15 (A3, C3)
- #16 (B1, C1)
- #17 (B1, C2)
- #18 (B1, C3)
- #19 (B2, C1)
- #20 (B2, C2)
- #21 (B2, C3)

Test set to satisfy pair-wise coverage:

- [A1, B1, C1] covers pairs #1, #3 and #19.
- [A1, B2, C2] covers pairs #2, #4 and #20.
- [A1, B1, C3] covers pairs #5 and #18. Pair #1 is already covered.
- [A2, B1, C2] covers pairs #6, #9 and #17.
- [A2, B2, C3] covers pairs #7, #10 and #21.
- [A2, B2, C1] covers pair #8. Pairs #7 and #19 are already covered.
- [A3, B1, C1] covers pairs #11, #13 and #16.
- [A3, B2, C2] covers pairs #12 and #14. Pair #20 is already covered.
- [A3, B1, C3] covers pair #15. Pairs #11 and #18 are already covered.

For further reading, interested readers can find out more about T-Wise coverage, base choice coverage and multiple base choices coverage.

Cost of Fixing Bugs

Bugs or defects found in an algorithm need to be fixed. The time and effort required to fix these issues brings up the total cost of development because fixing something at the end of development is a significant rework.

The best scenario in development is for an algorithm to work right the first time. Every time an issue is found, additional effort is required to fix the issue. If it happens after the development process is completed, a fix will trigger at least two testing activities: to verify the fix and to check if there is an impact because of the fix.

When a defect causes production incident, it causes operational loss to a business that uses the solution. The fix will trigger at least three testing activities: test the fix itself, test if it breaks something else within the solution (regression) and test if there is a downstream impact caused by the fix (integration). The cost of fixing bugs (or defects) increases exponentially the later it is discovered during software development life cycle.

Some costs associated with late discovery of a bug or defect:
- Effort to analyse and consistently reproduce an issue.
- Effort to understand the code to be fixed. This might be necessary if a defect is found long after a software engineer completed its development. Complex algorithm takes some time to figure out when it is no longer fresh in mind.
- Effort to fix the issue.
- Effort to implement the fix.
- Effort to re-test the failed functionality (testing the fix).
- Effort to check if the fix causes another issue (regression).
- Effort to check if the fix causes downstream impact (integration).
- Costs associated with change management to deploy fix to production.
- Costs associated with operational loss caused by an incident, especially for business-critical systems.
- Costs associated with lost business or lost opportunity.
- Costs associated with damaged reputation and relationships.
- Costs associated with lost development time.

Many bugs and defects will cost more than the cost to prevent them. Fixing an issue in a complex algorithm may only need trivial effort when development process is still in progress.

Possible strategies to catch bugs early:
- Practice the *detect early, detect often* mindset.
- Try to detect issues before merging code to main development branch.
- Implement *test-driven development*. With this approach, a team would focus on writing unit test cases before even writing the algorithm or code. Software developer then uses these test cases as guideline in designing the algorithm.
- Implement *continuous integration*. Smaller frequent changes are more manageable (and testable) than infrequent big bang change.
- Write and implement *test automation* from development phase, not after development is completed.
- Use the principles of algorithm testing introduced in this chapter during development process to write better algorithms.

10. BEYOND BASIC ALGORITHMS

Throughout the preceding chapters of this book, fundamental concepts, techniques, and problem-solving strategies have been introduced, covering wide spectrum of computational challenges. From sorting algorithms to search tree, these topics have been discussed with step-by-step examples, providing readers with solid understanding on those topics. This final chapter aims to give a brief introduction to some popular topics that extends beyond the realm of basic algorithms.

Database Queries

In the world of modern computing, data is the foundation of many applications, enabling them to perform different tasks from doing simple calculation to presenting analysis for business decisions. Central to the harnessing stored data is the ability to retrieve and manipulate information effectively.

Structured Query Language (SQL) is the standard language for database manipulation. It covers commands for data definition (creating data structure), query (retrieving data), manipulation (adding, editing, or deleting data), control (restricting access to data) and transaction control (commit and rollback).

Imagine walking through an extensive library with incredible collection of books, each containing valuable story or information. To find something, someone would need to systematically scan the shelves and examine the book covers. Queries work in a similar fashion in database systems. They silently loop through records in database tables, evaluating each row against given criteria to retrieve the requested data. This silent loop powers all data-driven applications in modern computing.

Observe the below simplified syntax of SELECT query:

```
SELECT <fields> FROM <table> WHERE <filter conditions>
    ORDER BY <sorting>
```

This query instructs a database engine to perform a loop through a table, which is comparable to an array of records, and find all rows (array element) that meets the filter conditions (`if` branch) and then sort it using the given criteria. All concepts of algorithm to execute this instruction has been discussed in this book.

A query with `JOIN` clause basically asks database engine to loop through multiple tables and compared records in different tables. This involves loops and optimised searching algorithm. `UPDATE` query requires a database engine to search certain records (searching for some values within an array of data) and then change some values in the rows that meet the criteria.

Companies behind popular database engines implement various advanced techniques to ensure that the algorithms to execute queries are as efficient as possible to handle complex relational database with large amount of data. These techniques have significant improvements compared to some pseudocodes presented in earlier chapters. However, the basic principles remain the same.

Having a strong understanding on how iterations algorithmic complexity (time and resource) work will help a software engineer to design a better and more efficient queries to interact with database systems. This would improve the overall quality of a solution.

Libraries and Frameworks

In software development, time is highly valued, and efficiency is critical. Software developers working on large solution with complex algorithms will soon realise that there are many repetitive tasks and having access to some reusable functions will help them to improve speed, focus and work quality.

Imagine cooking pasta for dinner using store-bought pasta compared to making the pasta from scratch. Sure, an expert could probably make better pasta from scratch, but the availability of commercially produced pasta enables more households to prepare pasta dinner with ease without having to spend too much time and effort.

Libraries and frameworks are created to provide some pre-built, reusable components, functions, and structures to help software engineers to better use their time. These tools also introduce further benefits that they enforce best practices and reduce issues. Examples of popular libraries and frameworks include Vue.js, jQuery, React, Node.js, Angular, .Net, Pandas, NumPy, TensorFlow and Scikit Learn.

Even though the terms library and framework are often used interchangeably in software development, there are some important differences between them. A *library* is a collection of reusable code written to help software developers to perform common tasks. It can contain modules, objects, classes, or functions. Libraries can be added to existing solution to add some capabilities and can also be replaced by others without significant rework. Software engineers uses some modules or methods in a library by calling them from their algorithms.

A *framework* takes things to another level. It aims to be the foundation of an application by offering the full package, including predefined approach to development, APIs, support applications, compilers, or even libraries. Instead of simply offering reusable code, framework inverses the control. It tells software developers what they need. Developer-supplied code becomes part of the main application controlled by framework, not the other way around.

It is considered not practical to replace a framework for an existing solution just like it is hard to replace house foundation once the house is built. Framework offers significantly faster development time at the cost of reduced flexibility because it sets many rules and guidelines.

While using libraries and framework is certainly beneficial to produce better solutions within shorter development time, it also comes with some risks and limitations. Over reliance could transform a software engineer into a "user" of those tools instead of being a full-fledged creator. Just like many other aspects in life, there needs to be a balance between using tools and knowing how to do things without them.

Low Code Platforms

Traditional programming requires specific skillsets in software development. The process to develop a solution takes time and demand extensive skill set. As businesses strive to adapt and innovate, the demand for applications and solutions has increased, but not all of them could justify significant investment (time and money) on building custom solution to meet their business process. This creates a new push people with varying levels of technical expertise to create common solutions that be customised without the intricacies of developing and testing conventional code.

Low code platforms are services to simplify application development. It uses visual tools and configurable common functionalities to reduce traditional programming activities. This new service allows software developers to build a solution at very fast rate, or non-programmers with some level of technical knowledge (often referred to as "citizen developers") to create solutions.

Some examples of popular low-code platforms include Microsoft Power Apps, Google App Maker, Oracle Application Express, Salesforce Lightning, ServiceNow Creator Workflows, SAP Build, Zoho Creator, Pega, Appian, OutSystems, Mendix and Quickbase. These platforms help companies to obtain new solutions and improve them at a rapid rate.

Proper knowledge on how traditional algorithms work can still be very beneficial in developing applications using low code platform. Even though the text-based syntax is replaced by drag-and-drop UI, the fundamentals of an algorithm flow remain the same. Loops and branches optimisations are still applicable to a varying degree.

Artificial Intelligence

Even though a lot of computing devices have the word smart in their names, computers are not smart at all. As the name implies, a computer is a device that computes. It executes instructions and performs calculations exactly as per defined by an algorithm, but it does so at incredible speed far above what humans can achieve.

The study of *artificial intelligence* (often abbreviated as AI) uses complex algorithms and calculations to allow computer to perform tasks that require human intelligence. This is achieved through one of these AI branches, or by combining some of them:
- Machine learning
- Artificial neural network
- Computer vision
- Natural language processing
- Robotics
- Fuzzy logic

Machine learning is one of the prominent branches of AI that is often confused by the term AI itself. In simplistic terms, machine learning focuses on using existing data to enable computers to perform tasks without being explicitly programmed. This study is a popular subset of AI, there are several other streams that fall under the umbrella of AI.

Supervised learning technique in machine learning uses labelled data to train an algorithm. It uses the labels of each data entity to find patterns that can be used to label/classify future input data. In *unsupervised learning*, the training data does not contain labels. This technique attempts to find meaningful correlations between data (including hidden patterns) without some predefined classifications (labels).

Reinforcement learning is another machine learning technique that uses trial and error method to learn instead of using training data. An algorithm interacts with its environment, makes actions, receive feedback or reward, and then learns to make better actions for the next step based on the positive or negative feedback obtained.

Deep learning is a subset of machine learning. It combines traditional principles of machine learning with artificial neural network to make intelligent decisions on its own. To achieve this goal, deep learning requires significantly larger training data and longer training duration to make non-linear and complex correlations.

There are two subsets of deep learning: discriminative AI and generative AI. *Discriminative AI* uses training data to classify new input data. *Generative AI* uses training data to create new data based on the patterns from data it was trained on.

Artificial neural network is a branch of AI that uses neurology (biology discipline studying nervous systems in human brain) and attempts to replicate some characteristics of it. This method is commonly used in implementations related to predictions, such as sales forecasting, stock exchange analysis, facial recognition, handwriting recognition, and many others.

Computer vision is a study of AI to extract meaningful information from digital images and videos. It attempts to simulate the way humans can understand the environments around them from things they see and hear.

As the name suggest, *natural language processing* is an AI branch to enable computers to communicate using natural human language that does not follow some restrictive syntax in traditional programming. This allows humans to interact with computer in a conversational method instead of having to learn specific instructions.

The study of *robotics* focuses on designing and constructing robots. This field has overlaps with mechanical engineering, electrical engineering, and other disciplines.

Fuzzy logic technique is a branch of AI that studies how computer can handle uncertain information. Instead of classifying every situation as 1 or 0 (computer representation of Boolean *true* or *false*), fuzzy logic adds degree of truth between these absolute values.

Popular services of AI, such as OpenAI's ChatGPT, Microsoft's Bing or Google's Bard are mainly generative AI that incorporates other AI branches to extend their capabilities. For example, to receive requests from users, they use principles from natural language processing. Their deep learning algorithms include some techniques from artificial neural network to help with predicting desired response. Other services like Jasper Art, Dall-E 2, Starry AI and Pictory combine deep learning with computer vision to generate new images and videos.

The impact of AI is evident in many aspects of modern society. Artificial intelligence opens a whole new set of possibilities of what can be achieved using computers. Several aspects still need our attention, such as ethics, risks, and regulations. If humans make the right choices with the future of AI, collaboration with technology will open new chapters in human civilizations.

Maybe one day, just maybe, all those bots can finally get through Captchas on their own.

INDEX

0

0/1 knapsack problem, 88, 153

A

abstract data type, 35
active clause coverage, 263
adjacency matrix, 42
ADT, 35
algorithm, 8
all combinations coverage, 267
all-defs coverage, 259
all-du-paths coverage, 260
all-uses coverage, 259
argument, 26
array, 14
artificial intelligence (AI), 274
artificial neural network, 275

B

backtracking technique, 200
base case, 32
Big O notation, 236
binary, 8
binary encoding, 170
binary search, 81
binary tree, 39
black-box testing, 252
Boolean, 14
bottom-up testing, 252
bounded knapsack problem, 88
branch, 10
branch and bound, 206
branching, 17
breadth-first search, 189, 196
bubble sort, 55
bug, 252
byte, 14

C

char, 14
child node, 38

chromatic number, 106
clause, 261
clause coverage, 261
coin change problem, 121
combinational coverage, 262
complete path coverage, 255
compound, 17
computer vision, 275
conditional statement, 17
constant complexity, 237
continuous integration, 269
control flow coverage, 254
control flow graph, 253
correct algorithm, 8
cost matrix, 45
coverage criteria, 252

D

data compression, 169
data flow coverage, 259
decision making tree, 181
deep learning, 275
defect, 252
depth-first search, 185, 192
development framework, 273
development library, 273
directed graph, 41
discriminative AI, 275
divide and conquer, 49
domain modelling, 266
dynamic programming, 115

E

each choice coverage, 267
edge, 38
edge colouring, 106
edge coverage, 254
edge-pair coverage, 254
element, 14
else if, 18
external node, 40

F

G

H

I

J

K

L

M

N

O

P

partial search tree, 200
pivot point, 76
post-order traversal, 185
predicate, 261
predicate coverage, 261
pre-order traversal, 184
Prim-Dijkstra algorithm, 97
prime numbers algorithm, 240
prime path coverage, 254
propagation, 252
pseudocode, 9

Q

quadratic complexity, 238
queue, 37, 189, 196
quick sort, 75

R

reachability, 252
record, 17
recursion, 32
recursive path, 32
reduced cost matrix, 206
region colouring, 107
reinforcement learning, 275
repeat-until, 24
resource complexity, 239
return value, 30
RIP model, 252
robotics, 276
root, 38

S

search tree, 181
SELECT query, 272
selection, 10, 17
selection sort, 50
self-balancing binary search tree, 40
sequence, 10
sequential search, 80
short integer, 14
shortest path problem, 94
sieve of Erathosthenes, 243

simple path, 254
sink node, 42
source node, 42
stack, 35, 185, 192
statement, 9
stopping state, 32
string, 16
structure, 17
Structured Query Language (SQL), 271
superlinear complexity, 238
supervised learning, 275
switch-case, 20
syntax, 9

T

test-driven development, 269
testing, 251
Theta notation, 237
time complexity, 236
top-down testing, 252
travelling salesperson problem, 160,
    206
tree, 38
tree traversal, 183
truth table, 20, 261

U

unbounded knapsack problem, 88
undirected graph, 41
unicode, 170
unsupervised learning, 275
unweighted graph, 42

V

validation, 251
variable, 10, 13
verification, 251

W

weighted graph, 42
Welsh and Powell algorithm, 109
while-do, 25
white-box testing, 252

REFERENCES

A. Levitin. *Introduction to the Design & Analysis of Algorithms (3rd Edition)*. Pearson. 2011.

A. Wah, H. Picciotto. *Algebra: Themes, Tools, Concepts*. Creative Publications. 1994.

C. A. Horstmann, G. Cornell. *Core Java: Fundamentals (9th Edition)*. Pearson. 2011.

D. A. Huffmann. *A Method for the Construction of Minimum-Redundancy Codes*. Proceedings of the IRE. 1952.

D. Graham, R. Black, E. van Veenendaal. *Foundations of Software Testing*. Cengage Learning. 2019.

E Horowitz, S. Sahni, S. Rajasekaran. Computer Algorithms (2nd Edition). Silicon Pr. 2007.

E. D. Taillard. *Design of Heuristic Algorithms for Hard Optimization*. Springer. 2022.

I. H. Witten, E. Frank, M. A. Hall. *Data Mining: Practical Machine Learning Tools and Techniques*. Elsevier Science. 2011.

J. Bather. *Decision Theory: An Intoduction to Dynamic Programming and Sequential Decisions*. Wiley. 2000.

J. R. Alfonsín. *The Diophantine Frobenius problem*. Oxford University Press. 2005.

J. Wengrow. *A Common Sense Guide to Data Structures and Algorithms (2nd Edition)*. Pragmatic Bookshelf. 2020.

M. A Weiss. *Data Structure and Algorithm Analysis in C++ (4th Edition)*. Pearson. 2013.

M. L Fredman, R. E Tarjan. *Fibonacci heaps and their uses in improved network optimization algorithms*. IEEE 25th Annual Symposium on Foundations of Computer Science. 1984.

M. S. Jenkins. *Abstract Data Types in Java*. McGraw-Hill. 1997.

P. Ammann, J Offutt. *Introduction to Software Testing*. Cambridge University Press. 2008.

P. Simon. *Low-Code/No-Code: Citizens Developers and the Surprising Future of Business Applications*. Racket Publishing. 2022.

R. E. Neapolitan, X. Jiang. *Artificial Intelligence: With and Introduction to Machine Learning (2nd Edition)*. Routledge. 2020.

R. M. Shah. Decoding JavaScript: *A Simple Guide for the Not-so-Simple JavaScript Concepts, Libraries, Tools, and Frameworks*. BPB Publications. 2021.

R. Sedgewick. *Algorithms in C++ (3rd Edition)*. Computer Science Press. 1998.

R. Setiadi. *Algorithm is Easy* (translated title). Prima Infosarana Media. 2008.

T. H. Cormen, C. E. Leiserson, R. L. Rivest, C. Stein. *Introduction to Algorithms (3rd Edition)*. MIT Press. 2009.

T. Roughgarden. *Algorithms Illuminated: Part 1 The Basics*. Soundlikeyourself Publishing. 2017.

T. Roughgarden. *Algorithms Illuminated: Part 2 Graph Algorithms and Data Structures*. Soundlikeyourself Publishing. 2018.

T. Roughgarden. *Algorithms Illuminated: Part 3 Greedy Algorithms and Dynamic Programming*. Soundlikeyourself Publishing. 2019.

V. S. Tanaev, Y. N. Sotskov, V. A. Strusevich. *Scheduling Theory: Multi-Stage Systems*. Springer. 2012.

W. Kruskal, W. A. Wallis. *Use of ranks in one-criterion variance analysis*. Journal of the American Statistical Association. 1952.

Online References

Cited between Sep 2021 to May 2022, or between Jul 2023 to Sep 2023

- https://courses.cs.vt.edu/~csonline/Algorithms/Lessons/index.html
- https://deepsource.com/blog/exponential-cost-of-fixing-bugs
- https://flexiple.com/algorithms/big-o-notation-cheat-sheet cited Sep 2023
- https://heracleia.uta.edu/~sharifara/5321/3_isp.pdf
- https://learn.microsoft.com/en-us/dotnet/csharp/language-reference/builtin-types/integral-numeric-types
- https://math.stackexchange.com/questions/58799/why-in-sieve-of-erastothenes-of-n-number-you-need-to-check-and-cross-out-numbe
- https://medium.com/dataseries/how-to-calculate-time-complexity-with-big-o-notation-9afe33aa4c46
- https://powerapps.microsoft.com/en-au/
- https://www.analyticssteps.com/blogs/6-major-branches-artificial-intelligence-ai
- https://www.baeldung.com/cs/sieve-of-eratosthenes
- https://www.bigocheatsheet.com/
- https://www.cs.cornell.edu/courses/cs5154/2021sp/resources/InputSpacePartitioning.pdf
- https://www.cs.utexas.edu/users/mitra/csSpring2017/cs303/lectures/algo.html
- https://www.freecodecamp.org/news/big-o-notation-why-it-matters-and-why-it-doesnt-1674cfa8a23c/
- https://www.geeksforgeeks.org/analysis-algorithms-big-o-analysis/
- https://www.javatpoint.com/traveling-salesperson-problem-using-branch-and-bound
- https://www.sencha.com/blog/difference-between-framework-vs-library-snc/
- https://www.techiedelight.com/travelling-salesman-problem-using-branch-and-bound/
- https://www.techrepublic.com/article/low-code-platforms-a-cheat-sheet/

Disclaimer & Credits

- ChatGPT (https://chat.openai.com) is used to assist with a small portion of this book, influencing less than 5% of the content. No AI response was used as-is without manual verification and editing.
- Part of cover design uses free license image by rawpixel.com on Freepik.

this page intentionally left blank

ABOUT THE AUTHOR

Robert Setiadi is an author, proud father, seasoned IT professional, project manager and Certified Lean Six Sigma Black Belt (ICBB) with over 15 years of experience in the corporate world. As the author of *Making Sense of Programming Algorithms Foundations*, he aims to share his extensive knowledge, providing amateur and experienced programmers with solid foundations and step-by-step examples to demystify the world of algorithms.

Robert hopes to provide a concise and comprehensive companion guide that empowers students, new learners, and experienced developers with essential knowledge for designing efficient algorithms and discovering the joys of coding.

With a PhD in software testing & quality assurance, a master's degree in software systems engineering, and over a dozen professional certifications, Robert is dedicated to helping readers from all backgrounds develop valuable technical skills for their careers and hobbies. For more information, visit his website at: www.robertsetiadi.com